Guide to America's Outdoors

Middle Atlantic

Guide to America's Outdoors
Middle Atlantic

By Ann Jones
Photography by Skip Brown

NATIONAL
GEOGRAPHIC
WASHINGTON, D.C.

Contents

Cover: Forbes State Forest, Pennsylvania
Page 1: Pony, Assateague Island National Seashore, Maryland
Pages 2-3: Sailboats on Lake George, New York
Opposite: Fall Foliage, Delaware Water Gap, New Jersey

Treading Lightly in the Wild

Water grasses, Erie NWR

NATIONAL GEOGRAPHIC GUIDE TO AMER-
ICA'S OUTDOORS: MIDDLE ATLANTIC takes
you from the ocean's coastline over ancient
mountains, including the Appalachians and
the Adirondacks, to the shores of great inland
lakes. With its plentiful parks, forests, wilderness areas, waterways, and wildlife refuges,
this densely populated region is a delightful
surprise for the outdoors enthusiast.

Visitors who care about this region know
they must tread lightly on the land. Ecosystems can be damaged, even destroyed, by
thoughtless misuse. Many have already suffered from the impact of
tourism. The marks are clear: litter-strewn acres, polluted waters, tram-
pled vegetation, and disturbed wildlife. You can do your part to preserve
these places for yourself, your children, and all other nature travelers.
Before embarking on a backcountry visit or a camping adventure, learn
some basic conservation dos and don'ts. Leave No Trace, a national edu-
cational program, recommends the following:

Plan ahead and prepare for your trip. If you know what to expect in
terms of climate, conditions, and hazards, you can pack for general
needs, extreme weather, and emergencies. Do yourself and the land a
favor by visiting if possible during off-peak months and limiting your
group to no more than four to six people. To keep trash or litter to a
minimum, repackage food into reusable containers or bags. And rather
than using cairns, flags, or paint cues that mar the environment to mark
your way, bring a map and compass.

Travel and camp on solid surfaces. In popular areas, stay within
established trails and campsites. Travel single file in the middle of the trail,
even when it's wet or muddy, to avoid trampling vegetation. Be particularly sensitive in boggy or coastal areas, and avoid stepping on mussels, sea
stars, and the like. When exploring off the trail in pristine, lightly traveled
areas, have your group spread out to lessen impact. Good campsites are
found, not made. Travel and camp on sand, gravel, or rock, or on dry
grasses, pine needles, or snow. Remember to stay at least 200 feet from
waterways. After you've broken camp, leave the site as you found it.

Pack out what you pack in—and that means *everything* except human
waste, which should be deposited in a hole dug away from water, camp,
or trail, then covered and concealed. When washing dishes, clothes, or
yourself, use small amounts of biodegradable soap and scatter the water
away from lakes and streams.

Be sure to leave all items—plants, rocks, artifacts—as you find them.
Avoid potential disaster by neither introducing nor transporting non-
native species. Also, don't build or carve out structures that will alter the

environment. A don't-touch policy not only preserves resources for future generations; it also gives the next guy a crack at the discovery experience.

Keep fires to a minimum. It may be unthinkable to camp without a campfire, but depletion of firewood harms the backcountry. When you can, try a gas-fueled camp stove and a candle lantern. If you choose to build a fire, first consider regulations, weather, skill, and firewood availability. At the beach, build your fire below the next high-tide line, where the traces will be washed away. Where possible, employ existing fire rings; elsewhere, use fire pans or mound fires. Keep your fire small, use only sticks from the ground, burn the fire down to ash, and don't leave the site until it's cold.

Respect wildlife. Watch animals from a distance (bring binoculars or a telephoto lens for close-ups), but never approach, feed, or follow them. Feeding weakens an animal's ability to fend for itself in the wild. If you can't keep your pets under control, leave them at home.

Finally, be mindful of other visitors. Yield to fellow travelers on the trail, and keep noise levels low so that all the sounds of nature can be heard.

With these points in mind, you have only to chart your course. Enjoy your explorations. Let natural places quiet your mind, refresh your spirit, and remain as you found them. Just remember, leave behind no trace. ∎

MAP KEY and ABBREVIATIONS

National Park	N.P.	
Forest Park	F.P.	
National Battlefield	N.B.	
National Historical Park	N.H.P.	
National Historic Site	N.H.S.	
National Military Park	N.M.P.	
National Monument	NAT. MON.	
National Recreation Area	N.R.A.	
National Reserve		
National Seashore	N.S.	
National Forest	N.F.	
State Forest	S.F.	
National Wildlife Refuge	N.W.R.	
Conservation Area	C.A.	
National Conservation Area	N.C.A.	
Natural Area	N.A.	
Natural Environment Area	N.E.A.	
State Wildlife Management Area	S.W.M.A.	
Wildlife Management Area	W.M.A.	
Wildlife Research Center	W.R.C.	
Wildlife Area	W.A.	
Wildlife Sanctuary		
State Park	S.P.	
State Historical Park	S.H.P.	
State Historic Site	S.H.S.	
State Marine Park	S.M.P.	
State Park Preserve		
Recreation Area	R.A.	
Indian Reservation	I.R.	
Military Reservation		
National Wild & Scenic River	N.W. & S.R.	
State Scenic River		

POPULATION

● **PHILADELPHIA**	above 500,000
● **Jersey City**	50,000 to 500,000
● Annapolis	10,000 to 50,000
● Newcomb	under 10,000

ADDITIONAL ABBREVIATIONS

B.	Bay
Br.	Branch
BLVD.	Boulevard
Cr.	Creek
Ctr.	Center
DR.	Drive
E.	East
EXPWY.	Expressway
Fk.	Fork
HWY.	Highway
I.-s.	Island-s
L.	Lake
MEM.	Memorial
Mid.	Middle
Mt.-s.	Mount-ain-s
N.	North
N.S.T.	National Scenic Trail
Pk.	Peak
PKWY.	Parkway
Pt.	Point
RD.	Road
Res.	Reservoir
S.	South
TR.	Trail
W.	West
WILD.	Wilderness

U.S. Interstate, Trans-Canada Highway: 95 7
U.S. Federal, State and Canadian Provincial Highways: 50 1 2
Other Road: 563

Trail
Canal
Abandoned Canal

BOUNDARIES

STATE or NATIONAL   FOREST   S.P.   WILD.

□ Point of Interest
⊛ State capital
⊛ National capital
+ Elevation
≍ Pass

╫ Falls
⊰ Dam
Swamp or Marsh
△ Campground

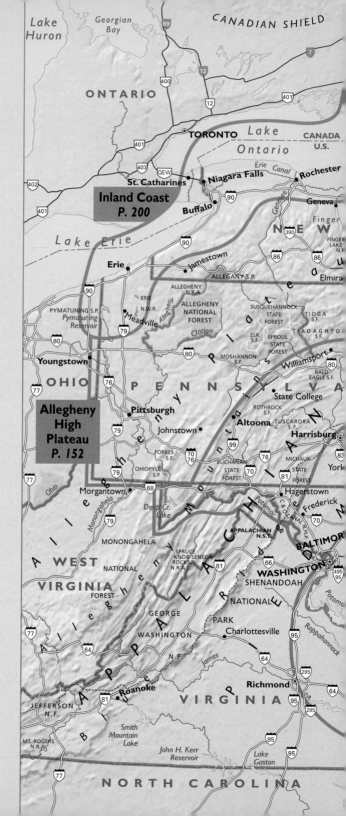

Lake Huron

Georgian Bay

CANADIAN SHIELD

69

12

ONTARIO

400

12

401

TORONTO

Lake Ontario

CANADA U.S.

7

401

403

QEW

St. Catharines

Niagara Falls

Erie Canal

Rochester

402

Inland Coast P. 200

Buffalo

90

Geneva

Finger

N E W

390

FINGER LAKE N.F.

Lake Erie

90

Elmira

Erie

Jamestown

86

86

ALLEGANY S.P.

90

ERIE N.W.R.

ALLEGHENY N.R.A

PYMATUNING S.P.
Pymatuning Reservoir

Meadville

Allegheny

ALLEGHENY NATIONAL FOREST

SUSQUEHANNOCK STATE FOREST

TIOGA S.F.

TIADAGHTO

80

Clarion

ELK S.F.

SPROUL STATE FOREST

MOSHANNON S.F.

Williamsport

80

79

80

Youngstown

76

P E N N S Y L V A

BALD EAGLE S.F.

State College

77

OHIO

Pittsburgh

ROTHROCK S.F.

Altoona

TUSCARORA S.F.

Harrisburg

Allegheny High Plateau P. 152

79

Johnstown

99

76

MICHAUX STATE FOREST

83

York

FORBES S.F.

70 76

BUCHANAN STATE FOREST

70

81

81

77

79

OHIOPYLE S.P.

Morgantown

68

Ohio

Monongahela

79

Deep Cr. Lake

A P P A L A C H I A N

Hagerstown

C & O CANAL N.H.P.

Frederick

70

MONONGAHELA

SPRUCE KNOB-SENECA ROCKS N.R.A.

APPALACHIAN N.S.T.

Potomac

C & O CANAL N.H.P.

BALTIMORE

M

495 95

WEST

NATIONAL

81

66

WASHINGTON

VIRGINIA

FOREST

SHENANDOAH

M D

GEORGE

NATIONAL

Potomac

WASHINGTON

PARK

Charlottesville

Rappahannock

64

N.F.

James

95

295

JEFFERSON N.F.

81

Roanoke

V I R G I N I A

64

Richmond

95

64

77

64

295

B

MT. ROGERS N.R.A.

Smith Mountain Lake

John H. Kerr Reservoir

85

Lake Gaston

Potomac

95

77

N O R T H   C A R O L I N A

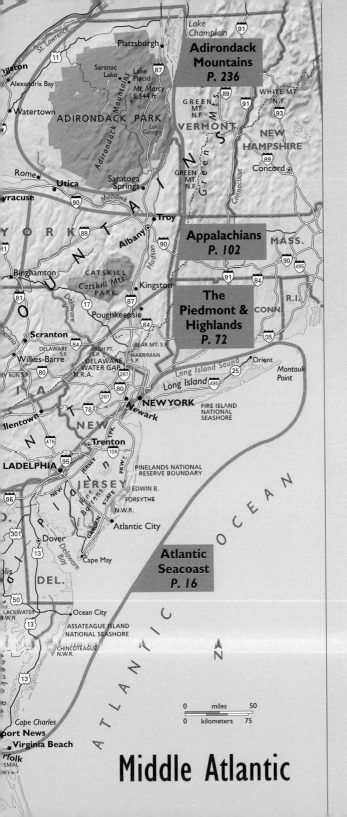

Middle Atlantic

Adirondack Mountains
P. 236

Appalachians
P. 102

The Piedmont & Highlands
P. 72

Atlantic Seacoast
P. 16

Lake Champlain

Plattsburgh

Saranac Lake

Lake Placid

Mt. Marcy 5,344 ft

ADIRONDACK PARK

Adirondack Mountains

Lake George

ngston

Alexandria Bay

Watertown

Rome

Utica

yracuse

Saratoga Springs

Mohawk

GREEN MT. N.F.

VERMONT

GREEN MT. N.F.

Green Mts.

WHITE MT. N.F.

NEW HAMPSHIRE

Concord

Connecticut

Troy

Albany

Hudson

MASS.

YORK

Binghamton

CATSKILL S.F.

Catskill Mts.

PARK

Kingston

Poughkeepsie

CONN.

R.I.

Delaware

Scranton

DELAWARE S.F.

HIGH PT. S.P.

BEAR MT. S.P.

HARRIMAN S.P.

Wilkes-Barre

DELAWARE WATER GAP N.R.A.

RUN S.P.

Long Island Sound

Orient

Montauk Point

Long Island

FIRE ISLAND NATIONAL SEASHORE

NEW YORK

Newark

llentown

NEW JERSEY

Trenton

LADELPHIA

PINELANDS NATIONAL RESERVE BOUNDARY

EDWIN B. FORSYTHE N.W.R.

Atlantic City

Dover

Cape May

ATLANTIC OCEAN

DEL.

Delaware Bay

LACKWATER .W.R.

Ocean City

ASSATEAGUE ISLAND NATIONAL SEASHORE

CHINCOTEAGUE N.W.R.

Cape Charles

port News

Virginia Beach

rfolk

ATLANTIC

N

miles 0 50
kilometers 0 75

The Gift of the Land

I LIVED DEEP in the concrete canyons of New York City for more than 20 years. Summer meant opera, Shakespeare, and Diana Ross in Central Park, bodysurfing the beaches of Long Island's southern shore, and running to catch the last ferry back from Fire Island. Fall was the season for tramping along the Hudson River and hiking the smoldering golden forests upstate. Winter brought solitary windswept jaunts along the beach at Montauk Point, ice skating at Wollman Rink, and cross-country skiing on the Great Lawn of Central Park (try riding the subway with skis!).

I went farther afield, too, meeting friends for weekends away from the city at the seaside or in the mountains. I canoed the lakes and rivers, and climbed Mt. Marcy, the Adirondacks' highest peak. Simply by living there, I saw many highlights of the middle Atlantic region, but I thought of it merely as my own front yard—the place where I lived.

"Real" exploration of the outdoors always began with a subway trip to John F. Kennedy Airport. "Real" trips took me to all the world's continents—to Antarctica, central Asia, South America, Africa. I went to live in other countries and in other parts of the United States. In remote spots around the globe and across the country, I studied the lay of the land. I learned the names of strange plants and animals, and how they lived. Little by little, I came to appreciate the intricate workings of natural processes, and the kinship of all life.

Camping, Promised Land State Park, Pennsylvania

When I set out to revisit the middle Atlantic states for this book, I saw the region with new eyes. As I looked at the rocks and the slope of the mountains, the shape of the drainages, the course of the waterways, the color and texture of the soils, I saw the land whole. I perceived why Native Americans and early Americans settled where they did, why they fought over the land, and even why the victors plundered the region's resources so, believing that such bounty must be boundless.

The region's highlights still drew me, but beyond them I found unexpected and amazing corners. I also learned lessons about the disastrous effects of unlimited "American ingenuity, industry, and progress" on the land we profess to love. Forests clear-cut, rivers silted up or polluted, animals exterminated—all devastation wreaked by hardworking Americans trying to make a living. Traveling the area today, you will find evidence of a different sort of painstaking effort: Government agencies, environmental organizations, and concerned citizens are toiling to restore some of what we lost. Just around the corner, however, the ruination continues.

For all the pleasures this land offers me, it is not intended merely for my amusement; it requires that I give something in return. Having rediscovered the mid-Atlantic, I moved back to a little shack in the Hudson Valley. Just beyond my windows, deer browse wild apple trees and the blue Catskills rise. Here I walk gently, eyes wide open, cherishing the gift of this land. I invite you to do the same.

Ann Jones

From Sea to Inland Sea

TAKE A METROLINER from New York City to Washington, D.C., and you may think there's little more to the middle Atlantic states than cities and suburbs. The great eastern cities—New York, Philadelphia, Baltimore, Washington—stand elbow to elbow along the Atlantic seaboard, forming one of the most densely populated stretches of landscape in the country. But each city grew tall beside a great river flowing southeastward to the sea—the Hudson, the Delaware, the Susquehanna, the Potomac—just at the point where the inland high ground falls away to the coastal plain. That fall line marks the centuries-old navigational limit of seagoing ships, the place where colonial seaports rose.

Even today, downstream to the east of the fall line and the urban corridor that spreads along its margins lies a magnificent seacoast, hedged by barrier islands. Upstream to the west extend miles of upland valleys and ridges, mountains, and a vast plateau fringed with forests. In this cradle of America's urban life—the middle Atlantic states—America's outdoors still flourishes with amazing diversity.

In earlier years of nation building, the great mid-Atlantic forests—chestnut, cherry, cypress, fir, hickory, oak, and pine—fell as New York State took the lead in timber production. Mines were opened and rivers dammed to power the mills and factories of burgeoning cities. Today a system of state and national parks and seashores, wildlife refuges, and recreational areas protects wild landscapes and allows formerly settled areas to return to their wild state.

In some cases, yesterday's technological innovation has become today's outdoor playground: Bicyclists, hikers, and trail riders now enjoy the 184.5-mile towpath beside the old Chesapeake and Ohio Canal, an engineering marvel that once served industry and commerce. Here and there throughout the region, disused railroad cuts are being converted to bike paths and hiking trails. Soon it will be possible to pedal along a bike path all the way from Pittsburgh to the nation's capital. And even though little virgin forest stands anywhere in the mid-Atlantic states, the region's outdoors is better protected and more accessible than it was a century ago.

The backbone of the middle Atlantic region is the Appalachian Mountains. Lying along the east coast of North America from Newfoundland in the north to Alabama in the south, the mountains we know collectively as the Appalachians include many ranges, from Vermont's Green Mountains to Virginia's Blue Ridge. Generations of American schoolchildren learned to describe the Appalachians as "old, worn-down mountains," reduced by erosion to the status of big hills.

A far more dramatic story of their formation, however, has been pieced together by modern geologists applying the theory of plate tectonics. Between 450 million and 260 million years ago, they surmise, crustal plates collided in three great episodes of mountain building, known as

Higbee Beach, Cape May, New Jersey

orogenies—the Taconic, the Acadian, and the Alleghany. These collisions buckled the edge of North America, folded it, thrust the folds inland, and uplifted the land to form Appalachians as high as the Alps or the Himalaya. Over the next 250 million years or so, erosion fashioned a gentler topography—a Ridge and Valley province consisting of numerous long, linear mountain ridges separating equally elongated valleys. Erosion-resistant sandstones underlie the ridges, whereas less resistant limestones and shales form the valley floors.

The Appalachians form the central part of this book (Chapter 3), which is organized more or less like the landscape it describes into six biogeographic sections. These chapters do not conform precisely to the complicated pattern of nature's handiwork, but they do make rough sense: They describe areas of similar latitude, altitude, vegetation, geology, and climate.

To the east of the Appalachians lies the Piedmont—literally, "the foot of the mountains" (Chapter 2). True to their name, gentle foothills cloaked in farmlands and deciduous forest slope steadily eastward from elevations of more than 1,000 feet to only a few hundred feet at the fall line, where rivers and streams plunge from the hard upland rocks to the sedimentary coastal plain. The Atlantic Seacoast region (Chapter 1) is a broad, flat plain that widens southward from New York City, pierced by the Delaware and Chesapeake Bays. Laced with estuaries, bays, lagoons, and salt marshes and protected by long barrier islands, the coast is a haven for waterfowl and migratory birds in spectacular numbers.

To the west of the Appalachians, the upland Allegheny Plateau (Chapter 4) stretches west across southern New York State and Pennsylvania to the shores of Lakes Ontario and Erie and into Ohio. It's a sprawling region of hills and declivities rich in forests, glens, and streams, and it encompasses the dramatically glaciated Finger Lakes region of New York. The plateau falls away to the northwest, where it is edged by the Inland Coast (Chapter 5)—that is, the shores of Lakes Erie and Ontario and the island-dotted St. Lawrence River flowing northeast to the Atlantic.

The far north of the middle Atlantic states—northeastern New York State—is the special realm of the Adirondack Mountains (Chapter 6). The ancient roots of the Adirondacks may be 1.5 billion years old; the peaks began to rise some 60 to 50 million years ago. Composed of erosion-resistant metamorphic Grenville rock, they are among the highest mountains in the East. In the High Peaks region of the Adirondacks, for example, more than 40 peaks rise above 4,000 feet, topped by Mt. Marcy at 5,344 feet. Here are mountains, forests, lakes, and streams—a wilderness unsurpassed.

These northern reaches of the mid-Atlantic region were scoured by ancient ice sheets during successive ice ages. When the ice withdrew only about 12,000 years ago, it left its telltale prints on the land of New York State and northern New Jersey and Pennsylvania. It left lakes and gorges and spectacular waterfalls. It left eskers and drumlins, U-shaped valleys and cirques, kettle ponds, and perhaps the most fashionable aggregation of terminal moraines in the world—New York's Long Island.

Add to all these features a climate that can go to extremes. Prevailing westerly winds bring most middle Atlantic weather in alternating sequences of high pressure (fair weather) and low pressure (clouds and storms), each lasting a few days. But Arctic air from the northwest routinely drops 5 feet of snow on upstate New York in winter, while the entire mid-Atlantic region is blasted each year by "nor'easters"—storms brewed in offshore low-pressure systems and delivered with a punch by northeasterly winds. The Gulf Stream carries warm, moist, potentially stormy air northward along the coast; in summer, southerly winds blow in from the Bermuda High—a huge high-pressure system in the tropical part of the central Atlantic—to bring long, hot, hazy, lazy days.

Such diversity of landscape and season invites year-round exploration. Indeed, there are great things to see and do outdoors in America's middle Atlantic. This book presents some highlights—from the thunderous wonder of Niagara Falls to the subtler beauty of a cypress swamp or a cranberry bog—but it cannot contain all the manifest riches of the region. It leaves to you the the pleasure of discovering many other wonderful places for yourself. But the sites presented here are arranged to help you understand how the land fits together, how we have sacrificed it to our own imperfect schemes, and how, with greater awareness, we can protect and partially restore it. So let the following pages get you started; then let your own inclinations guide you to the abundant beauties of the middle Atlantic. ■

Rowing on the Potomac River near Fletcher's Boathouse

Atlantic
Seacoast

Montauk Point Lighthouse, New York

LIKE THE EAGER SUMMERTIME VISITORS of today, substantial
bits and pieces of the ancient Appalachian Mountains
headed for the beach. But that was a long, slow geologic
journey, for the seashore originated in some of the
oldest processes of the Earth's formation. Long before
its remarkably transformative river trip, borne along
by rain and streams to the edge of the sea, the sand
itself—where today we happily spread our beach
towels—was part of the weathered and decaying rock

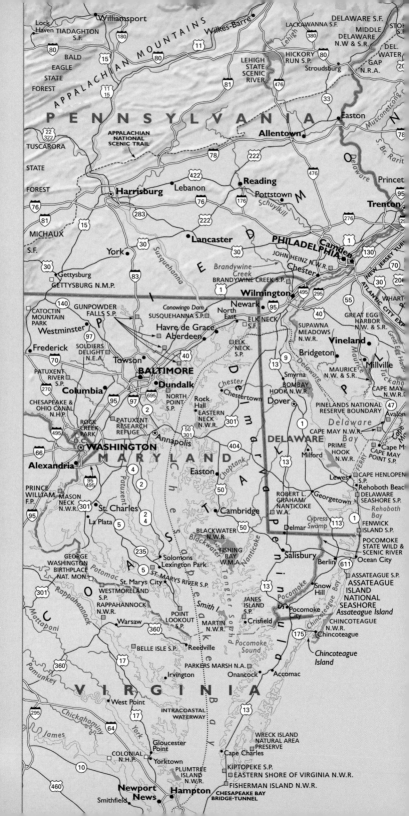

of Appalachian high peaks. During hundreds of millions of years, erosional processes worked away at the mountains and spread soft sediments to the east to form a broad, flat plain. The sea rose over this plain many times and receded again into its basin, each time leaving behind on the shore a wash of sediments and the bodies of sea creatures.

When the last of the glacial ice sheets began to melt about 18,000 years ago, the sea—then 300 feet below it present level—began to rise once more. Over thousands of years, the Atlantic rose to define the coastline of today. Underwater, beyond the seam where sea laps shore, lies a great expanse of submerged coastal plain 50 to 80 miles wide: the continental shelf. The seashore is still subject to incessant change, suddenly wrought by storms or slowly traced along the arc of geologic time. The line where sea meets shore today is the vital edge of ecosystems where wind, water, and weather still ceaselessly work.

When seawaters rose at the end of the Ice Age, they also flooded and covered over the mouths of old rivers that once flowed all the way across the coastal plain to a distant ocean. In this way the Susquehanna River lost one-third of its length, which disappeared beneath Atlantic waters to form Maryland's Chesapeake Bay—not really a bay at all, but a drowned river, or estuary. The great shallow expanses of the Chesapeake Bay and Delaware Bay (another estuary to the north) are among the most distinctive features of the middle Atlantic coast. Both bodies of water are so rich in aquatic life that they have been called "protein factories."

From the outflow of the Chesapeake Bay, the mid-Atlantic coast stretches north through Delaware and New Jersey in a long strand of sandy beaches. Behind the beaches spread salt marshes, swamps, and sandy-floored pine barrens, while just offshore lie the long, skinny barrier islands that shelter the beach and give this coast its uniquely serene character. To the north, the coastline makes a sharp right turn and New York's Long Island points out to sea, like a boat breaking free of its moorings. As with its companion barrier islands, Long Island is famous for its broad, sandy beaches, but it is in fact an Ice Age deposit of glacial moraines and outwash—shards of Canada and New England dumped by a receding ice sheet. The end of one of those moraines, the Ronkakama, pokes out on the island's easternmost tip at New York's Montauk Point—a distinctive, lonely outcrop along the whole expansive sandy shore of the middle Atlantic.

The gentle slope of the coastal plain, the sandy beach, the moderate tides, and the shelter of the barrier islands combine to make the middle Atlantic coast a subtle shore. As pioneering conservationist Rachel Carson observed in her 1955 classic *The Edge of the Sea,* the region's shoreline offers the visitor "a sense of antiquity" that is missing from rockier, more dramatic coasts; "the sea and the land lie here in a relation established gradually, over millions of years."

Today the serene shore is a summer playground. Much of the coast, in every state, is crowded with summer estates, cottages, condos, and simple shanties. When summer humidity rises and temperatures soar, waterfront

Chesapeake Bay marsh

near cities is carpeted with wall-to-wall beach blankets: Holidaymakers
flock to the boardwalks of Ocean City, Maryland; Atlantic City, New Jersey;
and Coney Island, New York. Yet many areas—from the National
Seashores on Fire Island in the north to Assatcague Island in the south—
have been set aside for the protection of aerial, terrestrial, and marine
wildlife and habitats. The configuration of the Piedmont region and coastal
plain—with several major river valleys cutting paths southeastward to
the sea—lays a natural path for migratory birds that congregate on middle
Atlantic beaches in spring and fall in incredible numbers, joining year-
round residents. Plover and sandpipers dart along beaches washed by
Sargassan kelp, while farther back in the hollow of dunes, migrating
swallows and warblers roost in thickets of bayberry and beach plum. In
saltmarshes where ocean waters meet fresh inland streams, Canada geese
and tundra swans make a meal of cordgrass, while blue herons and snowy
egrets patrol the shallow banks of freshwater creeks. Sheltered from the sea
by the outlying barrier islands, mid-Atlantic beaches and wetlands beckon
summer sun worshipers, surfers, crabbers, and anglers. Spring and fall
bring flocks of birders. And in winter, when a low sun silvers the sea and
black-backed gulls still stalk the surf's edge, dedicated beachcombers may
have miles of windswept shoreline to themselves. ◼

Chesapeake Bay

■ 3,200 square miles ■ Between continental coastline of Maryland and Virginia and Delmarva Peninsula ■ Year-round ■ Camping, boating, sailing, fishing, crabbing, biking, horseback riding, bird-watching, wildlife viewing ■ Contact Maryland Department of Natural Resources, Tawes Office Building, Annapolis, MD 21401; phone 877-620-8367. www.dnr.state.md.us

THE IMMENSE BODY OF WATER that splits Maryland and reaches southward into Virginia can be described only in superlatives. It's the longest bay in the United States (195 miles) and the largest (3,200 square miles). It has more miles of shoreline (4,600) than the entire West Coast of the United States; if you include its 150 tributaries, the shoreline stretches to 8,100 miles. All told, the bay and its tributaries cover an area of 4,400 square miles and drain approximately 64,000 square miles from New York to southern Virginia and west to the middle of Pennsylvania.

Some 1,300 feet under the floor of the lower bay lies a crater 56 miles wide, caused by the impact of a meteor that hit the Earth 35 million years ago. That impact may have slightly depressed the Earth's crust, leaving a shallow basin to be filled in later by rising seawaters. But that's not the whole story. Strictly speaking, the Chesapeake Bay is not a bay at all. It's an estuary—a river valley drowned by a rising sea. The river in this case is the Susquehanna, which originates in upstate New York and flows southward across Pennsylvania before entering the bay at its northern end. Other large rivers—the Potomac, James, Patuxent, Rappahannock, and York—flow into the bay from the west, while the Choptank and several smaller rivers enter the bay from the east. These latter rivers are considered tributaries of the Susquehanna, though their confluences have long been lost under the waters of the bay; technically, the estuary is that of the mighty Susquehanna alone. Here in the bay, river and sea meet and marry. The river's current pushes against the ocean's tide, which periodically pushes back. Fresh water and salt water mix to form brackish water of varying degrees of salinity, all the saltier near the wide mouth of the bay.

Surprisingly, this immense bay has an average depth of only 25 feet. Its shallowness makes it an enormous petri dish, filled with a sun-warmed soup in which phytoplankton, algae, and aquatic vegetation simmer and photosynthesize. Fed by nutrients from river, wetland, and tide, the bay and marshlands annually produce an astonishing mass of organic matter, calculated in tons per acre. A rich resting and feeding ground for hundreds of thousands of migrating shorebirds and waterfowl, this is also an abundant hatchery, nursery, and eatery for more than 250 species of fish, including striped bass, bluefish, sea trout, American shad, menhaden, spot, croaker, and drum. It's even more productive of shellfish: clams, mussels, oysters, and crabs. Long before the arrival of Europeans, the Algonquian people named these waters Chesepiooc, or "great shellfish bay." Today two million pounds of seafood are taken from the bay each year, including nearly a million pounds of blue crabs—worth about a billion dollars.

Sailing on the Chesapeake near Annapolis, Maryland

The delicate balance of this immensely productive ecosystem is badly threatened by development, deforestation, overfishing, overuse, and pollution. Fresh water is the lifeblood of the estuary, but with 15 million people now living in the watershed of the Chesapeake Bay, the rivers carry far less fresh, unpolluted water; New York fertilizer, West Virginia sewage, and Pennsylvania bathwater all find their way into the Chesapeake Bay. For this and other reasons that are still only vaguely understood, populations of striped bass, canvasback ducks, and oysters have dramatically declined. The bad news is that when this once beautiful and bountifully productive body of water was subjected to an ecological review in the 1990s, it received a rating of only 28 points out of a possible 100. The good news is that the evaluating organization, the Chesapeake Bay Foundation, is just one of many public and privately funded groups working all out to restore the bay to its full and former glory.

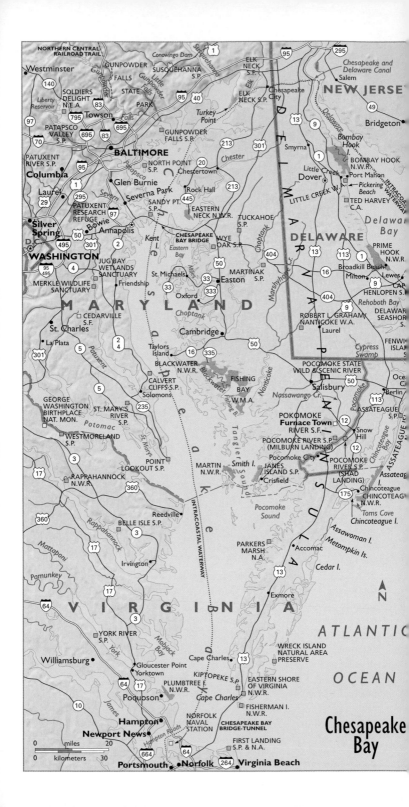
Chesapeake Bay

What to See and Do

On the Water

The Chesapeake Bay is best seen—and appreciated—by boat. Part of the Intracoastal Waterway, it is an important thoroughfare for watercraft of all descriptions. The bay's shore hosts the U.S. Naval Academy at Annapolis, Maryland, and the world's largest naval base at Hampton Roads, Virginia. With more than 500 harbors and countless boat launches and marinas, it's also home to more than a quarter million fishing and pleasure boats. Many local residents like to sail into natural areas on the fringes of the bay and explore by canoe, a pastime named "gunk-holing" for the muddy bottom you hit when you jump out of your boat.

If you plan to bring your own sail- or powerboat, as many visitors do, call the Maryland Department of Natural Resources, Fisheries Service *(800-688-3467)* and request "A Fisherman's Guide to Maryland Piers & Boat Ramps," a complete and compact map. You may want to head for one of the favorite large marinas on the bay, such as Herrington Harbour in Friendship, Zahniser's Yachting Center or Spring Cove Marina in Solomons, Somers Cove in Crisfield, the Annapolis City Marina, the Inner Harbor Marina in Baltimore (all in Maryland), or the York River Yacht Haven in Gloucester Point, Virginia. If you prefer a smaller marina, set your course in Maryland for the St. Michaels Town Dock Marina, Mears Yacht Haven in Oxford, Worton Creek Marina in Chestertown, or the Spring Cove Marina,

the Lankford Bay Marina, or the Sailing Emporium, all in Rock Hall. In Virginia, try the Tides Marinas in Irvington.

On the important question of where the fish bite, every angler has an opinion, and a few secrets. The answer is long and complicated because it depends upon a thorough knowledge of how different species of fish move around the bay at different seasons. That's before you get to the issues of what bait to use, and which technique. But the short answer is: the **Chesapeake Bay Bridge** and the **Chesapeake Bay Bridge-Tunnel.** The submerged parts of these engineering feats serve as artificial reefs, attracting crowds of fish. At the bridge, try for rockfish in spring, white perch and spot in summer, rockfish and gray trout in the fall. At the bridge-tunnel, fish for rockfish, flounder, bluefish, and black drum. If you prefer open water fishing, the broad flats and

Preferred Ports

For cruisers in need of supplies, repairs, service, good restaurants, and shoreside fun, Chesapeake Bay boaters give high marks to Solomons Island, Maryland, on the northern edge of the mouth of the Patuxent River (Western Shore); St. Michaels, Maryland, about midway along the bay's Eastern Shore (on the western bank of the Miles River); and, of course, Annapolis and Baltimore.

Woman's Work

Built in 1833, the Turkey Point Lighthouse is one of the highest on the Chesapeake Bay; the light is 129 feet above the water and visible for 13 miles. After the death of her lighthouse keeper husband, Fannie May Salter was appointed to the job in 1926 by President Calvin Coolidge. She maintained the light for 21 years, while raising three children. She used an oil lamp until the lighthouse was electrified in 1942; it was automated after she retired in 1947. Fannie May Salter was the last female lighthouse keeper in America.

deep channels of **Tangier Sound** are legendary. For river fishing, you won't do better than the **Potomac River,** revitalized after passage of the Clean Water Act of 1972. For 50 miles upriver of La Plata, Maryland, you'll find rockfish, channel catfish, largemouth bass, crappie, and white and yellow perch.

To fish in Maryland, you'll need a license and the current catch-and-release and size regulations. Contact Maryland Department of Natural Resources, Fisheries Services *(800-688-3467. www.dnr.state .md.us).* You'll also need a license to catch the legendary blue crab—plus a string, some raw chicken necks, a dip net, and considerable speed and coordination. Naturalists at **Janes Island State Park** will give you a hand getting started. A good rule: Take home only as many crabs as you can eat at your next meal.

If you have no boat of your own, don't despair. Chartered fishing party boats regularly set out from most of the ports named; alternatively, you can rent a fishing or sight-seeing boat at almost any town with a dock. State parks at waterfront locations rent rowboats, canoes, kayaks, and paddleboats, or they can direct you to nearby outfitters who offer private rentals, instruction, or guided trips. You might even consider opting for a learning holiday; the sailing schools of Annapolis are justly famous.

Be warned that the bay is not as tranquil as it often appears. It's stirred by tricky currents and subject to sudden storms. Know your abilities, and check with the Coast Guard for boating and weather information *(U.S. Coast Guard Boating Safety Hotline 800-368-5647).*

The Western Shore

Highways parallel the Chesapeake Bay only a few miles from its shores, so it's easy for landlubbers (or boat launchers) to travel the surrounding coastal plain and gain access to the bay itself down many a side road.

On the Western Shore, you'll find some particularly beautiful green getaways along the **Patuxent River** southeast of Washington. **Merkle Wildlife Sanctuary** *(Off US 301, Prince George's County. 301-888-1410)* is an important wetland, a preferred fall feeding ground for thousands of Canada geese, and a year-round haven for waterfowl and woodland birds. With binoculars at the ready, hike or mountain bike the 8.5-mile system of trails that meander

Great blue heron, Maryland's Eastern Shore

through the preserve's 1,670 acres of riverside marshlands and deciduous forests.

Nearby **Patuxent River State Park** *(between Md. 27 and Md. 97, Howard and Montgomery Counties, 301-924-2127)* is an undeveloped park where you can canoe, fish for trout, hike, mountain bike, or ride your horse through 6,648 acres. Or head for **Jug Bay Wetlands Sanctuary** *(1361 Wrighton Rd., Lothian. 410-741-9330)*, 622 acres of designated state wildland protecting a particularly beautiful stretch of the Patuxent River. Scan the river from the pier near the park office, then take a stroll on the **Black Walnut Creek Boardwalk Trail,** a mile-long loop through marsh, cypress swamp, and oak forest.

Northeast of Washington, midway along the Baltimore-Washington corridor, you'll find a surprising island of peace in the midst of the urban multimegaplex. **Patuxent Research Refuge** *(Laurel, Md. 301-497-5580)* is the only national wildlife refuge established to conduct wildlife research.

Because its mission is to study and test techniques to maintain and improve wildlife habitats, the 12,750-acre refuge is a mecca for environmental scientists—and an amazingly diverse resource for nature lovers. More than 50 ponds, impoundments, and natural wetlands are scattered among hardwood forests and piney woodlands. All are rich in wildlife. Stop at the **National Visitor Center** in the **South Tract** (south side of the Patuxent River) to see its state-of-the-art interactive displays on global environmental issues, then drive the 9-mile wildlife loop through the **North Tract** and hike or bike on more than 20 miles of trails.

Northeast of Baltimore in Harford and Baltimore Counties, **Gunpowder Falls State Park** *(2813 Jerusalem Rd., Kingsville. 410-592-2897)* follows the valleys of **Gunpowder Falls** and **Little Gunpowder Falls** rivers and their convergence in the Gunpowder River. This popular recreation center offers almost everything, from camping and horseback riding to trout fishing and wind-surfing. Its 16,000 acres, divided into several sections, is crossed by more than 100 miles of trails. The park also contains a 20-mile section of the hike-and-bike **Northern Central Railroad Trail,** connecting with the York County Heritage Rail-Trail in Pennsylvania.

At the head of the Chesapeake Bay, turn north into the scenic valley of the lower Susquehanna. You can camp and fish in 2,639 protected acres on the river's west bank—before it enters the bay—at **Susquehanna State Park** (*Off Md. 155, 3 miles N of Harve de Grace. 410-557-7994*). You may see the park's bald eagles fishing, too, at Conowingo Dam. Then head south again and east onto the Delmarva (Delaware/Maryland/Virginia) Peninsula to the Eastern Shore.

The Eastern Shore

If you're uncomfortable in the heavy metropolitan traffic unavoidable along the Baltimore-Washington corridor, head directly for the more rural Eastern Shore of Maryland. The most scenic roads lie in this region, which retains some of the isolated character and spaciousness it enjoyed before the Chesapeake Bay Bridge and the Chesapeake Bay Bridge-Tunnel connected it to the "mainland." With its scenic rivers, beautiful wildlife management areas, and active wildlife refuges (see entries pp. 29-45), it is an especially rewarding sector of the bay area. ■

Getting Snippy

Every one of the Chesapeake Bay's famous blue crabs (*Callinectes sapidus*) begins its life near the mouth of the bay as a microscopic free-floating zoea. After several moltings—shedding its shell to replace it with a larger one—the zoea reaches larval stage. Looking like a tiny cross between a crab and a lobster, the larva is known as a megalops. It drifts into the ocean for about six weeks, returning to the bay to molt again and become the "first crab." This minuscule creature, no bigger than a pellet of birdshot, begins migrating north into the tidal rivers and upper reaches of the bay. In 12 to 18 months, the crab grows to measure 5 inches across its back. Then the green-backed adult crab is recognizable by the blue coloring on its large claw. It also reaches sexual maturity and

mates to begin the life cycle anew. After mating, the males remain in the fresher waters of the bay. The females migrate south, arriving by fall at the spawning grounds at the mouth of the bay, where the eggs will hatch the following summer. Although each female carries an egg mass of about two million eggs, fewer than one percent of them will reach maturity. Many immature crabs will provide food for rays, striped bass, bluefish, gulls, and wading birds. Mature crabs are best known for their role as food for people. Commercial crabbers in the Chesapeake Bay take 80 million pounds of crabs each year (in crab pots and by dredging the bottom); recreational crabbers may harvest almost as much. The crab's fate is all in its name. The word *Callinectes* in its scientific handle means "beautiful swimmer," but *sapidus* means "tasty."

Elk Neck State Park

Elk Neck State Park

■ 2,188 acres ■ North end of Chesapeake Bay, south of I-95 and US 40 on Md. 272 S ■ Best months April-Oct. ■ Camping, hiking, boating, canoeing, swimming, fishing, biking, bird-watching, wildlife viewing, wildflower viewing ■ Adm. fee ■ Contact the park, 4395 Turkey Point Rd., North East, MD 21901; phone 410-287-5333. elkneckstatepark.com

THE SKINNY FINGER OF LAND—Elk Neck—lying between the Chesapeake Bay and the Elk River is the northernmost of the many peninsulas that jut into the bay. This location, verging on the Piedmont, helps explain its unusual topographical features: hills and sea cliffs. At **Elk Neck State Forest** near the base of the peninsula and Elk Neck State Park at its point, the rolling hills are heavily wooded with oak, hickory, tulip poplar, and abundant mountain laurel. No, you won't sight elk here—elk were killed off in Maryland and Virginia before 1840—but you will see white-tailed deer.

The park offers 278 campsites and 13 cabins, including some fronting the Elk River. It has a swimming beach; a boat-launching site where you can rent boats, paddle boats, kayaks, and canoes; and 7 miles of trails leading through varied wildlife habitats. Don't miss the 2-mile (round-trip) **Blue Trail,** which leads through forest and hilltop meadows to the old **Turkey Point Lighthouse** (see sidebar p. 26) atop a 100-foot bluff at the southern tip of the peninsula, with fine views of the Chesapeake Bay. Each fall, Turkey Point is the site of a Hawk Watch. Ospreys pass through in September, followed in October by sharp-shinned, broad-winged, and red-tailed hawks, merlins, kestrels, bald eagles, and vultures, all taking wing with resident falcons and harriers.

One sad feature is that a housing development, complete with close-clipped lawns in place of natural vegetation, has somehow insinuated itself between the body of the park and Turkey Point; you therefore have to drive through a suburban enclave to reach the forest trail to the light-house. This unexpected dose of "civilization" comes as a shock—and as a reminder of the importance of conservation. ■

Eastern Neck National Wildlife Refuge

■ 2,285 acres ■ Eastern Maryland on Eastern Neck Island, 6 miles south of Rock Hall, MD ■ Best months late Oct.–March ■ Hiking, boating, fishing, crab-bing, biking, bird-watching, wildlife viewing ■ Contact the refuge, 1730 Eastern Neck Rd., Rock Hall, MD 21661; phone 410-639-7056

EASTERN NECK ISLAND was a fishing ground for Native Americans, as shell middens and stone artifacts found there testify, and subsequently for Chesapeake watermen. Strategically located at the confluence of the Chester River and Chesapeake Bay, it was among the first places settled in the New World. After being cleared and cultivated, by the late 17th cen-tury it had become the estate of Kent County's most successful citizen, Joseph Wickes. Parceled out in small farms, orchards, and woodlots, the island remained in the hands of Wickes family heirs until 1902. Over the next 50 years, some plots were sold to wealthy outsiders for hunting lodges. When a developer planned a subdivision of 293 houses in the 1950s, however, the local community prevailed upon the Fish and Wildlife Service to acquire the island for wildlife preservation.

Today Eastern Neck is a place you have to want to get to. Although it's only 15 miles from Annapolis as the crow flies, it's 50 miles from the Chesapeake Bay Bridge—on secondary roads down the long peninsula. Eastern Neck is on the way to nowhere but itself, yet it is well worth the trip. Crossing the arching bridge over **Eastern Neck Narrows** to the island has the effect of a brief space flight to a far better place—a place of grasslands and spartina marshes, hedgerows and fields, sweet gum and tulip poplar trees, holly and pawpaw, great blue herons and red foxes, fal-

Tundra Swans

Winter brings to the Chesapeake Bay the weird piercing yodel of the tundra swan (Cygnus columbianus). Hunted during the 18th and 19th centuries for its fine white feathers and its meat, the tundra swan was almost exterminated. Now it's staging a comeback, appearing in big vocal numbers each fall to winter around the Chesapeake Bay as well as along the Atlantic coast as far south as North Carolina.

With signs of spring, usually in late February or early March, tundra swans foregather at staging areas, massing for the long flight to the coastal regions of the high Arctic and Alaska, where they breed in summer. The lower Sus-quehanna River just north of the Chesapeake Bay is one such staging area, where come March you might see 12,000 tundra swans waiting for a warm wind north.

You can't miss these glorious birds. The adults—pure white except for their black feet and bills and a tiny yellow spot in front of each eye—measure 4.25 feet from head to tail and weigh approximately 20 pounds. Their wingspan is 7 feet. Occasionally, when they are flying low, you can hear the steady whoosh, whoosh, whoosh of their wings. And when you see these great white fliers catching the last light against a deepening winter sky, it puts you in mind of the flight of angels.

cons and woodpeckers, bluebirds and chickadees, 33 kinds of waterfowl, and dozens of species of butterflies. This is a place where, in late October, the air fills with tundra swans (see sidebar) arriving for the winter.

Explore the island for yourself by driving, hiking, or biking its 6 miles of roads and trails. Although there's no driving loop, as there is on many national wildlife refuges, several county roads cut across the island, and Eastern Neck Road passes right down the center. The island's four designated nature trails are short but rewarding, especially the **Tubby Cove Boardwalk Trail;** after a few hundred yards it culminates in an observation platform that overlooks the Chesapeake Bay. With luck, you'll get a glimpse of some of the more famous species in residence here: the bald eagle, the peregrine falcon, and the endangered bushy-tailed Delmarva Peninsula fox squirrel (see sidebar p. 34). To explore the 1,000 acres of tidal marsh that surround the island, launch your boat, canoe, or kayak at historic **Bogles Wharf Landing,** where packet boats docked from colonial times until 1924.

Spring and fall are the best times to see migratory birds. Songbird numbers peak in late April and again in late September, when masses of waterfowl move onto the refuge as well. Winter brings a special peace—and a profusion of birds. Peak years have numbers reaching 20,000 Canada geese, 15,000 canvasbacks, and 7,000 tundra swans, plus countless mallard, wigeons, black ducks, lesser scaup, pintail, redheads, teal, buffleheads, oldsquaws, and white-winged scoters. January is the time, too, to look for eagles and great horned owls, busy building nests. ■

Blackwater National Wildlife Refuge

■ 25,000 acres ■ Eastern Shore of Maryland, 12 miles south of Cambridge
■ Best seasons fall-spring ■ Hiking, boating, fishing, biking, bird-watching, wildlife
viewing ■ Adm. fee ■ Contact the refuge, 2145 Key Wallace Dr., Cambridge, MD
21613; phone 410-228-2677. blackwater.fws.gov/

IN BLACKWATER'S FORESTS AND MARSHES, shaggy loblolly pines and tall
Olney "three-square" bulrushes reach the northern limit of their ranges,
lending a distinct southern flair to the landscape. The open forests,
cleared of undergrowth by seasonal flooding, the sprawling marshes, and
the broad expanse of the Blackwater River and the Chesapeake Bay seem
infinitely spacious. Seen on a misty morning or under a red sunset,
Blackwater is as beautiful as it is important in the great scheme of natural
things. Set up in 1933 mainly to protect a stopover for migrating ducks,
it now hosts one of the largest populations of nesting bald eagles—up
to 200 spend the winter here. It's also the chief wintering ground for

Kayaking on Blackwater River, Blackwater NWR

migrating Canada geese, which must have noticed that 6,000 of their brethren residing here year-round are comfortably fat. Migrants first appear in September and reach their maximum numbers by early November: 35,000 Canada geese and 15,000 ducks. From mid-October to mid-March, peak viewing season for wintering waterfowl, you'll see mallard, black ducks, blue-winged teal, green-winged teal, wood ducks, wigeon, pintail, and more than a dozen other duck species as well as snow geese and tundra swans. Year-round residents in the woodlands include owls, woodpeckers, bobwhites, woodcocks, and turkeys; warblers, orioles, flycatchers, and vireos are annual summer visitors. The refuge's official bird list names 287 regular species. In the woodlands, too, are white-tailed deer and sika deer—actually a small species of Asian elk introduced to area islands in 1916—and some of the few remaining highly endangered Delmarva Peninsula fox squirrels (see sidebar p. 34).

The Fish and Wildlife Service manages Blackwater, as it does all national wildlife refuges, to protect wildlife and habitats. Blackwater also administers **Martin National Wildlife Refuge,** located to the south on Smith Island. Refuge managers manipulate water levels in freshwater impoundments to suit the seasonal needs of various species; they seed

The Delmarva Peninsula Fox Squirrel

Larger than the common gray squirrel, the Delmarva Peninsula fox squirrel is usually pale gray—almost white in the case of older animals—and possesses a great bushy tail, like a fox. It likes to nest in large old trees; and prefers open forest with little shrubbery because it travels and feeds on the ground. The squirrel also feeds in farmlands on corn, soybeans, and other crops.

Once its range included the whole Delmarva Peninsula, the Eastern Shore of Virginia, southeastern Pennsylvania, and southern New Jersey, but today the squirrel is found only in Maryland's Kent, Queen Anne's, Talbot, and Dorchester Counties, in Delaware, and in Virginia's Chincoteague National Wildlife Refuge (see pp. 40-41), where it was introduced. Intensive lumbering and development are blamed for its decline. The Fish and Wildlife Service and others are working on saving the squirrel. As you walk through the forests of the Eastern Shore, be on the lookout for this lovely vanishing breed.

more than 600 acres in millet, buckwheat, winter rye, and other grains to help refuel migratory waterfowl.

Sadly, since the 1940s, the refuge has lost about 7,000 acres of marshland to "natural" causes—rising water levels, subsidence, erosion, and the presence of the non-native nutria, a rodent that eats the vegetation's roots—aggravated by development and pollution. Normally the marsh would regenerate itself farther upstream, but development outside the refuge already blocks any natural movement of the marsh, making what remains of these wetlands all the more valuable.

Although Blackwater abuts the Chesapeake Bay, the area open to the public lies about 10 miles inland. Begin your visit at the visitor center (*Key Wallace Dr.*) to pick up interpretive leaflets for the refuge's driving loop and trails. Then slowly cruise the 6.5-mile **Wildlife Drive** past freshwater ponds and fields, through woodlands, and along the edge of the marshes. Walking and biking are permitted on the road, but you will get closer to wildlife by using your vehicle as a kind of mobile blind.

Along the drive you'll find trailheads for hikes. The short (onethird-mile), wheelchair-accessible **Marsh Edge Trail** provides a good close-up introduction to Blackwater's habitats on the very edge, where oak and loblolly pine forests give way in the transition zone to shrubby wax myrtle and bayberry; these in turn yield to the marsh's cattails and three-square bulrushes. The half-mile **Woods Trail** circles through open pine and oak woodlands where you may see Delmarva Peninsula fox squirrels which live here in their largest concentration. When leaving the refuge, turn into nearby Shorters Wharf Road; though mainly outside Blackwater's boundaries, it cuts across it, affording interesting perspectives on the differences between preservation and "progress." ■

Janes Island State Park

■ 3,147 acres ■ Southeast Maryland ■ Best seasons spring and fall ■ Camping, boating, kayaking, canoeing, fishing, crabbing, biking, bird-watching, wildlife viewing ■ Contact the park, 26280 Alfred Lawson Dr., Crisfield, MD 21817; phone 410-968-1565 or 888-432-2267 (camping reservations). www.dnr.state.md.us/publiclands/eastern/janesisland.html

ALTHOUGH A SLICE OF JANES ISLAND STATE PARK hugs the mainland shore of the Little Annemessex River *(Md. 413, near Crisfield, Md.),* most of the park (2,900 acres) is an island—or rather an island-shaped maze of tidal marshes about 6 miles long and 1.5 miles wide. In other words, it's more or less under water a good deal. This is not the place for a hike.

The island wasn't always so soggy; it once had high ground and residents, before the Chesapeake Bay rose to reclaim its own. The whole point of the present park is to give you a personal view of those recovered wetlands. To that end, the park is a key player in a new nature tourism program of the Maryland Department of Natural Resources; by special agreement, the DNR authorizes private outfitters to operate within the park, thereby increasing recreational opportunities for visitors (see Resources, p. 281).

The park itself provides 25 boat slips (first-come, first-served) and rents motorboats, canoes, and kayaks. It also maintains six well-marked and mapped interlocking water trails—30 miles in all—laid out around and through the marsh. On these you're likely to see otters, muskrat, raccoons, water snakes, and an array of waterfowl and shorebirds from gadwalls to glossy ibises. You might catch your dinner, too, for the island lies in **Tangier Sound**—prime fishing and crabbing waters. Four water trails follow the island's small creeks and interior waterways. Sheltered from wind and waves, these routes require little paddling experience. They range in length from 2.5 to 4 miles. Two longer trails (5 miles and 12.5 miles) entail paddling along the western shore of the island in the open water of Tangier Sound— a trickier enterprise calling for some expertise. Approximate paddling times range from 90 minutes on novice trails to eight hours for open water routes. Outfitters are available if you prefer paddling with a guide or want to venture farther afield. Luckily there's just enough dry land at the Janes Island mainland site to provide 104 water-view campsites, as well as rental cabins sheltered among loblolly pines. ■

Cabin in the pines, Janes Island State Park

Pocomoke Wild and Scenic River

■ 73 miles long ■ Delmarva Peninsula, access at Snow Hill or Pocomoke City ■ Best seasons spring and fall. Hunting activity in state forest Sept.-April ■ Camping, hiking, boating, canoeing, kayaking, fishing, biking, bird-watching, wildlife viewing ■ Contact Pocomoke River State Forest and Park, 3461 Worcester Hwy., Snow Hill, MD 21863; phone 410-632-2566. www.dnr.state. md/publiclands/pocomokeriver.html or Worcester County Tourism, 113 Franklin St., Snow Hill, MD 21863; phone 800-852-0335 or 410-632-3617

THE PEACEFUL POCOMOKE RIVER rises in the Cypress Swamp in Delaware, flows southwesterly across Maryland, and empties into Pocomoke Sound at the Chesapeake Bay. In the east it's a narrow stream overarched by riverine trees and creepers, but as it flows west it broadens into an open river, perhaps 200 yards wide in some stretches, watched over by soaring bald eagles. The river is subject to bay tides of nearly 3 feet, but it brews its color inland from the tannic acid of decaying cypress and oak leaves— the rich, clear mahogany of strong tea. (The tides, treacherous currents, and surprising depth of the river—up to 45 feet—make swimming inadvisable.) Snowy egrets, ospreys, and great blue herons dwell in the wetlands that fringe the river's 73-mile course; pileated woodpeckers and the rare and beautiful prothonotary warblers haunt the swampy woodlands, where cypress knees breach the surface like knobby periscopes. All told, birders have spotted more than 150 species.

Between Snow Hill and Pocomoke City, the river flows through the loblolly pines and cypress swamps of 14,753-acre **Pocomoke River State Forest and Park.** Here two areas, **Milburn Landing** on the north side of the river and **Shad Landing** on the south, provide campgrounds, cabins, picnic grounds, and boat landings. The larger Shad Landing area also offers canoe and boat rentals, a nature center, and a 25-meter swimming pool. Either one makes a fine base camp for exploring the Pocomoke.

What to See and Do

Hiking and Biking Trails

A good place to start is **Furnace Town** *(410-632-2032),* in the heart of Pocomoke Forest about 5 miles northwest of Snow Hill off Md. 12. Named for a gigantic smelting furnace (a National Historic Mechanical Engineering Landmark), Furnace Town replicates the 19th-century town that once clustered around it. The town processed bog iron—that is, iron ore dissolved by the acidic water of the cypress swamps and deposited along boggy creek banks. In the heyday of the bog iron industry (1828-1850), smelted ore was shipped down Nassawango Creek to the Pocomoke River and the Chesapeake Bay.

Today the lands along the creek from Furnace Town to the Pocomoke (some 3,000 acres) are protected by the Nature Conservancy,

Bald Cypress, Pocomoke River

which maintains the **Paul Liefer Nature Trail** at Furnace Town. Do walk this beautiful mile-long trail, along the old canal towpath and on boardwalks through the cypress swamp—it will give you a deeper sense of the natural environment and of the ways people have interacted with it.

The **Bald Cypress Nature Trail** at Milburn Landing also provides a good introduction to Pocomoke habitats, encompassing in the space of a mile a loblolly pine grove, a mixed hardwood forest, and a bald cypress swamp. There are other hiking trails in the state forest as well, and a 4-mile nature-exercise trail at Pocomoke City.

For cyclists, the well-marked, 100-mile **View Trail 100** cuts away from the river and traces a big loop to the north and south of it through the gentle fields and forests of Worcester County. For a map, contact Worcester County Tourism.

Canoeing and Boating

Today the head of the navigable Nassawango Creek lies 1.6 miles south of Furnace Town at Red House Road—a popular put-in point for canoes and kayaks on the **Bogiron Trail.** From there it's an easy 2.5-mile paddle to the Pocomoke River, where you can choose to head upstream to Snow Hill (2 miles) or downstream to Shad Landing (2 miles). Either way can be an easy trip—depending, of course, upon the tide.

For a map of these and other water trails, contact Worcester County Tourism. For tidal information, you can check the National Oceanic and Atmospheric Administration's website at www.co-ops.nos.noaa.gov). The Pocomoke River Canoe Company *(312 N. Washington St., Snow Hill, MD 21863. 410-632-3971)* can also advise you about tides, as well as rent you canoes, kayaks, and boats at both Shad Landing and Snow Hill. In addition, it offers instruction, trips, guide and shuttle service, and canoeing inn to inn.

A shorter, easy paddle ideal for beginners or families is the **Corkers Creek Canoe Trail,** a 1.5-mile loop nature trail that begins and ends at Shad Landing. (With north or west winds, do the loop clockwise; with south or east winds, head the other way.)

Other paddling trips—for nature study or just for fun—are regularly offered by the park and outfitted by Pocomoke River Canoe Company. An option for those who don't want to paddle their own canoe is the excursion boat; it makes the round-trip from Snow Hill to Shad Landing several times a day. *(Call Captain Carmine 410-623-3003 or 888-568-3003.)*

Fishing

From boat or bank, here's what you might catch: yellow or white perch, eel, gar, sunfish, pickerel, catfish, crappie, bluegill, herring, spot, croaker, bluefish, and largemouth bass. Unless you fish from one of the designated free fishing areas on the riverbank, you'll need a Chesapeake Bay sport fishing license. You can get information and a fishing license at the state park. For information, licenses, and fishing gear, check in with the friendly folk at Sea Hawk Sports Center in Pocomoke City *(643 Ocean Hwy. 410-957-0198).* ∎

Assateague beach

Assateague Island

■ 48,000 acres ■ Barrier island off coast of Maryland and Virginia ■ Best seasons spring and fall ■ Camping, hiking, boating, kayaking, canoeing, swimming, surfing, surf-fishing, biking, bird-watching, wildlife viewing, wild ponies ■ Adm. fee for refuge and national seashore. Adm. fee for state park in summer ■ Contact Assateague Island National Seashore, 7206 National Seashore Ln., Berlin, MD 21811; phone 410-641-1441 www.nps.gov/asis. Assateague Island SP, 7307 Stephen Decatur Hwy., Berlin, MD 21811; phone 410-641-2120. www.dnr .state.md.us/publiclands/eastern/assateague.html. Chincoteague NWR, P.O. Box 62, Chincoteague Island, VA 23336; phone 757-336-6122. http://chinco.fws.gov

LYING OFF THE COAST of Maryland and Virginia, Assateague is one of the longest Atlantic barrier islands—currently 37 miles—and arguably one of the wildest and most beautiful. It once adjoined Ocean City, Maryland, but in 1933 a hurricane opened an inlet through the land and cut Assateague loose. Since then the northern end of the island (in Maryland)

Barrier Islands

Very few of the world's coasts are cloaked by barrier islands, but the Atlantic seaboard from New York to central Florida is one of them. Long, skinny islands lying parallel to the coastline, 1 to 8 miles offshore, these barriers safeguard the mainland from the open ocean.

Barrier islands are never found along rocky or precipitous shores, for they are born on gentle sedimentary slopes like that of the Atlantic coastal plain and continental shelf. Precisely how they form, though, is a matter of geological speculation. They consist roughly of five zones: a broad oceanside beach; a range of primary dunes held in place by beach grasses; an "interdune" leeward depression where beach heather grows with scattered shrubs; a secondary dune ridge that may support forests of pine and oak; and a bayside shore fringed with salt marshes and penetrated by tidal creeks. In the forest zone of some islands, such as Assateague, low-lying hollows expose the water table in freshwater ponds. Formed originally of nothing but sand, the barrier islands are works in progress—subject to daily revision by wind, wave, and storm.

has marched about 1,000 feet closer to the mainland, while the hook at the south end (in Virginia) has grown by a couple of miles.

Created by one storm, Assateague was saved by another. In the 1950s developers paved a 15-mile stretch of "Baltimore Boulevard" from the north end of Assateague to the Virginia state line and laid out 9,000 building lots on more than 130 cross streets. When a storm in 1962 literally blew away the infant subdivision, the Park Service was persuaded to create **Assateague Island National Seashore** in its place. Today a few street signs and weathered chunks of Baltimore Boulevard may still be seen along the **Dune Walk Trail**—reminders of the island's narrow escape. The sunbaked asphalt is useful only to gulls, who crack clams and crabs by dropping them on the rock-hard surface.

Near the island's north end, the national seashore abuts a second, much smaller park: **Assateague Island State Park** (680 acres), operated by the Maryland Department of Natural Resources. The National Park Service maintains the **Barrier Island Visitor Center** on Md. 611 on the mainland just before the bridge to the island. Entrances to both the state park and the national seashore lie just over the bridge.

The southern, or Virginia, part of the island was preserved earlier—purchased with Duck Stamp revenues (see p. 71) and designated in 1943 as **Chincoteague National Wildlife Refuge.** (Don't be confused by the fact that Chincoteague refuge is mainly on Assateague Island, not—as you might expect—on neighboring Chincoteague Island.) The 14,000-plus acre refuge also encompasses nearby Assawoman Island, Morris Island, and parts of Chincoteague, Metompkin, and Cedar Islands. Originally established to save wintering waterfowl, with an emphasis on the greater snow goose, the refuge now restores and manages habitat for hundreds of species of migratory and resident coastal wildlife. The U.S. Fish and Wildlife Service maintains a visitor center at the south end of the refuge, while the Park Service runs the **Toms Cove Visitor Center** at the south end of the beach.

Here's the catch: To get from the public-use facilities at the north end of the island to those at the south end, you can walk or paddle 26 miles, or you can drive 55 miles on the mainland. The recommended route from north to south is: Md. 611 to Md. 376 west to Berlin; US 113 south to the Snow Hill vicinity; Md. 12 to the Virginia line, where the road becomes Va. 679; Va. 175 east across Chincoteague Island to Assateague Island. That sounds more complicated than it is, but be prepared for traffic jams on summer holiday weekends: Assateague Island is less than a day's drive away from 37 million people. The national seashore and the wildlife refuge are among the most visited facilities of their kind in the nation. Two and a half million migratory *Homo sapiens* touch down at Assateague each year, most of them in the summer, sunburned, and reeking of bug spray. But because to this day there is no "Baltimore Boulevard" to facilitate transit up and down the island, dedicated beachcombers can still find a wild and pristine piece of it for themselves alone.

What to See and Do

From the Beach

In summer, lifeguarded swimming beaches with bathhouses and changing facilities are maintained on both ends of the island—at the national seashore and the state park in Maryland, and at the Toms Cove beach in Virginia. The beach at the state park also offers surfboarding and surf fishing.

The rule for surf-fishing is catch and release—except for what you can eat—and it's permitted almost everywhere except the guarded swimming beaches. In Maryland, a license is required only for night fishing; in Virginia the requisite permit is available at the Toms Cove Visitor Center. Naturalists give summertime demonstrations for those new to the sport.

The bay is the place for shellfishing. The preferred method for catching clams is to rake the bottom, whereas crabs are usually caught with a baited line (chicken necks are a favorite) and a scoop net. The rule is to take only what you can eat promptly. Combing the beach for shells, another popular pastime, is best done after a storm at the southern beaches of **Toms Cove** hook.

The shallow waters of Chincoteague Bay at the Maryland end are perfect for canoeing and give access to four bayside backcountry camps maintained by the Park Service. Canoes can be rented on weekends in April, May, September, and October (daily in summer) from concessionaires located at the Bayside picnic area in Maryland. Call the national seashore for information.

At the Virginia end, boats are permitted to land only at **Fishing Point** but never from mid-March through August, when threatened

Assateague Island marsh

piping plover are nesting on the beach.

On the Island

Assateague Island State Park has a comfortable campground (more than 300 sites) on the ocean side, with bathhouses equipped with flush toilets and hot showers. Call ahead for reservations May through September.

The national seashore has two spacious campgrounds at the Maryland end, Oceanside and Bayside, with more than 100 sites. They are officially "primitive" (chemical toilets and cold showers). At Oceanside some spaces are reserved for walk-in tent campers only, and it's hard to beat these beautiful, widely spaced sites set among bayberry shrubs just behind the dunes. Reservations can be made from mid-May through October *(800-365-2267)*.

No camping is permitted on the southern part of Assateague Island, but there are private

campgrounds not far from the Chincoteague National Wildlife Refuge, on Chincoteague Island *(Chincoteague Island Chamber of Commerce 757 336 6161)*

To get away from it all, head for one of the designated backcountry campsites on the Maryland end. Three ocean sites are open to hikers year-round, as are four sites on the bay (accessible by canoe). Be forewarned: The ocean campsite closest to a parking lot is a 4-mile walk. You'll need a use permit,

issued at the national seashore (north end) or Toms Cove Visitor Center (south end).

A word of advice: Camping for the first time at the seashore may be a rough surprise. In summertime, factor in hot sun, high winds, blowing sand, and the stickiness of salt water—all part of the romance of seaside camping for the initiated, but no fun for the hot, sticky, sunburned first-time beach camper chasing his tent over the dunes. Plan accordingly—and

Assateague pony

Assateague's Ponies

Misty of Chincoteague, the gentle pony of Marguerite Henry's award-winning book, captured the hearts of generations of American children. Today Misty's friends and relatives—not ponies, actually, but horses—freely roam Assateague Island. Most are bigger than Misty, thanks to western mustangs introduced to the island in the 1970s to diversify blood lines. The mustangs died in the first year, but not before spreading some tall genes. Paint, sorrel, and golden buckskin, the horses are easily spotted grazing on cordgrass in a salt marsh or nibbling rosehips in the interdune scrub.

According to legend, the horses' ancestors swam ashore from a wrecked Spanish galleon. Historians say it's more likely they strayed from colonists' herds put to graze offshore to escape the taxman. Two herds, each numbering about 150 feral horses, live on the island today, separated by a fence at the Maryland-Virginia state line. The Park Service manages the Maryland herd. The Virginia herd (known as Chincoteague ponies) is owned by the Chincoteague Volunteer Fire Company and grazes by special-use permit on the national wildlife refuge. On the last Wednesday and Thursday in July—Pony Penning—firemen-cowboys round up the animals and make them swim the channel to Chincoteague Island. There, on the following day, foals and yearlings are sold at public auction. Thousands of spectators are drawn to Chincoteague and Assateague each year to witness the pony swim, and many pay up to $7,000 for the privilege of owning one of the famous breed (*Chincoteague Chamber of Commerce 757-336-6161*).

Warning: Because the feral horses are wild, they may behave in unpredictable ways. Every year many visitors are kicked or bitten—and horses conditioned to seek roadside handouts are killed by cars. Observe the ponies as you would any wild animal: from a distance.

don't forget an extra supply of drinking water.

Jump start your island exploration at the north end by taking the **nature trails** of the national seashore. Three self-guided half-mile trails are located within a mile of the entrance station (3 miles past the visitor center). These introduce the plant communities of dune, marsh, and forest—very different from their counterparts on the mainland just across the bay—and some of the creatures that inhabit them. Hiking the windswept endless beaches to the northern tip or south toward Virginia is limited only by your own stamina.

From the entrance station some 3 miles of paved paths give cyclists access to the nature trails. Bikes can be rented in summer from concessionaires located at the Bayside Picnic Area in Maryland. Call the national seashore for information.

At the south end, about 14 miles of trails thread the forests and marshes of the 14,000-acre wildlife refuge, more than half open to bicycles. A 3.2-mile self-guided **wildlife loop** is open all day to hikers and cyclists, and after 3 P.M. to vehicles as well. It circles freshwater impoundments and rides the edge between freshwater marsh and maritime forest.

Serious hikers can walk the length of the island on the beach. Because you can't camp in Virginia, it's best to start at the south end (*register at Toms Cove Visitor Center*) and cover the 13-plus miles to the first oceanside backcountry camp in Maryland while you're fresh. Also recommended is the 7 miles of wild beach north of Assateague State Park to the Ocean City Inlet.

In summer, naturalists at both ends of the island offer many bird, wildlife, and nature walks. (*Consult the visitor centers for programs.*) All of the national wildlife refuge's 14 miles of accessible trails provide excellent opportunities for bird-watching, wildlife viewing, and nature photography. More than 320 species of birds have been tallied at the refuge, the most conspicuous summer residents being the varieties of egrets, herons, and ibises. In late summer empty beaches fill with more than 40 species of migrating shorebirds. In September and October come kestrels, hawks, falcons, and merlins. Thousands of snow geese, black ducks, mallard, and pintail winter on the refuge.

Among land dwellers, white-tailed deer and Sika elk are easiest to spot. More evasive are the smaller residents: red foxes, opossums, raccoons, muskrat, cottontail rabbits, meadow jumping mice, toads, snakes (none poisonous), and a population of endangered Delmarva Peninsula fox squirrels (see sidebar p. 34) introduced here to save the species. From the beaches, you might even see common or bottlenose dolphins.

The Chincoteague National Wildlife Refuge is planning to open an education and administrative center in March, 2003—the 100th birthday of the national wildlife refuge system. In addition to interactive exhibits and a teacher resource room, the building will house an large auditorium. ■

Cape Henlopen State Park

■ 5,000 acres ■ Delaware coast ■ Best seasons spring-fall ■ Camping, hiking, swimming, surfing, fishing, surf-fishing, biking, bird-watching, wildlife viewing ■ Adm. fee in summer ■ Contact the park, 42 Cape Henlopen Dr., Lewes, DE 19958; phone 302-645-8983. www.destateparks.com/chsp/chsp.htm or Delaware Division of Parks and Recreation, P.O. Box 1401, Dover, DE 19903; phone 302-739-4702

DELAWARE'S SEACOAST IS ONLY 25 miles long, but it is the setting for three state parks where the Atlantic rolls in to break upon fine, broad beaches. Del. 1 runs straight through the middle of two long, thin parks—3-mile-long **Fenwick Island State Park** *(302-539-9060)* in southern Delaware and 7-mile-long **Delaware Seashore State Park** *(302-227-2800)* midway up the coast—making their beaches convenient if not exactly remote from civilization. Farther north, where the Atlantic pours into Delaware Bay, stands the largest of these coastal parks, Cape Henlopen State Park. Like the Chesapeake Bay, 50-mile-long Delaware Bay is not a true bay but an estuary—of the Delaware River. Cape Henlopen occupies the broad, sandy hook at its mouth, enjoying the best of both the estuarine and the maritime worlds: a quarter-mile-long fishing pier extending into the bay

Cape Henlopen Lighthouse near Rehoboth

on one side and 2 miles of Atlantic beach on the other.

Its strategic location thrust Cape Henlopen into military history long before it became a park in 1964. Gun emplacements, bunkers, and observation towers remaining from its World War II days as Fort Miles cast a somber shadow; still, the bunker atop the Great Dune and the single observation tower open to the public provide sweeping views of the bay and ocean. Hiking trails pass through grassy dunes and salt marsh and along the edge of the woods beside a brackish pond. The most common starting point for these trails as well as the 2-mile bike path is the nature center *(0.5 mile from park entrance)*. The campground's 158 campsites under the pines are sized like the state—very tiny. But most visitors to Cape Henlopen come for the swimming, surfing, and fishing on the Atlantic.

In summer, all three parks draw crowds of swimmers, sun worshipers, surfers, surf casters, and in Rehoboth Bay, "behind" Delaware Seashore State Park, sailors and windsurfers. Off-season for people is high season for birds and the desolate beauty of empty beaches. Bird-watchers in the know come to these stopovers for migratory songbirds, shorebirds, waterfowl, and raptors on the Atlantic flyway—the first (or last) landfall on the way from (or to) Cape May on the other side of Delaware Bay. Look for hawks and songbirds in spring and autumn; ducks, brant, and cormorants in winter; breeding terns and red knots in spring. ■

Of Shorebirds and Horseshoe Crabs

FOUR BIRD FAMILIES count as shorebirds: sandpipers, plovers, avocets and stilts, and oystercatchers. Mostly they're small—about robin size—and they forage on sandy beaches and mudflats. Some stay year-round in Central and South America, but many fly north for summer in the Arctic, where there are few predators, plenty of daylight foraging time, and millions of tasty insects. Their round-trip flight may cover 20,000 miles. That's an effort equivalent to a cyclist riding a bike at 10 miles per hour for 2,000 hours without stopping.

A million shorebirds or more pause to refuel at Delaware Bay in May. Plover, sanderlings, ruddy turnstones, and semipalmated sandpipers make up 95 percent of the crowd. Some arrive almost starving, like the red knots who fly nonstop from South America—4,000 miles in 60 hours. For red knots and ruddy turnstones, the bay is their only stopover; 80 percent of the total hemispheric population of red knots and 30 percent of sanderlings show up here in May. Others among the 11 shorebird species of regular visitors are dunlins, willet, greater yellowlegs, short-billed dowitchers, and semipalmated and black-bellied plovers.

They all come for the springtime horseshoe crab buffet. The horseshoe crab, which looks like some sci-fi armored space vehicle, is not a crab at all but an arthropod—a prehistoric relative of spiders and scorpions little changed in 300 million years. Each spring (April-June) at the new and full moons, the big females come ashore by the thousands, dragging little males behind them to fertilize the eggs they bury in the sand. Each female repeats the process as many as 20 times, laying altogether about 80,000 tiny blue-green eggs. Many eggs are safely buried too deep even for the long probing beaks of dowitchers; but in the melee, enough eggs are scuffed to the surface to satisfy scarfing shorebirds. Scientists say a sanderling will eat one egg every five seconds, 14 hours a day, for days on end. In two weeks, eating about 9,000 eggs apiece each day, most shorebirds will add half again to their body weight, thus getting ready for the long flight to their Arctic breeding grounds.

Horseshoe crabs are valuable to people, too. The scientific study of horseshoe crabs has increased understanding of human diseases such as AIDS, Alzheimer's, arteriosclerosis, arthritis, cancer, and schizophrenia—and it has led to three Nobel Prizes. We learn about the human eye by studying the horseshoe crab, which has nine. We use chitin from its shell to coat sutures and burn dressings to accelerate healing. We use a clotting agent (lysate) from its copper blue blood to test quickly for meningitis and to check every new pharmaceutical drug for bacterial toxins. At one time, the crabs were also ground into fertilizer, a big business that caused a decline in the horseshoe crab population. Commercial fisherman use thousands of the critters as bait.

The relationship between shorebirds and horseshoe crabs is probably almost as old as the bay itself. But in the last ten years, the number of both birds and crabs has dramatically declined. The sanderling population is down 80 percent. Among the suspected causes are pesticides in the birds' wintering grounds, loss of

Horseshoe crabs, Cooks Beach, New Jersey

coastal wetlands along migration routes, and human predation of crabs. New Jersey, Delaware, and Maryland have limited the taking of crabs, and other seaboard states, Virginia among them, are following suit. Worst-case scenario: An oil spill in Upper Delaware Bay, the second largest petrochemical port in the country.

The primeval spectacle of horseshoe crab spawning peaks in mid-May, and you can watch at many prime viewing spots. To make the most of the experience, visit the New Jersey locations on weekends when naturalists are present or join a Cape May Bird Observatory trip (see p. 55). This is a fragile process. Bring binoculars or a scope and watch from a distance; *never* walk out on dunes or beaches.

In **New Jersey**, take US 9 north from Cape May to N.J. 47, turning west at County Road 603 and north at County Road 642 for **Norburys Landing**. Another site, **Reeds Beach** may be reached by turning west off N.J. 47 at County Road 655 (Reeds Beach Rd.).

In **Delaware,** Del. 9 in the vicinity of Little Creek, east of Dover and about 12 miles south of Bombay Hook National Wildlife Refuge, leads to the **Ted Harvey Conservation Area** *(turn E off Del. 9 on Cty. Rd. 68).* For **Pickering Beach,** turn east off Del. 9 at County Road 349. For the **Little Creek Wildlife Area,** turn east off Del. 9 at the access road, 1.5 miles south of the town of Little Creek. For **Port Mahon** turn east on Cty. Rd. 89 (Port Mahon Rd.) in the town of Little Creek. ■

Delaware Bay Wildlife Refuges

- 10,000 acres (Prime Hook NWR); 15,978 acres (Bombay Hook NWR)
- Delaware Bay ■ Best seasons spring and fall ■ Hiking, boating, kayaking, canoeing, fishing, hunting, biking, bird-watching, wildlife viewing, wildflower viewing
- Adm. fee for Bombay Hook ■ Contact Prime Hook NWR, RD 3, Box 195, Milton, DE 19968; phone 302-684-8419 or Bombay Hook NWR, 2591 Whitehall Neck Rd., Smyrna, DE 19977; phone 302-653-6872

BIRDS MIGRATING LONG DISTANCES to winter homes or summer breeding grounds, like any long-distance travelers, need stops to refuel and regain strength. **Prime Hook** and **Bombay Hook National Wildlife Refuges** were established (in 1963 and 1937 respectively) to meet that need. Like several other eastern wildlife refuges and wildlife management areas, they lie along the Atlantic flyway, the preferred migratory path of eastern birds. The mandate of both refuges is to preserve critical migratory bird habitat: wetlands on Delaware Bay. Prime Hook stands about 10 miles from the mouth of the bay *(from Del. 1 turn E on Broadkill Rd. toward Broadkill Beach, then N on Turkle Pond Rd.)*. Bombay Hook is some 40 miles farther north, closer to the head of the estuary and reached via Del. 1 and Del. 9.

Snow Geese, Bombay Hook National Wildlife Refuge

Most of Prime Hook's 10,000 acres consist of freshwater marsh, tidal marsh, and open water, including a 2,500-acre freshwater impoundment. The management plan calls for careful seasonal manipulation of water levels on 4,200 acres of these wetlands to suit various visiting species. Some 1,000 acres of the refuge are wooded, providing essential habitats for the endangered Delmarva Peninsula fox squirrel (see sidebar page 34), and 1,300 acres are given over to grasslands and grain crops that feed wintering waterfowl. Similarly, Bombay Hook's nearly 16,000 acres encompass some upland forests, cultivated croplands, and about 1,100 acres of freshwater impoundments, but 80 percent of the refuge is tidal salt marsh. By all means enjoy the privilege of viewing the wildlife in its natural habitat, but use common sense, too—be respectful and keep some distance.

Time your visit as the birds do. Autumn brings more than 100,000 ducks—including pintail, teal, black ducks, mallard, gadwalls, shovelers, and wood ducks—to each refuge. More than 150,000 snow geese descend on Prime Hook and another 100,000-plus settle upon Bombay Hook. Both spring and fall bring a million shorebirds to Delaware Bay; willet, dunlins, red knots, ruddy turnstones, and sandpipers flock to the refuges. Spring also brings warblers in bright breeding plumage. Avid birders have noted more than 300 species. In summer, egrets and herons take up residence.

Hunting on the Refuges

It sounds contradictory, but national wildlife refuges, including Prime Hook and Bombay Hook, permit hunting in season for waterfowl, upland game, and deer. Hunting is one of the six "compatible wildlife-dependent recreational uses" as defined by the Refuge System Improvement Act of 1997. The others are fishing, wildlife observation, wildlife photography, environmental education, and environmental interpretation.

Wildlife managers say the flocks must be thinned because there are too many birds for the refuges to support, though a snow goose headed south over New Jersey and looking for a place to land would surely see the problem as too many people. For information about the special hunting regulations that apply, contact the refuges or the Fish and Wildlife Service at 800-344-9453 or www.fws.gov.

Summer also brings heat and throngs of biting bugs—a dietary delight for birds, but seriously pesky to people.

Bombay Hook is the easier refuge to visit. From the visitor center, a 12-mile **self-guided driving tour** leads past four impoundments reflecting a range of habitats from marsh to woody swamp to freshwater pond. It also gives access to nature trails. The half-mile **boardwalk trail** leads from a freshwater, brackish pond spouting bulrushes to a salt marsh thick with cordgrass.

The quarter-mile-long **Bear Swamp Trail** (half of which is handicapped accessible) takes you through sweet gum forest and freshwater impoundment to a 30-foot observation tower offering an eagle's-eye view of fish and turtles as well as birds at **Bear Swamp Pool.** The driving route is also open to bicycles and walkers. No boating is permitted at Bombay Hook.

Prime Hook takes a little more work. Although there is no formal driving tour, you can drive, bike, or walk across the refuge on three public roads running east from Del. 1 to Delaware Bay. (A fourth, **Slaughter Beach Road,** forms the refuge's northern border.) The southernmost of these—**Broadkill Beach Road,** or Del. 16—leads to the refuge visitor center. **Prime Hook Beach Road** and **Fowler Beach Road** are farther north off Del. 1. Settlement has cut the refuge from the bay, so each road ends in private property. Prime Hook also offers four short instructive nature trails. The best of these is the half-mile **boardwalk trail** through bird-busy woodlands and marshes mounded with muskrat huts.

The key to Prime Hook lies along 7 miles of meandering creeks and swamps open to canoes, kayaks, and—if you must make noise—powerboats of 25 horsepower or less (there's a boat launch behind refuge headquarters). Just off Del. 1, where it crosses Prime Hook Creek, is a put-in for a self-guided **canoe trail** that starts among woodlands of red maple and sweetbay magnolia and winds 7 miles into the heart of the marsh. You can fish, too, on the tidal creeks and two freshwater ponds. ∎

Nature trail, Cape May Point State Park

Cape May

■ Southern New Jersey, where the Atlantic Ocean meets Delaware Bay ■ Best seasons spring-fall ■ Walking, fishing, biking, bird-watching, whale-watching, wildlife viewing, wildflower viewing ■ Contact Cape May County Department of Tourism, 4 More Rd., Cape May Court House, NJ 08210; phone 800-227-2297 or 609-463-6415. www.beachcomber.com/Capemay/tourism.html

CAPE MAY HAS BEEN POPULAR with tourists for two centuries—ever since 1800, when health-conscious Americans donned long black woolen costumes to wade into the ocean for the invigorating effects of "seabathing." Its 19th-century Victorian cottages and hotels are collectively a national historic landmark. Today summer tourists still flock here to enjoy the water, swim at beaches on the Atlantic Ocean and on Delaware Bay, and to sightsee, whale-watch, or go deep-sea fishing. Others are drawn by the historic interest of the place.

For outdoor enthusiasts, Cape May's top attraction is its birdlife. This is one of the top birding spots in North America, and quite possibly the best. Four hundred species have been spotted here—as many as 200 in a single day. Less celebrated but equally beautiful are the smaller residents and migrants who pass through the cape—the monarch and 107 other species of butterflies, as well as bats and dragonflies.

Just as people are guided by landmarks, migrating birds seem to use the visual cue of a shoreline or watercourse. Birds southbound over New Jersey follow the coastline on the east or the Delaware River Valley and Delaware Bay on the west. Inevitably, the topography funnels them all to Cape May, where they rest before undertaking the next stage of their journey. For northbound migrants, Cape May is an attractive landfall after the 13-mile flight across Delaware Bay. Great masses of shorebirds in the spring and raptors in the fall are met at Cape May by thousands of dedicated bird-watchers. Nonbirders may be surprised to learn that bird-

Sanderlings

watching is now America's fastest growing leisure pastime, more popular than baseball or golf. One in three adults admits to ogling or feeding wild birds; more than 18 million Americans take trips each year specifically to bird-watch. For non-bird-watchers curious to see what the fuss is about, there's no better place to start than Cape May. In autumn, there are a whole lot of birds, and a lot of them are big.

The entire county is called Cape May, including Cape Island, separated from the Cape May Peninsula by the Intracoastal Waterway. There

What to See and Do

Cape May Point State Park

Summer visitors to this 215-acre state park (*off southern end of Garden State Pkwy. 609-884-2159. www.state.nj.us/dep/forestry/parks/capemay.htm*) enjoy the ocean beach, the panoramic view from the lighthouse (*fee*), and especially the **nature trails** through freshwater marsh and woods. These trails are centered in the park's 153-acre **Cape May Point Natural Area** (*maps available at visitor center*). Park naturalists regularly conduct walks, including some for beginning birders. In September the annual Hawkwatch gets under way at a large viewing platform east of the parking lot; it continues through November. As a rule of

nature prey animals outnumber predators, so hawks and other raptors are seldom seen—except when they migrate en masse.

Cape May Point has earned the title "Raptor Capital of America"; during Hawkwatch an average of 60,000 raptors are counted each year. Regular visitors include members of the hawk genus *Accipiter*, such as the sharp-shinned hawk, Cooper's hawk, and northern goshawk; members of the hawk genus *Buteo*, such as the red-tailed hawk, red-shouldered hawk, broad-winged hawk, rough-legged hawk, and Swainson's hawk; and falcons such as the peregrine, merlin, and American kestrel. Bald and golden eagles, ospreys, and harriers are often seen as well. Counters from the Cape May Bird Observatory (CMBO) make the official tally, and naturalists are on hand (often with live birds of prey) to give amateur birders information and help. For best viewing you need good binoculars, a good field guide, and northwest winds following a cold front.

Cape May Bird Observatory

Serious ornithological studies have been under way at Cape May since 1808, when Alexander Wilson first described in Cape May Meadows the bird now called Wilson's plover. John James Audubon and Roger Tory Peterson both studied birds here. In this tradition the New Jersey Audubon Society established the CMBO in 1975 to carry on applied research, environmental education, and bird conservation,

and to support recreational birding. **Northwood Center** (*just N of Cape May Point SP, off Lighthouse Rd. 609-884-2736. www.njaudubon.org*) serves the latter purpose, offering visitors birding information, great field trips, books, and birding equipment. (They'll even check and clean your binoculars—for free.) Serious birders or wannabes should ask about the CMBO's daily walks, special programs, and three-, four-, and five-day birding workshops. CMBO also maintains the annual Hawkwatch at Cape May Point State Park (*Sept.-Nov.*) and a Seawatch (*mid-Sept.–mid-Dec.*) at 7th Street and the beach in nearby Avalon.

South Cape May Meadows

This beautiful 180-acre meadow (*contact the Nature Conservancy, Delaware Bayshores Office, 2350*

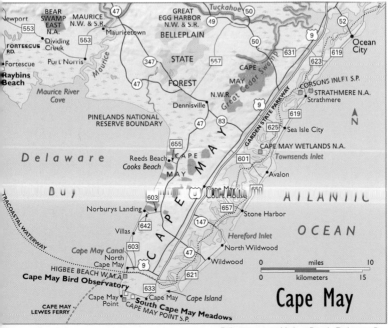

Following pages: Higbee Beach, Delaware Bay

Route 47, Delmont, NJ 08314. 609-861-0600), stretching along the south side of Sunset Boulevard to the beach, preserves a thin slice of what must once have been a paradise for shorebirds, wading birds, and gulls. Along the path from street to shore you might see egrets, herons, plover, sandpipers, and marsh wrens—and wonder how many more there would be if the meadows had not been reduced to this one exquisite field.

Higbee Beach Wildlife Management Area

In the urbanized setting of Cape Island, **Higbee Beach** is a breath of fresh air—416 acres without a visitor center, roads, or maps. Located off New England Road between Cape May Point and the Intracoastal Waterway, this is still wild enough to get lost amid a mix of habitats: bay beach, dunes, fields, and windswept woodlands. This variety gives haven to a great range of resident species and seasonal migrants, from woodcocks to warblers. And butterflies, too—seen in great numbers spring to fall.

Cape May National Wildlife Refuge

This is a place to keep tabs on. Established in 1989, it has limited public-use facilities and at 10,000 acres is less than half its projected size. However, it offers foot trails through various refuge habitats, including the short **Woodcock Trail.** Spring and fall are best for viewing the refuge's 317 bird species, 42 mammal species, and 55 reptile and amphibian species. The refuge *(609-463-0994)* is divided into two separate areas. The **Delaware Bay Division** extends along 5 miles of the Delaware Bay in Middle Township, while the **Great Cedar Swamp Division** encompasses inland areas in Dennis and Upper Townships. It is sure to grow in importance as valuable habitat disappears to development. ∎

World Series of Birding

Who says bird-watchers aren't serious athletes? Competition is stiff for one day each year in May, when the World Series of Birding takes place in New Jersey under the auspices of the New Jersey Audubon Society. Operating in teams with a minimum of three people, birders spot and identify as many species as they can in a 24-hour period. Tactics? Some roam New Jersey; others stay in one area. In the millennial World Series, 63 teams—10 of them youth teams—gave it their best. Two teams tied for first with 219 species each. (There's no play-off.)

The cumulative total of species spotted—263—included everything from a ruby-throated hummingbird to a turkey vulture. (One less ambitious team loitered on the Cape May golf course and tallied 72.) The real payoff: Pledges from team sponsors go to environmental organizations of the team's choosing. For more information or to participate, contact the Cape May Bird Observatory *(701 E. Lake Dr., Cape May Point, NJ 08212. 609-884-2736. www.worldseriesofbirding.org).*

Batsto Natural Area, Wharton State Forest

The Pine Barrens

■ 1.1 million acres, including 1,100 acres of Wharton State Forest ■ Southern New Jersey ■ Year-round ■ Camping, primitive camping, hiking, kayaking, canoeing, swimming, fishing, mountain biking, horseback riding, bird-watching, wildflower viewing ■ Contact the Pinelands Commission, P.O. Box 7, New Lisbon, NJ 08064; phone 609-894-7300. www.state.nj.us/pinelands/

THE MOST DENSELY POPULATED STATE in the country, New Jersey is the last place you'd expect to find a wilderness area. But there it is: the Pine Barrens, so named for its poor acidic soil, unsuitable for crops, and the pine that flourish instead. A thick layer of sandy soil covers a good part of New Jersey south of Asbury Park, extending from the coast halfway across the state. Once the whole area was covered in evergreen forest: pitch pine, shortleaf pine, and (along watercourses and swamps) tall Atlantic white cedars. Farmers left it alone, and the forest became an industrial area: the center of timbering and the bog iron business, producing ammunition for the American Revolution and the War of 1812. Later, glass- and paper-making industries came then petered out, and the Pine Barrens remained.

In his book *The Pine Barrens* (1968), writer John McPhee celebrates the way of life of the area's isolated 20th-century residents: growing cranberries and blueberries, gathering wild huckleberries and sphagnum moss, cutting cedar, hunting white-tailed deer and pheasant. Today the Pine Barrens are recognized as a botanist's dream: some 1,500 plants, a mix of

Sand road, Wharton State Forest

northern species carried in by Ice Age cooling trends (when glaciers also kindly deposited a few gravel hills) and southern species moving north with the warming climate. You can find remarkable plants here, such as the flowering bog asphodel, 23 kinds of orchids—including the arethusa and the rose pogonia—and carnivorous bog plants: sundews, bladderworts, and pitcher plants.

Sadly, the pinelands are shrinking and fragmenting under pressure from encroaching development. Still, a big piece in the heart of the Pine Barrens—the largest single track in the New Jersey state park system—is preserved in **Wharton State Forest** *(4110 Nesco Rd., Batsto, Hammonton. 609-561-0024),* roughly 20 miles northwest of Atlantic City. Some people find the Pine Barrens monotonous—mile after mile of the same pine trees along the same straight roads over the same flat land. To make the most of your visit, look beneath the trees, especially in spring and early summer when wildflowers such as pink lady's slipper and turkey beard abound. Then take to the trails, the rivers, and the sandy roads.

What to See and Do

From 1766 to 1867, **Batsto Village** *(Cty. Rd. 542, 5 miles E of Hammonton. 609-561-0024)* was a bog iron and glass-making industrial center. Today 33 historic buildings on the site suggest how people once made their living from this land. It's worth a visit in summer, when craftspeople are on hand to demonstrate how things were done.

You can pick up a plant list and information about the forest at the Batsto Village visitor center. The nature trail beside **Batsto Lake**

provides a preview of the subtle complexity of the Pine Barrens. In May, for example, you are treated to soggy bogs, carpets of golden heather, clouds of deep pink sheep laurel, cascades of trailing arbutus, goldfinches and flickers darting among oaks and pines, and a marsh hawk overhead—all underscored by the minimalist music of spring peepers.

Take time to visit the **Oswego River Natural Area** (1,927 acres), on the east side of the state forest

Carranza Memorial

Near the northern edge of Wharton State Forest, a stone monument honors Cap. Emilio Carranza of the Mexican Army Air Corps. In 1928, on behalf of his country, the 23-year-old Carranza made a celebrated solo good-will flight to the United States. On his return flight from New York, July 12, 1928, he crashed during a storm in the Pine Barrens. Men from the Mount Holly post of the American Legion recovered his body and in 1933 erected a monument of stones sent from Mexico. Since 1929, on the first Saturday after July 4, the legion post holds ceremonies of remembrance here.

off County Road 679. It's here in the old white cedar forests and freshwater wetlands along the **Oswego River** that you might come upon the bog asphodel or encounter the equally rare Pine Barrens treefrog. You can reach the area by canoe on the Oswego River, or pick up the **Batona Trail** (see below) where it crosses County Road 679 and walk through.

For pleasant lakeside camping with hot showers, head for the north side of Atsion Lake at **Atsion Recreation Area** *(609-268-0444)*. Nine rustic cabins (for four to eight people) are also for rent here. On the south side of the lake is the forest's only lifeguarded swimming beach and bathhouse. For primitive camping the forest maintains seven campsites in more

remote areas; the best are Mullica on the Mullica River and Lower Forge on the Batsto River, both accessible only by canoe, foot, or horseback. Godfrey Bridge Camp can be reached by canoe on the West Branch of Wading River or by car on County Road 563.

Four clear, cedar-dark rivers rich in tannin flow through the forest. Because all the rivers of the state forest rise within the barrens, they're clean as can be, and perfect for canoeing. You can get a list of local canoe outfitters at the Batsto Village visitor center. Beginners should head for the flat **Mullica River** (below Atsion Lake) or **Batsto River;** the Oswego and the **West Branch of Wading River** are a bit twistier and call for some paddling experience.

If you have a mountain bike or trail horse, bring it (or him/her)—you can't rent either one here—and take off on the forest's 500 miles of sand roads. If you have to make do with a motor vehicle, by all means get off the asphalt and into the woods. Be on the lookout for owls, turkeys, foxes, and white-tailed deer; scan the skies for hawks, ospreys, and bald eagles.

A word of caution: It's easy to get lost in the pine barrens. Take a detailed map *(available at Batsto Village visitor center);* if you're traveling by bike, horse, or on foot, take a compass just in case.

Batona Trail

Hikers should have a go at the Batona (BAck-TO-NAture) Trail, or at least part of it. Started in 1961 by the Batona Hiking Club and completed in 1987, the trail stretches north from Batsto 31.6

miles to **Lebanon State Forest** *(609-726-1191)* and southeast another 17.9 miles to **Bass River State Forest** *(609-296-1114)*, making a through hike (if you start from one end or the other) just shy of 50 miles. Hikers can camp *(by permit only)* at designated sites in each of the three state forests.

If you're not up to the whole 50 miles, it's easy to hike a piece of the trail or to hike it in stages; it intersects many roads along the way, including N.J. 70 and 72. One particularly good shorter hike is the stretch from the **Carranza Memorial** (see sidebar opposite) to **Apple Pie Hill.** It culminates in a climb of about 100 feet to the highest point of the Pine Barrens—205 feet above sea level. Round-trip from the Carranza Memorial

is an 8.2-mile hike; or you can leave a car on County Road 532 where it intersects the trail and continue hiking past Apple Pie Hill for a one-way of 5.2 miles.

Just about anybody can hike the whole Batona. The trail is flat, save for Apple Pie and a few other gentle hills, and well marked by pink blazes. The forest—mostly pine or mixed pine and oak woodland—is open and offers no worse challenge than wet feet in some boggy areas. At any season, the forest is astir with woodland birds; spring brings a noisy mating chorus of swifts, swallows, martins, warblers, flycatchers, cuckoos, whip-poor-wills, and night hawks—and the visual delight of wildflowers and flowering shrubs. Summer brings hikers the

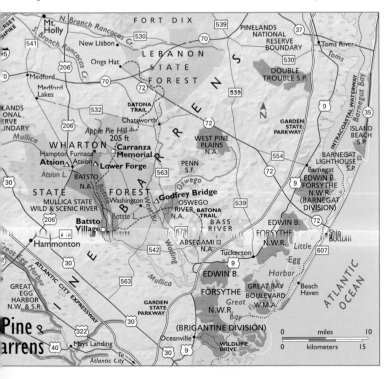

singular pleasure of highbush blueberries, ripe for the picking along the trail.

Driving Tour

For a short loop on sand roads entirely within the piney woods, go northeast from Batsto on the Batsto-Washington Road to Washington and take the Tuckerton Road northwest to High Crossing, where you can see the Carranza Memorial (see sidebar p. 62). Turn west on High Crossing Road to Hampton Furnace and continue southwest on Hampton Road to Atsion. Then take Quaker Bridge Road to Quaker Bridge and beyond, bearing right back onto the Batsto-Quaker Bridge Road to return to Batsto.

This is the quintessential Pine Barrens experience: woods as repetitious as wallpaper—and as fascinating as your keen eye and imagination can conceive. ■

Edwin B. Forsythe National Wildlife Refuge

■ 43,000 acres ■ Great Bay, southern New Jersey ■ Best seasons spring and fall ■ Fishing, crabbing, hunting, bird-watching, wildlife viewing, photography ■ Adm. fee ■ Contact the refuge's Brigantine Division, Great Creek Rd., P.O. Box 72, Oceanville, NJ 08231; phone 609-652-1665. www.fws.gov/r5ebfnwr/

THE MULLICA RIVER of the Pine Barrens meets the Atlantic Ocean in Great Bay, a small estuary ringed by wetlands, often referred to as the **Tuckerton Marshes.** Large tracts of the salt marsh lie within the Edwin B. Forsythe National Wildlife Refuge, along with some upland fields, pine and oak woodlands, and islands—more than 43,000 acres in all. (Other large tracts of the Tuckerton Marshes fall within the adjoining Great Bay Boulevard Wildlife Management Area, administered by the state.) To the north of Great Bay, near the town of Barnegat, the Holgate Unit (comprising the bulk of the **Barnegat Division**) is closed to the public for the sake of breeding piping plover, black skimmers, least terns, and other beach-nesting birds greatly endangered by loss of habitat.

Public use of the refuge mainly revolves around the beautiful **Brigantine Division,** off Great Creek Road east of the town of Oceanville, although even here activities are limited to walking and driving on prescribed paths. Still, Brigantine is well worth all the time you can give it. Seasonal fishing, crabbing, and hunting are also allowed in specified areas, subject to special regulations *(call refuge for information).*

The main job of both divisions is to provide habitat for migratory waterbirds, with special attention to the Atlantic brant and the American black duck—species in trouble because of major habitat loss. The lovely tidal salt meadows and marshes interspersed with bays and coves that make up 80 percent of the Brigantine Division serve that purpose. The refuge also manages a system of dikes to create 1,415 acres of freshwater and brackish water marsh habitat.

Atop the dikes runs the refuge's birding highlight—the 8-mile, self-guided **Wildlife Drive,** with splendid views of both the impoundments and the tidal salt marshes. (On clear days, Atlantic City glitters on the horizon, a reminder of the sprawl that necessitates these refuges.) Spring and fall are peak bird-watching seasons. In late March, northbound ducks and geese arrive and tuneful frogs go a'courting. Late in April, just when Canada goslings are hatching, come the wading birds: great and snowy egrets, glossy ibises, and great blue herons. May brings warblers to the uplands, and ruddy turnstones arrive to forage on horseshoe crab eggs (see pp. 48-49). In June come ducklings; in August, shorebirds and warblers head south. Fall and early winter bring flights of brant, snow geese, mallard, and black ducks. By November and into December there may be 100,000 ducks and geese on the refuge, many heading south, some staying to winter.

Don't leave without walking the **Leeds Eco-Trail,** a half-mile loop that illustrates "life on the edge," where salt marsh and woodland meet. The trail passes from woodland pitch pine and black cherry, strung with trailing arbutus and Virginia creeper, through sassafras and marsh elder shrubs to the cordgrass of the salt marsh. From boardwalks leading over the marsh you get a privileged view of fiddler crabs, marsh wrens, egrets, and herons. ∎

Wetlands, Not Wastelands

Lands that are flooded or saturated for part or all of the growing season are called wetlands. Bogs, swamps, marshes, and shallow watery areas along rivers, lakes, and ponds are all wetlands. For a long time, such wetlands were thought to be useless. Americans drained and filled them for agriculture, housing, commercial buildings, and highways—all in the name of progress.

Now we know that wetlands are immensely valuable. They prevent flooding by absorbing storm surges. Wetlands act as natural filters, cleansing runoff water as well as playing an essential part in recharging depleted aquifers. Critical areas of biological diversity, these areas generally support more life-forms than either land or water alone. And they are essential to the life cycle of one-third of all North American birds, two-thirds of commercially valuable fish and shellfish, and 43 percent of currently endangered animal species. Millions of people depend upon them, too: for recreation such as fishing, boating, birding, and hunting, and often—as in the case of commercial fishermen—for their livelihood.

Nevertheless, we have already destroyed the lion's share of the country's irreplaceable wetlands. An estimated 200 million acres of wetlands covered the country in colonial times. Now less than half that acreage remains, and thousands of acres are still destroyed each year. Everyone can help by buying an annual popular collectible— Federal Duck Stamps (see sidebar p. 71). Proceeds go to purchase and preserve additional wetlands.

Jacob Riis Park, Jamaica Bay, Gateway NRA

Gateway National Recreation Area

■ 26,000 acres ■ Northern New Jersey and southern New York, around New York Harbor ■ Best seasons spring-fall ■ Hiking, boating, kayaking, swimming, fishing, surf-fishing, biking, horseback riding, bird-watching, wildlife viewing, wildflower viewing ■ Contact the recreation area, 210 New York Ave., Staten Island, NY 10305; 732-872-5970 (Sandy Hook Unit), 718-318-4340 (Jamaica Bay Wildlife Refuge). www.nps.gov/gate

WHERE IN AMERICA CAN you swim, kayak, hike, cycle, fish, watch birds, and groove to the classic Del-Satins, all in one day? The answer is the 26,000-acre Gateway National Recreation Area, a combination of three unusual places—**Sandy Hook, Jamaica Bay,** and portions of the south shore of **Staten Island.** Established in 1972 and still in process, Gateway is one of the country's first urban national parks, and possibly the only one to offer rock-and-roll concerts. It also marks an entrance to the biggest city and the busiest urban complex in the country. (History buffs will be interested in the country's oldest lighthouse, at Sandy Hook, and old military fortifications at all the park's segments, reflecting its strategic location.)

Geographically, the three areas are distinctive. Just where New Jersey's 90-mile shoreline wraps around the corner from Raritan Bay to the Atlantic Ocean at the entrance to New York Harbor, it pokes a long, skinny finger of beach northward toward New York City in the land's equivalent of a rude gesture. This is Sandy Hook, a 1,665-acre barrier-beach peninsula. On the other side of New York Bay, along the shores of Brooklyn and Queens, lie lonely expanses of marshland in and around a smaller bay named Jamaica, sheltered by the long arm of Rockaway Peninsula. West of these two points, at the entrance to New York's inner harbor, stands Staten Island.

What to See and Do

Sandy Hook

The **Old Dune Trail** is a mile-long loop near the Sandy Hook Visitor Center, where you can pick up a trail guide. It provides an instructive introduction to dune ecology, wandering through the grasses, sedges, heathers, and prickly pears of the dunes to beach-plum thickets and a surprising forest of American holly containing trees 150 years old. Look for woodpeckers and warblers along the way.

Put what you've learned to the test on another, longer dune trail starting at **Fishing Beach.** Hike, beachcomb, or surf cast on 7 miles of beautiful Atlantic beach, and swim in summer at five lifeguarded oceanside beaches. For birding, try the salt marsh at **Horseshoe Cove,** or the **Spermaceti Cove Boardwalk** across from the visitor center.

Jamaica Bay

Birders—not to mention frazzled city dwellers longing for a glimpse of nature—should take to the miles of trails in the 9,155-acre **Jamaica Bay Wildlife Refuge,** one of the largest bird sanctuaries in the northeast (off Cross Bay Blvd., Queens). You can try the 1.5-mile trail along **West Pond Dike,** an easy walk and usually a rewarding one for birders. As always along the Atlantic flyway, spring and fall are the best times. Some 330 different species have been sighted here, including showers of spring warblers in breeding plumage and hordes of wintering brant. Along the shore look for oystercatchers, black-crowned night-herons, and, on occasion, marbled godwits, Wilson's phalaropes, and bald eagles.

For another vantage point, explore the 18 square miles of bay salt marsh by kayak. Consult the visitor center and tide tables, and take a map and compass; it's easy to get lost in a marsh. Note: To protect nesting sites, kayakers are asked not to enter island interiors.

The best fishing and the best fish stories are at historic **Canarsie Pier.** The Rockaway Peninsula has more good birding and a view of the whole gateway at **Battery Harris East,** a viewing platform built atop an old gun emplacement at **Fort Tilden.** Nearby, **Jacob Riis Park,** New York's first seaside park, offers swimming, a historic bathhouse, and concerts.

Check Gateway's website for a list of nature programs, concerts, and other special events at the various visitor centers and facilities. Call or write for a program guide; it will include directions to reach all the far-flung parts of the park by car, bus, subway, and train. ■

Long Island

■ 1,800 square miles ■ Atlantic Ocean off New York City ■ Best season summer. Marinas open May–mid-Oct. Ferries run to Fire Island early May–Oct. (fee) ■ Camping, primitive camping, hiking, boating, kayaking, swimming, surfing, fishing, surf-fishing, biking, horseback riding, bird-watching ■ Adm. fee for Jones Beach State Park ■ Contact Fire Island National Seashore, 120 Laurel St., Patchogue, NY 11772; phone 516-289-4810. www.nps.gov/fis

THE COUNTRY'S BIGGEST ISLAND, Long Island is 120 miles long. Even omitting the New York City boroughs of Queens and Brooklyn, technically "on the island," Long Island has a population pushing three million. Unless you live in New York City, this is probably not your pick to enjoy the outdoors. Nevertheless, millions of people do just that. The island's eastern end is less crowded, but you have to run the gauntlet of commuting congestion to get there. Rule of thumb: Unless Steven Spielberg personally invites you, don't drive to Long Island on a summer weekend.

What to See and Do

Fire Island National Seashore

A classic barrier island (see sidebar p. 40), Fire Island stretches 32 miles along the south shore of Long Island, with **Great South Bay** at its back. It varies in width from half a mile to a few hundred feet; at its highest point, dunes soar to 30 feet above sea level.

The national seashore includes nearly all of the island, with four visitor centers; two are accessible by car, two by ferry from the mainland. Closest to New York City is the **Lighthouse Area**. The visitor center is next to the lighthouse, a half-mile walk from the parking lot; nearby is a half-mile self-guided **boardwalk trail** among dunes and cranberry bogs along the shore of Great South Bay, where the trees have been half-shorn by salt winds.

Adjoining the national seashore here is **Robert Moses State Park** (*West end of island. 631-669-0470*),

worth a visit for its beautiful beaches. The Wilderness Visitor Center serves the easternmost seven miles of the island, New York's only federally designated wilderness area. Primitive camping is permitted here in season (*May-Oct.*). In September, when the summer people have gone and birds are on the wing, it's just about perfect.

Arriving by ferry (*May-Oct.; fare*)—a half-hour trip across Great South Bay—adds a special thrill to reaching other areas of the seashore. Both **Sailors Haven** and **Watch Hill** offer lifeguarded swimming beaches and bathhouses; the Watch Hill area provides a family campground for those who submit applications well in advance (*send a self-addressed stamped envelope for an application in Feb. or March for a drawing in April*). Watch Hill also provides boaters with a 158-slip

Sunken Forest, Sailors Haven, Fire Island

Fire Island ferry

marina, open from May through the middle of October.

Sailors Haven is the site of the lovely, ancient **Sunken Forest.** In this dense, mysterious woodland, ancient holly, tupelo, sassafras, and shadblow rise to the level of the surrounding dunes; then, blasted by salt wind, they grow horizontally, as if to put a protective roof over the whole magical forest. Pass through it on the **boardwalk trail,** or linger to enjoy the shade on benches along the way.

Between the areas of the national seashore, 17 summer communities stand chockablock yet discrete, separated from one another by the particular character of each: sexy singles, young family, proudly gay, flauntingly rich, funky. By strolling the beaches or the boardwalks, you can take a sunny sociological hike from one part of the seashore to another. And you can surf cast along the beaches as you go for the island's signature bluefish and striped bass.

Jones Beach State Park

Named for Maj. Thomas Jones, an Irish soldier of fortune who established a whaling station here on the wild outer south shore of Long Island 300 years ago, **Jones Beach** *(Ocean Dr., Wantagh, NY 11793. 516-785-1600. nystateparks.state .ny.us/parks. Adm. fee)* opened in

1929—the grandiose dream (or nightmare) of urban planners.

The stats: 2,413 acres, 6.3 miles of ocean beach, seven ocean and one bay swimming areas, 250 lifeguards, two Olympic-size swimming pools, parking for 23,000 cars, plus a restaurant, numerous refreshment stands, a boardwalk, nature center, and theater. Only 33 miles from Manhattan, it's the city's most egalitarian beach, accessible in summer by train from Pennsylvania Station with special low round-trip fares to Freeport or Wantagh stations, where free shuttle buses wait.

Fishing is big here, at designated surf casting sections of beach and at piers on the bayside. But a day of swimming, sunning, hot dog (with mustard and onion) eating, and people-watching at Jones Beach is a quintessential New York experience: claustrophobic, harrowing, comradely fun. If you hate crowds, stay away. If you go on a summer weekend, get there by 9 a.m. or forget about it.

Montauk Point

Some say 132 miles is a long way to go for tacky motels and a view of the ocean. But there's a special remoteness about the windblown beaches on the tip of Long Island that captures the imagination of many visitors. Here you can swim and surf.

Anglers may try their luck surfcasting or fishing the freshwater pond in the **Montauk County Park** (*East Lake Dr., Montauk, NY 11954; 631-852-7878*). Bring your horse, or hire one in the county park and explore miles of bridle paths from the vantage point of

Duck Stamps

Duck stamps are not hunting licenses, but every migratory-bird hunter has been required to buy one and affix it to his or her license since Franklin Delano Roosevelt signed the Migratory Bird Hunting Stamp Act in 1934. Proceeds go to conservation. A major contest is held each year to choose the stamp's artwork, and today almost 15 percent of stamp sales are to nonhunters —collectors and concerned citizens appreciative of these beautiful annual stamps.

The program is a success: The federal government has purchased and safeguarded more than five million acres of wetlands and other migratory bird habitat with funds from the sale of duck stamps. (*Contact the Federal Duck Stamp Program. 877-887-5508.*)

the saddle. For those who like to beach camp, both the county park and **Hither Hills State Park** (*off Sunrise Hwy. 631-668-3781*), 4 miles west, offer sites by the water.

Hike, bike, and beachcomb to your heart's content, except during short seasons when diehards hunt duck in the fall and deer in winter. Spring and fall are good times to pay this beautiful area a visit, when the crowds are down and the birds are flying. Best of all are the lonely beaches and rocky bluffs of **Montauk Point State Park** (*off Sunrise Hwy. 631-668-3781. nyparks.state.ny.us/parks*) on a wild winter morning. ■

The Piedmont and Highlands

Kayaking the Streamers, Great Falls

HEAD WEST OR NORTH from the flat coastal plain of eastern Maryland, Delaware, southern New Jersey, and Long Island, and the land soon begins to rise. When the road becomes a gentle roller coaster carrying you inland from the ocean and upward to elevations of a few hundred to a thousand feet or so, you're in the Piedmont. That label—commonly applied to the broad area of gently rolling landscape that covers most of central Virginia and the Carolinas—suggests a pastoral landscape of

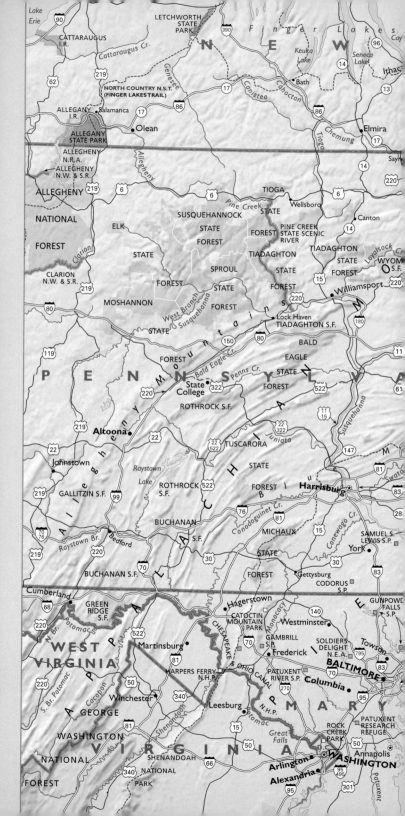

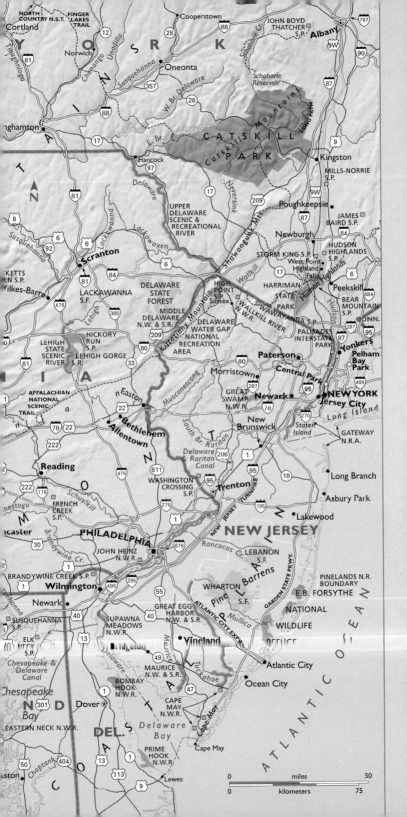

farmhouses and peaceful cows. But what is popularly referred to as the Piedmont extends northward as well—through central Maryland, eastern Pennsylvania, northern New Jersey, eastern New York, and on into most of southern New England.

Thousands of years ago in these northern reaches, the Piedmont landscape was periodically rearranged by bulldozing ice sheets and glaciers. As a result, much of today's northern Piedmont region appears rougher, steeper, and more abrupt than its southern counterpart. The layers of bedrock—metamorphic schist and gneiss, shale, and sandstone—more often break through the rich soils and surface greenery. Lonesome boulders stand here and there. Known as erratics, these chunks of rock were bred someplace to the north and hijacked to strange neighborhoods by glaciers on the run. A native Virginian might not recognize this ridged and rocky, low-lying plateau as the Piedmont, but the Piedmont it is, in its northern incarnation.

In the vicinity of New York City, the Piedmont plateau runs up against a complicated puzzle in a physiographic province known as the New England Uplands, and more specifically a subprovince called the Hudson Highlands. Another subprovince of the New England Uplands, the Manhattan Prong, underlies New York City itself. This jumble—as complex a geological area as you'll find anywhere in the United States— is the subject of intense interest, dispute, and speculation among professional geologists. (In fact, there are few better places than the palisades, cliffs, and highway roadcuts of the Hudson Highlands for amateurs to brush up on their fieldwork.) Generally it's said that the highlands are part of a northeast-trending mass of ridges and shallow valleys that extends from Pennsylvania to Connecticut.

Although not a strict geological example, the Manhattan skyline can serve as an analogy. At Wall Street, near the southern tip of Manhattan, and at midtown, towering skyscrapers stand anchored to bedrock ridges. In between, where the bedrock dips, the skyline dips as well— to the low-lying roofs of Greenwich Village, Little Italy, and Chinatown. Travel any uptown avenue in Manhattan and on the upper reaches of the island, somewhere north of 86th Street, you'll begin to get the feel of those ridges.

The hills of the highlands are the roots of ancient mountains laid down as sediments by Precambrian seas. As the sediments deepened, compressed, and heated over the course of millions of years, they metamorphosed into gneiss, marble, mica-rich schist, and the unusual gray metamorphic granite found so often in this area. The collision of tectonic plates caused new folds and gave birth to new mountains, but all the while the forces of erosion abraded and polished the land, leaving the low-lying "Highlands" landscape we see today. It is a peculiar rough-around-the-edges version of the Piedmont, pierced by unexpected cliffs, littered with odd rocks, punctuated by big erosion-resistant granite hills such as Storm King and Bear Mountain along the Hudson, and marked by trademark *roches moutonées* (sheepbacks)—smooth rock outcrops

Hudson River near Bear Mountain, New York

with rough southern sides, pummeled and polished eons ago by southbound glaciers.

Another characteristic of this highlands area is its long, straight valleys, eroded over the centuries along fracture or fault lines. Through the biggest of these straight valleys, the Hudson River flows to the Atlantic Ocean; the tides of the Atlantic, in turn, reach 160 miles back up the river to the city of Troy. Between today's cities of Peekskill and Newburgh, a glacier worked its way during the Pleistocene Ice Age, scouring a narrow, 15-mile-long gorge to new depths below sea level. Today the Hudson River flows here, continuing to carve the bedrock. That glacial gouging makes the lower Hudson a true fjord, like the famously beautiful coastal fjords of Norway. South of Maine, it's the only fjord on the East Coast.

The Piedmont has always been an appealing area. Settlers thought its climate more suitable to their needs than that of either the coastal plain to the east or the mountains to the west. Except for its southeast margin, most of the Piedmont was conveniently crossed by navigable rivers flowing to the sea. Its forests were tall and easily felled. Its wildlife was abundant, although its native bears, cougars, bison, wolves, elk, and moose are mostly now long gone. Its soils were rich, and its topography made for ease of cultivation—and, in later periods, canal and railroad building.

This long history of human settlement and exploitation of the Piedmont means that today most of its natural areas are restricted, recycled, and hemmed in by suburbs and cities. Its forests are second growth, its wetlands contracted, its waters recovering, and its surviving wildlife less diverse and in many cases scarce or threatened. Yet its beauties are still evident and well worth seeking out. ■

Chesapeake and Ohio Canal

■ 184.5 miles long ■ Maryland side of Potomac River from Washington, D.C. to Cumberland, Maryland ■ Best seasons spring-fall ■ Camping, primitive camping, hiking, rock climbing, boating, kayaking, canoeing, fishing, biking, horseback riding ■ Contact C & O Canal National Historical Park, P.O. Box 4, Sharpsburg, MD 21782; phone 301-739-4200. www.nps.gov/choh

AFTER SETTLERS CROSSED THE Appalachian Mountains to the Ohio Valley, the country faced a new problem: how to connect the resources of the new frontier to the established commerce of the East. In the mid-18th

Cycling the C & O Canal Towpath near Great Falls, Maryland

century, planners pinned their hopes on the Potomac, the only river that cut through the Appalachians. At first they tried to tame the river itself for navigation, but by 1824 they had given up that scheme and organized the Chesapeake and Ohio Canal Company to build a canal on the east side of the river from Washington, D.C., 360 miles to the Ohio River.

President John Quincy Adams himself turned the first spadeful of earth for this great national project on the Fourth of July, 1828. The company built 74 lift locks to raise the canal from sea level to 605 feet at Cumberland, Maryland, 184.5 miles away; 7 dams on the Potomac; 11 stone aqueducts to carry the canal over the Potomac's major tributaries; a 3,118-foot-long Paw Paw Tunnel to run the canal under a mountain;

and hundreds of lesser structures—all at a cost of 22 million dollars. The canal was 6 feet deep and ranged in width from 60 to 80 feet. By the time the builders reached Cumberland in 1850, however, the faster, cheaper Baltimore and Ohio Railroad had already moved into the Ohio Valley; plans to continue the waterway to Pittsburgh were dropped.

Along the truncated canal, coal, lumber, sand, gravel, limestone, corn, and wheat were shipped in 92-foot-long barges, each pulled by a two-mule team walking along the towpath. It was slow work and hard, and it never turned much of a profit; after a damaging flood in 1924, the canal shut down altogether. Eventually the abandoned waterway was turned over to the government, which unveiled a myopic plan in the 1950s to pave it over as a scenic highway. Fortunately, William O. Douglas, Associate Justice of the U. S. Supreme Court and an ardent conservationist, led an effort to have the C & O declared a national monument. In 1971, federal legislation was passed to create what is now known as the Chesapeake and Ohio Canal National Historical Park.

Today the C & O Canal is an immensely popular scenic and recreational site for Washingtonians and visitors alike. Some parts of the waterway are still navigable by kayak and canoe; others lie in interesting ruins. But the towpath is as good as new. It follows the old canal and the scenic river from Georgetown to the Great Falls of the Potomac, across the rolling Piedmont, and into the Ridge and Valley province of the Appalachian Mountains. The Allegheny Trail Alliance is coordinating efforts to complete the bike path from Cumberland to Pittsburgh, extending the canal—or the path, anyway—all the way to the Ohio at last.

What to See and Do

The **Potomac River** marks the boundary between Maryland on one side and Virginia and West Virginia on the other, sparking debate among local residents about which side of the river is more beautiful. The river is certainly seen to advantage from the Virginia side at **Great Falls Park** *(703-285-2965)* and **Riverbend Park** *(703-759-9018)*, and from West Virginia at **Harpers Ferry National Historical Park** *(304-535-6223)*. There the Shenandoah River cuts through the Blue Ridge to join the Potomac as its largest tributary; the **Appalachian Trail** (see pp. 120-21), following the Blue Ridge, crosses over both

rivers above the confluence. The spectacular views awaiting at the confluence should not be missed.

The canal and towpath lie entirely on the Maryland side of the Potomac, which should be the focus of your visit. Because highways flank the river and canal, you can dip into the park at almost any point. Park Service visitor centers, providing information about the park and ranger-led programs, are located at Georgetown, D.C. and Great Falls Tavern, Williamsport, Hancock, and Cumberland, Md. Any one of these centers would make a good place to begin your visit, but if you plan to touch down at only one point on the

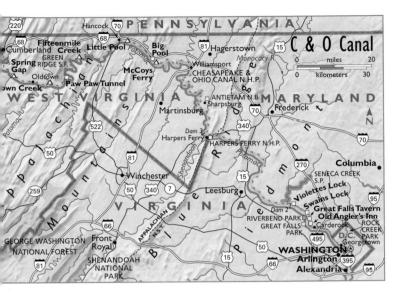

canal, do make it Great Falls, without a doubt one of the most scenic spots on the entire Potomac River.

Great Falls of the Potomac

The real star of the show at Great Falls is the river. Only 14 miles from Washington, the river descends some 200 feet, gradually narrowing as it rushes from the Piedmont toward the coastal plain. Then, at greatly accelerated speed, it drops through a long series of rapids collectively known as Great Falls, and plunges through a steep-sided canyon called **Mather Gorge.** Officially Class VI (risk of life), the rapids entice semisuicidal kayakers to desperate fun. Two to three drownings occur every year—take the posted restrictions and warnings seriously.

Stop at the visitor center in historic **Great Falls Tavern,** which served from 1831 to 1938 as a popular hostelry for canal travelers. Take a one-hour trip in a mule-drawn canal boat *(fare)* to get a taste of another century *(canal boat trips also offered in Georgetown).* Stroll north along the towpath for possible sightings of resident barred owls, woodpeckers, painted turtles, and muskrats.

Hiking

A safe view of the rapids can be had from the **Great Falls Overlook Trail.** This signposted, half-mile trail starts from the towpath just downstream from Great Falls Tavern. It carries you over a footbridge above the fish ladder, a skinny chute of rushing water, and on to **Falls Island.** Here boardwalks cross the fragile ecosystem of a bedrock terrace forest where pine, oak, and river birch cling to precarious footholds.

The trail carries on to **Olmsted Island** in mid-river and the **Great Falls Overlook.** From here you can feel the full force of the river's power. Watch for eagles soaring over the water and great blue herons standing casually in the shelter of midstream rocks on the lookout for dazed fish.

For a view of Mather Gorge, vigorous hikers can pick up the aptly named **Billy Goat Trail** about half a mile downstream from Great Falls Tavern, which stands beside Lock 16. This blue-blazed trail follows the river edge for 2 miles, joining up with the towpath for the additional 6 miles downstream to Carderock. (You can make a 4-mile loop by hiking the first 2 miles of the trail on **Bear Island,** along Mather Gorge, and returning 2 miles on the tow-path.) Be sure to be prepared for a strenuous scramble over boulders and some precipitous slopes—30 percent of all the park's accidents occur on this trail.

Behind Great Falls Tavern a network of interlooped trails climbs through pleasant wooded uplands around the site of an old gold mine. An easy, level trail, the disused **Berma Road,** parallels the canal for 2 miles southward from Great Falls Tavern to Old Angler's Inn, a popular bar and restaurant. Several branches of the **Gold Mine Trail** network connect to the Berma Road, making it possible to devise a woodland hiking loop to suit yourself.

Hiking and Biking

You can get onto the towpath almost anywhere between George-town and Cumberland for a round-trip hike or bike ride, or by working out a shuttle, for a point-to-point trip as long or as short as you want. The 12-foot-wide towpath is virtually level all the way, except for an 8-foot rise at each lock, so it makes little differ-ence in terms of exertion whether you travel up- or downriver.

If you're ambitious enough to go the canal's whole distance (184.5 miles), as many people do, start at the southern end. Traveling up the canal, you'll be tracing the chronological drift of history and settlement, moving away from the urbanized East toward the more scenic mountain "frontier." Perhaps understandably, the farther you go from Washington, the less traffic you'll meet on the towpath. You can also skip the urban section and start at Great Falls.

Boating, Canoeing, and Kayaking

The longest watered section of the canal extends from Georgetown to **Violettes Lock** (Lock 23) above Great Falls. Canoes have to portage around the locks. Above Violettes Lock there are only short sections for canoeing at **Big Pool, Little Pool,** and a 4.5-mile stretch from Town Creek to Oldtown. For boats, nothing larger than an elec-tric trolling motor is allowed in these short sections. (Canoes and boats can be rented at the boat houses listed in Resources, p. 281.)

The Park Service provides boat-launching sites on the Potomac, but it strongly discourages boating and canoeing on the river for all but the most experienced, espe-cially at Great Falls and in the dangerous areas between Little Falls Dam and Chain Bridge, and between Dam 3 and the US 340 bridge downstream from Harpers Ferry. Take these warnings seriously —drownings occur annually.

Risk-loving, highly experienced kayakers, however, should head for

Potomac River off C & O Canal, Glen Echo, Maryland

Virginia bluebells along C & O Canal

Little Falls and Great Falls. The rapids just across from Old Angler's Inn are a popular play spot for kayakers and canoeists of all levels.

Above Great Falls, you will find the Potomac to be a peaceful river. A 7-mile stretch of flat water backs up behind Feeder Dam 2 (near Violettes Lock). Known as the **Seneca Slackwater,** this is a popular spot for waterskiing, power-boating, and fishing.

Horseback Riding

Although you can't hire horses in the area, you can enjoy a ride on your own horse anywhere on the towpath from Swains Lock to Cumberland, except through the Paw Paw Tunnel. There are a few rules, however. Your party cannot exceed five in number, and you must keep your horses at least 50 feet away from campgrounds and picnic areas. An important safety tip: Don't bring a horse that spooks at bicycles.

Camping

Hikers and bikers will find campgrounds every 5 miles or so above Swains Lock; only the Marsden Tract site requires a permit, available for no cost at Great Falls Tavern. Vehicles can drive in to primitive campsites at McCoys Ferry, Fifteen Mile Creek, and Spring Gap, but be sure to bring your own drinking water.

Fishing

You'll see anglers up and down both banks of the Potomac, using every kind of tackle from state-of-the-art fly-fishing rods to old cane poles. Whatever the gear, certain areas are popular for large- and smallmouth bass, perch, and bluegill. Among the many spots to try are the stretch just above Little Falls, the waters near **Bealls Island** just below Swains Lock, or the Seneca Slackwater.

Rock Climbing

The Virginia side is popular with climbers. From the Great Falls Overlook in Maryland, you'll sometimes glimpse them spread-eagled on the rock faces of Great Falls Park, across the river. If you want to try it yourself, head downriver along the Billy Goat Trail for the rock faces opposite Bear Island. Or try the **Carderock** area, just above Milepost 10.4 on the towpath, thought to be the best rock climbing on the Maryland side of the Potomac. ■

John Heinz National Wildlife Refuge

■ 1,200 acres ■ Southeast Pennsylvania, near Philadelphia International Airport
■ Best seasons spring and fall ■ Wildlife viewing, hiking, photography ■ Contact
John Heinz NWR at Tinicum, 2 International Plaza, Suite 104, Philadelphia, PA
19113; phone 215-365-3118

THE WETLANDS KNOWN AS THE Tinicum Marsh once covered an area of 6,000 acres just southeast of Philadelphia. Then came urban sprawl. By 1955, when the city of Philadelphia created a wildlife preserve on 145 donated acres, it encompassed most of what remained of the Tinicum Marsh. Highways and a landfill were proposed for the surrounding land, but Pennsylvania Senator John Heinz joined a citizen effort to save the area for wildlife. The effort culminated in Congress establishing the John Heinz National Wildlife Refuge in 1972. Since then the refuge has grown to 1,200 acres, including woodlands, fields, and 250 acres of tidal marsh. **Darby Creek** leads from the marsh to the Delaware River and carries back its tides—but the marsh is too far from the ocean to become salt. This is a freshwater marsh of cattails, duckweed, and spatterdock, the largest remaining freshwater marsh in Pennsylvania and literally one of the last refuges of red-bellied turtles and leopard frogs. Yet, oddly enough, this is also the nation's most urban national wildlife refuge, standing between the roaring jet traffic of Philadelphia airport and the heart of the city only a few miles away. Scan the marsh for herons, egrets, and killdeer and you'll see the city towers just beyond.

Enter the refuge at 86th Street and Lindberg Boulevard, following signs to the new $5 million **environmental education center.** Built to serve visitors and the thousands of Philadelphia students for whom the refuge is a science classroom, it is worth a stop. Then take to the trails. Near the visitor center is the trailhead for the 10-mile-loop **Dike Trail** with boardwalked spurs leading into the marsh, the highlight of the refuge. (Connectors between trails let you tailor the length of your hike.) Another easy walk is the level 3.3-mile trail around the East Impoundment, especially interesting in spring and fall when migratory waterfowl come through. Be alert, too, for white-tailed deer.

Even better, if you have a canoe, kayak, or rowboat *(no motors allowed),* you can enter Darby Creek at the boat launch behind the visitor center, near the trailheads. A silent watercraft is the perfect vantage point for wildlife viewing, but beware of low tide—you might get stuck in the mud. ■

Leopard frog

Great Swamp National Wildlife Refuge

■ 7,500 acres ■ Northern New Jersey, near New York City ■ Best months April and May ■ Walking, bird-watching, wildflower viewing, wildlife viewing, auto tour ■ Contact the refuge, 152 Pleasant Plains Rd., Basking Ridge, NJ 07920; phone 973-425-1222

TWENTY-SIX MILES SOUTH of New York City's Times Square and smack in the midst of densely populated suburbia stands the Great Swamp National Wildlife Refuge. This small refuge—7 miles long and 3 miles wide—is the improbable vestige of Lake Passaic, a 30-mile-long inland sea left behind about 25,000 years ago by the receding Wisconsin glacier. In modern times, parts of the area were logged and drained; because it had become a swamp, however, it survived while surrounding higher ground sprouted suburban split-levels. When the Port Authority of New York and New Jersey announced plans in 1959 to build an international jetport on the "wasteland," irate citizens raised more than a million dollars to buy 3,000 acres, which they donated to the Department of the Interior. From that nucleus grew the Great Swamp refuge. In 1968, its eastern half was named the first national wilderness area.

Today the area provides nesting and feeding habitats for migrating warblers and waterfowl. Mallard, teal, pintail, shovelers, black ducks, and wood ducks are common transients, and many stay to nest. In the western half of the refuge, woodlands, grasslands, and wetlands are intensely managed to provide diverse habitats for a great variety of species, including the scarce eastern bluebird.

Bird-watch from your vehicle along the 1.5-mile **wildlife observation auto tour** (*Long Hill Rd. near Pleasant Plains Rd.*) or the overlook on Pleasant Plains Road (*200 yards from headquarters*). Then stroll the boardwalk interpretive trail at the **Wildlife Observation Center** (*Long Hill Rd.*). Best times are early morning, for the grand chorus of warblers, or early evening, when the peepers pipe up to drown out the distant traffic. The trail's observation blinds are good places to wait for wildlife to come to you. Scan the swamp and lowlands for birds (222 species have been counted), but look, too, for bog turtles, bull frogs, and blue-spotted salamanders.

Wildflowers abound as well, including the rare swamp pink in April and early May. Motor vehicles are prohibited in the wilderness, but you can park at well-designated areas on the periphery of the refuge and hike the more than 8 miles of footpaths that wind through the forests and grasslands. In addition, environmental education courses and guided tours are offered by the **Great Swamp Outdoor Education Center** (*Southern Blvd. 973-635-6629*) on the eastern side of the refuge, and by the **Environmental Education Center** (*Lord Stirling Park. 908-766-2489*) on the refuge's western side. ■

Interpretive trail, Great Swamp NWR

Boating, Central Park

Central Park

■ 843 acres ■ Manhattan Island from 59th Street to 110th Street ■ Best seasons spring-fall ■ Walking, boating, biking, horseback riding, bird watching, tennis, ice-skating ■ Contact the Central Park Conservancy, 14 East 60th St., New York, NY 10022; phone 212-310-6600

THE MOST IMPORTANT SLICE OF NATURE in New York City is not natural at all. It's the product of a design contest held in 1857 after poet and newspaper editor William Cullen Bryant persuaded city hall that New Yorkers needed a public park. Landscape designer Frederick Law Olmsted and architect Calvert Vaux, who won the contest, promised to "translate democratic ideas into trees and dirt." That meant carriage roads for the rich and walking paths for the poor, formal gardens for the upper class and rustic meadows for the masses.

Strongly influenced by romantic notions of nature, Olmsted and Vaux replaced a swamp and a city dump with a lovely lake, a country woodland (the **Ramble),** a castle, and a meadow full of sheep. They built sunken roadways so that crosstown traffic would not sully the views within their pastoral park. They intended Central Park to be a quiet refuge from busy city life, and astonishingly, that's exactly what it still is. Well, maybe not totally quiet, but a much appreciated refuge from city life for the 15 million people who visit it each year. It is also popular for migratory birds on the Atlantic flyway, particularly songbirds and other land birds. More than 270 bird species have been recorded in the park, and in peak migratory seasons—April to May and September to October—you may see as many as a hundred in a single day. Thousands of warblers, flycatchers, swallows, thrushes, vireos, sparrows, and other migrants stop over here.

Central Park is big: Three blocks wide and 51 blocks long, its 843 acres stretch from midtown to Harlem. Many New Yorkers who live near the park use it every day to exercise, walk the dog, or take the kids to the playground, and most residents have their favorite spots to spend a beautiful spring day. For visitors there's also a lot to see. Start at the **Dairy** *(212-794-6564)*, a restored Victorian building that serves as a visitor center dispensing maps and information; you'll find it in the middle of the park, along the 65th Street pathway. South of the Dairy is the **Sheep Meadow,** the province of summertime sunbathers. North of the Dairy, **the Mall** is enclosed by a colonnade of American elms thought to be the largest remaining stand of this tree in the country. The graceful **Bethesda Fountain** marks the end of the mall, beyond which lie the Ramble, the **Delacorte Theater,** and the **Great Lawn**—where the Public Theater, the New York Philharmonic, and the Metropolitan Opera perform summer nights.

Runners should head for the entrance to the **Reservoir** at East 90th Street or contact the New York Road Runners Club *(212-860-4455)*, which often leads runs through the park. Bird-watchers will do well in the 33-acre Ramble. Bicycles, rowboats, or gondolas are available for rent at Loeb Boathouse on the lake *(E side of park, bet. 74th and 75th Sts. 212-517-2233)*. Or hire a horse from nearby Claremont Stables *(175 W. 89th St. 212-724-5100)* or a horse drawn carriage from the ranks on Central Park South. You can play tennis at the **Tennis House** on the west side of the park between 94th and 95th Streets. **Wollman Rink** *(E side of park, between 62nd and 63rd Sts. 212-396-1010)* offers in-line skating in summer and ice-skating in winter. **Strawberry Fields,** the memorial garden honoring John Lennon, is on the west side of the park between 71st and 74th Streets, opposite the Dakota, the apartment building where he lived.

Is it safe? Crimes are committed in Central Park, yet millions of people visit it—many every day—without incident. To play it safe, leave your flashy jewelry at home, don't go to the park alone, and don't go after dark, except to attend a public event. ■

Urban Bird Refuges

Public parks were created in large urban areas to provide havens of artificial "nature" for city dwellers. Ironically, they've now become sanctuaries of real nature—tiny islands of green in a sea of gray concrete for migrating birds on the Atlantic flyway.

In addition to Central Park, the New York Audubon Society lists three New York city parks as critical feeding, breeding, or nesting grounds for birds. Prospect Park (526 acres) in Brooklyn, another park designed by Olmsted and Vaux, is well forested, making it critical habitat for woodland birds. In the Bronx, Van Cortlandt Park (1,146 acres) and Pelham Bay Park (2,764 acres) support breeding communities of wood thrush, gray catbird, red-eyed vireo, chestnut-sided warbler, ovenbird, and eastern towhee. Pelham Bay also supports salt marsh birds, including a rookery of black-crowned night-herons, and is a well-known site for fall hawk-watching. As urban sprawl expands exponentially, these unnatural urban parks become increasingly valuable as the last natural refuges of birds.

Following pages: Sheep Meadow, Central Park

Palisades Interstate Park

■ 2,472 acres ■ Northern New Jersey along Hudson River ■ Year-round
■ Hiking, fishing, cross-country skiing ■ Adm. fee ■ Contact the Palisades
Interstate Park Commission, Bear Mountain, NY 10911; phone 845-786-2701.
www.nysparks.com or www.njpalisades.com

ORIGINALLY FORMED A CENTURY AGO to protect the Hudson River cliffs
known as the Palisades, the Palisades Interstate Park Commission, a joint
venture of New York and New Jersey, now oversees more than 100,000
acres of parkland in the Hudson Highlands on the west side of the Hudson
River between Fort Lee, New Jersey, and Kingston, New York. In addition
to the protected 13-mile section of the Palisades, the system now encompasses half a dozen historical sites from the Revolutionary War, including
Fort Lee; two preserves; 15 state parks, including Harriman and Bear Mountain State Parks (see pp. 94-100); and other small properties.

One, **Palisades Interstate Park,** is the ultimate linear park, stretching
13 miles long and averaging less than an eighth of a mile wide. Its most
significant distance, however, is vertical. It exists to protect the grandest
section of a unique rock wall that rises 530 feet from the west bank of the
Hudson River. The wall is called the Palisades after the resemblance its
peculiar vertical columns bear to the log palings of fortifications once
built by local Native Americans, the Lenni Lenape ("the real people"). It
begins at the Rahway River in New Jersey, crosses the western edge of
Staten Island, and follows the Hudson River through New Jersey into
Rockland County, New York, where it suddenly ends—a distance of
about 40 miles. This is an area of reddish brown sandstone, the kind that
faced the famous brownstone houses of old New York. But the Palisades
are a continuous sill, formed by the intrusion of molten rock into the
sandstone layers. Subsequent cooling caused the fractures that give the
sill its columnar appearance.

This beautiful and unusual cliff was heavily quarried in the 19th century, when the talus slopes at its base were hauled away as ship's ballast.
The red oak forest that crowned its ridge was felled for timber. About
1900, under citizen pressure, an Interstate Park Commission was organized to save this great geological treasure. The scenic **Palisades Interstate Parkway** (see sidebar p. 96), from which commercial vehicles are
banned, was built atop the cliff in 1958.

The Palisades can be glimpsed from the east side of the Hudson, but
to get a good look you'll want to walk the trails that pass under and over
the cliff. Just south of the George Washington Bridge, via either Fort Lee
Road or Hudson Terrace, the **Shore Trail** (13.5 miles long with white
blazes) is a broad, level path for most of its length, offering incomparable
neck-cricking views of the towering Palisades. If you'd rather leave the
driving to someone else, buses (*New York's Port Authority Terminal 212-
564-8484*) travel from New York and New Jersey to nearby Bridge Plaza;
Hudson Terrace and the park entrance are a block south. You'll pass by

New Jersey Palisades Interstate Park

old fields, fishing shacks, and woodlands of red oak and flowering dogwood. At **Forest View** (Milepost 11.5) the trail becomes rugged and enters its most scenic 2 miles, winding over talus slopes and climbing to the cliff top near the state line and State Line Lookout.

Along the cliff top runs a 12.7-mile section of the 300-mile-long, turquoise-blazed **Long Path** (see pp. 98-99), entered from Bridge Plaza at the end of the George Washington Bridge in Fort Lee. Although not far from the parkway and the sound of traffic, it often passes through "five oak" woodlands of red, black, white, scarlet, and chestnut oak trees. Five connector trails link the Long Path to the Shore Trail at intervals of a few miles, making shorter loop hikes possible. You can also intersect the Shore Trail by driving down the Englewood Approach Road to the Englewood or Alpine Boat Basins, both of which have parking. Alternatively, you can drive to the state line and walk either of the trails in reverse. ■

Bear Mountain and Harriman State Parks

■ 5,067 acres (Bear Mountain State Park); 47,000 acres (Harriman State Park)
■ Hudson River, southwest bank ■ Year-round ■ Camping, hiking, boating, swimming, fishing, biking, mountain biking, cross-country skiing, ice-skating, nature study ■ Adm. fee ■ Both parks: contact Bear Mountain SP, Bear Mountain, New York 10911; phone 845-786-0427 (Bear Mountain SP) or 845-786-2701 (Harriman SP)

BEAR MOUNTAIN STATE PARK and its big next-door neighbor, Harriman State Park, are two of the oldest and largest parks in the Hudson Highlands. Together they account for three-quarters of the acreage of the

Sunset at Lake Welch, Harriman State Park

interstate park system. Both parks were established in 1910, thanks largely to the generosity of Mary Averall Harriman, whose donations of land and money quashed a misguided state plan to crown beautiful Bear Mountain with what is now Sing Sing Prison.

Accessible by bus from New York's Port Authority Terminal *(212-564-8484)*, the two parks offer a great range of activities for city dwellers. Bear Mountain is more "domesticated" with its swimming pool, drive-in scenic overlook, clipped picnic grounds, winter ice-skating rink, and Bear Mountain Inn *(845-786-2731)*, a massive stone country hotel built in the 1920s that provides the only accommodation at Bear Mountain. Harriman State Park is wilder, with more than half its acreage forested and accessible mainly by foot trails. It offers lakeside camping at Beaver Pond Campground and cabin rentals at Lake Sebago. In either park you can hire a boat, go fishing, ride your bike, or enjoy a picnic. On a rainy day you can

Palisades Guide

The maze of roads and heavy traffic on the Palisades parkway can be daunting and confusing. To insure a good visit, stop at the visitor center (*between Lake Welch and Anthony Wayne exits. 845-786-5003*). It serves Bear Mountain and Harriman State Parks as well as the whole Palisades Interstate Park System, carrying the complete trail and road maps you'll need. Tackle and New York State fishing licenses are also for sale.

visit the **Trailside Museum and Nature Study Center** in Bear Mountain. (Children especially enjoy the rescued wild animals who live there.)

With more than 235 miles of trails, this is serious hiking country. Before you set off on a walk, however, be advised that these trails are not short, level, self-guided nature loops. Generally the distances given are one way, not because you're expected to return by the same path but because you're expected to patch together a return route on other trails—which is why you need that detailed map, guidebook, and ideally a compass. Be prepared.

Trails reach marshes, swamps, open fields, hardwood ridges, hemlock forests, streams, gorges, 36 lakes, and a scattering of abandoned iron mines. The forests of both parks are a mix of evergreens—red cedar, hemlock, and white pine—and deciduous trees such as hickory, ash, beech,

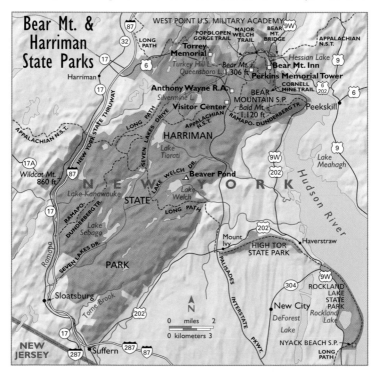

Turkey Hill Lake, Popolopen Gorge Trail, Bear Mountain State Park

and the predominant oaks and maples that kindle the brilliance of fall.

On the trails you very well may meet snakes, skinks, squirrels, raccoons, woodchucks, and white-tailed deer. With luck you might even spot a beaver, otter, mink, bobcat, or black bear. Of more than 240 bird species recorded in the parks, you're sure to see the summer regulars: catbirds, towhees, and turkey vultures. Watch, too, for great horned owls, wild turkeys, pileated woodpeckers, and brilliant scarlet tanagers.

Bear Mountain itself—together with Storm King to the north, and Breakneck Ridge—is one of the great sentinels of the Hudson River, which reaches its narrowest stretch here. That strategic fact explains why this area is a mecca for Revolutionary War history buffs. Many hike the Bicentennial Trails, blazed in 1975 for the country's birthday celebration, which follow the routes used by the British and American armies in 1777 and 1779 respectively.

The literal high point of a visit to Bear Mountain is a trip to its 1,284-foot summit for panoramic views of the Hudson Valley from the observation deck of the **Perkins Memorial Tower.** It's possible to drive to the summit on Perkins Memorial Drive (*off Seven Lakes Dr.*), but to earn the view take the **Major Welch Trail** (formerly part of the Appalachian Trail) behind Bear Mountain Inn. The 2.6-mile trail, blazed with a red dot on white, follows the asphalt path beside the western shore of Hessian Lake,

The Long Path

HIKING DEVOTEES built the first section of the Long Path—a trail meant to extend from New York City to White-face Mountain in the Adirondacks—along the top of the New Jersey Palisades in the 1930s. The Long Path was to be a largely unmarked route through a 10-mile north-south corridor; hikers were to bushwhack along the corridor using topographical maps. The project languished for 25 years, and by the time it was taken up again in the 1960s, suburbia had sprawled and the green corridor hard to find.

Planners abandoned the bushwhacking scheme and continued the Long Path as a marked trail. By 1995 it had reached its current status as a continuous 329-mile trail winding through every conceivable habitat of the region, from suburb to swamp, offering superb panoramic views along the way.

The Long Path begins at the New Jersey end of the George Washington Bridge, traces the top of the Palisades through Palisades park (see pp. 92-93), then follows the Palisades Escarpment to its end in Mount Ivy. Next it passes through Harriman State Park before descending to the Hudson River Valley, where for the next 50 miles it mainly follows country roads through densely populated Orange County.

It climbs Shunnemunk Mountain, follows an abandoned railroad track and rural roads, passes through Highland State Park, and scales the escarpment of the Shawangunk Mountains. Along the way the trail passes two Shawangunks sky lakes, traverses the Rondout Valley, and winds 95 miles through Catskill Park, climbing nine peaks higher than 3,500 feet. It continues beyond Catskill Park (see pp. 146-151), descends to the Schoharie Reservoir, and runs through the Schoharie Valley. In Middleburgh it crosses the Endless Mountains to the Helderberg Escarpment, which it follows north into John Boyd Thatcher State Park, 15 miles west of Albany.

Efforts are under way to find better routes for trail sections currently on roadways. The complete guide to the Long Path is available from the New York-New Jersey Trail Conference *(GPO Box 2250, New York, NY 10116)*, with updates on www.nynjtc.org. ∎

Torrey Memorial, Long Mountain, Long Path

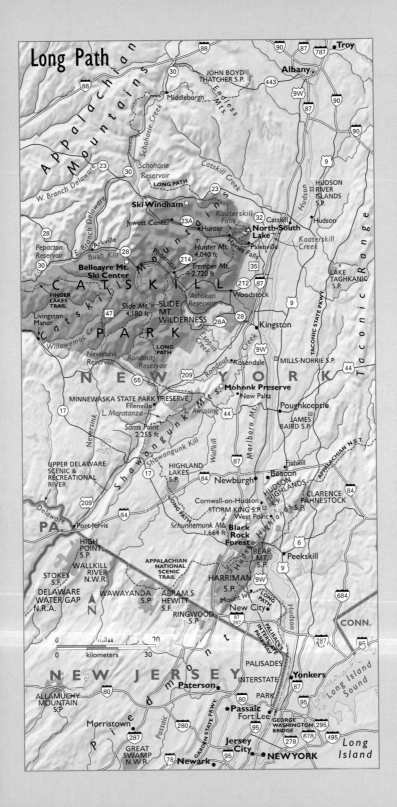

The Symbol of Storm King Mountain

Located on the Hudson River off US 9W between Highland Falls (West Point) and Cornwall-on-Hudson, Storm King Mountain *is* more than a beautiful state park. It was the center of a 17-year legal struggle that established the right of citizen groups to sue a government agency to protect natural resources and scenic beauty. The suit was brought in 1963 by groups ranging from the Nature Conservancy to the Hudson River Fishermen's Association after the Consolidated Edison power company announced plans to build a powerhouse in the state park at the base of Storm King Mountain and a reservoir in the Black Rock Forest Highlands beyond. The suit was settled out of court in 1980, a precedent-setting victory for conservation. Today the eastern end of Storm King Mountain rises more than 1,000 feet from the Hudson River—a wall broken only by the encircling line of N.Y. 218. The best views of Storm King are from Hudson Highlands across the river, near Peekskill, New York on N.Y 35. There are great views *from* Storm King, too, but its steep, rugged trails are recommended for experienced hikers only.

then turns sharply into the woods; it culminates in a steep, steady climb 900 feet to the observation tower at the summit. The way down, along a ridge on the south side of the mountain, offers more fine views. The trail ends on a lower section of Memorial Drive, where it meets the current **Appalachian Trail** (see pp. 120-21). If you've dreamed of testing yourself on the AT, this convenient section—more than 20 miles across the two parks, crossing nine summits, from N.Y. 17 to Bear Mountain Bridge—is your chance.

If you catch summit fever, try the **Cornell Mine Trail** (2.5 miles one way; blazed in blue), which begins about 100 yards behind and west of Bear Mountain Inn. It begins with an easy walk along old roads, ascends 1,000 feet in 1.5 woodland miles, then climbs the last steep half mile to the **Ramapo-Dunderberg Trail** between Dunderberg (Thunder Mountain) and Bald Mountain. Before returning, walk a short way west on the Ramapo-Dunderberg Trail to the abandoned Cornell Mine, a good vantage point for Bear Mountain and the Hudson River views.

For a less strenuous walk, try the **Popolopen Gorge Trail** (4.5 miles one way; blazed in red on white). The trail begins on US 9W, just before the Popolopen Gorge Bridge. To reach the trailhead, take the paved path behind Bear Mountain Inn along the east side of Hessian Lake and continue north past a traffic circle to US 9W. The trail follows the steep south side of the gorge of Popolopen Creek, passes through old hemlock forest, skirts the shores of Queensboro and Turkey Hill Lakes, and terminates at the **Long Path** (see pp. 98-99). Once you hit the Long Path, you can retrace your way back to the inn; or, if your feet are still itching, set off across the state. ■

Wallkill River National Wildlife Refuge

■ 4,373 acres ■ Northwest New Jersey-New York border ■ Best seasons spring and fall ■ Hiking, canoeing, fishing, bird-watching ■ No autos, bicycles, or pets ■ Contact the refuge, 1547 County Rte. 565, Sussex, New Jersey 07461; phone 973-702-7266. http://wallkill.fws.gov

ESTABLISHED IN 1990, this refuge embraces a 9-mile stretch of the Wallkill River, mostly in Sussex, New Jersey, and partly in Orange County, New York. The refuge is still growing toward a projected 7,500 acres, to include 4,200 acres of freshwater wetlands, 2,500 acres of grasslands and uplands, and 800 acres of hardwood forest. In the hilly Piedmont section of northwest New Jersey—just where New Jersey, New York, and Pennsylvania meet—the refuge occupies a strategic location squarely between two major migratory bird flight paths: the valleys of the Hudson River to the east and the Delaware River to the west.

The bottomlands of the Wallkill River floodplain, subject to seasonal flooding, were drained for farming in the 19th century. Now protected within the refuge and being restored to their natural state, these wetlands are the most important (and practically the only) remaining sizable habitat for migrating waterfowl in northern New Jersey. The spring and fall parade of migratory birds is especially diverse: 24 species of raptors and 125 species of songbirds. Along the Wallkill River and among the cattails of freshwater marshes lurk vocal bullfrogs, painted turtles, and threatened bog turtles as well as river otters and muskrat. The upland forests of sugar maple and mixed oaks are home to gray and red foxes, coyotes, white-tailed deer, and the occasional black bear. The river itself holds largemouth bass, pickerel, and bullheads.

The very best way to see these rich habitats and get close to wildlife is by canoe or kayak, floating through wet meadows and floodplain forest—though you must be prepared to get out occasionally and push. (There is no driving route through the refuge, and no biking is allowed.) You can also fish from access points at **Bassetts Bridge** and **Oil City Road.**

For the boatless, the refuge's two nature trails provide an easy stroll through varied habitats. The comfortable benches and photo blind along the 2-mile interpretive **Wood Duck Nature Trail** at the refuge's south end invite quiet contemplation and leisurely observation of nature. If birding is your passion, try the 2.5-mile **Liberty Loop** at the north end. Starting from Oil City Road in Pine Island, the trail is elevated in part on an old farm dike, offering good views of both grassland birds and waterfowl. A mile of the loop lies along the **Appalachian Trail.** ■

Mallard pair

Appalachians

Catskill Mountains near Woodstock, New York

ONE OF THE MOST DRAMATIC SCENARIOS in the annals of scientific conjecture culminated in the hills and valleys we know today as the Appalachian Mountains. Geologists theorize that beginning about 450 million years ago, in the Paleozoic era, a vast sea lying east of what is now the Appalachians began to shrink. A plate of the Earth's crust bearing the seafloor slid under the North American continental plate, a process involving a lot of bashing, scraping, and crumpling of both plates. That collision buckled

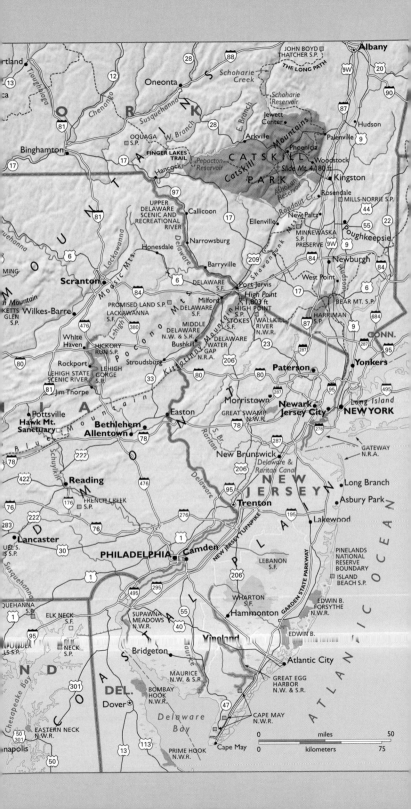

the North American landscape inland in the first episode of Appalachian mountain building, known as the Taconic orogeny. Then about 380 million years ago, the seafloor having completely subducted beneath it, North America collided with the British Isles and Scandinavia. This second crash, the Acadian orogeny, knocked the Appalachians galley-west and forced them higher.

But the best—the Allegheny orogeny—was still to come. About 260 million years ago North America smashed up again in this game of continental bumper cars—this time with North Africa and probably with South America as well, as these two crash victims were bound together at the time in the giant southern landmass called Gondwana. This final megawreck was so stupendous that it welded Gondwana to the North America-Europe landmass to produce the supercontinent Pangaea. You can imagine what it did to the Appalachians. About 125 million years ago, swelling along what is now called the Mid-Atlantic Ridge split apart the joined continents.

The Appalachians of today are the eroded remains of the rocks that were folded, faulted, and uplifted by the Allegheny orogeny. Large quantities of rock have been removed and deposited as sediment far from the Appalachians. Now aligned northeast-southwest between Alabama and Newfoundland, the modern Appalachians encompass the Great Smoky Mountains of North Carolina; the Blue Ridge of Virginia; the central area known as the Ridge and Valley province of western Maryland and central Pennsylvania; the Green Mountains of Vermont; and many other ridges and ranges.

Among all the Appalachian ranges, the Ridge and Valley province is the most distinctive. Its largest lowland, the Great Valley, extends from the Hudson River watershed through Virginia's Shenandoah Valley. Its most prominent ridge, appropriately named Endless Mountain by the Lenni Lenape people, is called the Shawangunk Mountains in New York, Kittatinny Mountain in New Jersey, and the Blue and Tuscarora Mountains in Pennsylvania.

The pattern of long, steep ridges divided by long, narrow valleys is explained by differential erosion: Some rocks wear away rapidly, some much slower. Less easily explained is the peculiar tendency of rivers in the Ridge and Valley province to cut paths through the ridges rather than flowing down the valleys like normal, well-behaved streams. The Delaware Water Gap and Pennsylvania's Lehigh Gorge are two places where rivers went their own way, with highly scenic results.

Despite the catchall name Appalachians, the mountains are not all of a piece. For one thing, glaciers scoured the northern reaches, leaving erratics, kettle ponds, sky lakes, and other geological mementos; the rest of the range went untouched by the ice sheets. Differences in soil, elevation, and climate produced variations in flora and fauna all through the range. Patterns of settlement and exploitation left various marks upon the land. For the most part, however, the middle Atlantic mountains are crowned with transition forest—the type found in a broad band across the northern United States from Minnesota to Maine, and in Canada across the southern parts of Ontario, Quebec, and the Maritime Provinces. Transition forest and even traces of boreal (northern conifer) forest extend southward over the cool, high elevations of the Appalachians.

As the name suggests, the transition forest contains a mix of trees found in both the deciduous forests to the south and the boreal forests to the north. Generally the species that can adapt to the widest range of conditions will predominate in any forest. In the Appalachians the red maple is king, sometimes almost alone among the hardwoods, but more often sharing dominion with yellow birch, American basswood, or beech. Less prominent are white ash, black cherry, aspen, paper birch, northern red oak, and American elm. Holding their own amid the hardwoods are such conifers as fast-growing white pine, shade-tolerant hemlock, and cold-tolerant red spruce.

Kaaterskill Falls

You can easily discern the mixed elements of the transition forest on a mountainside during its autumn glory, the evergreens scattered darkly among the gold and orange of aspen and oak and the fiery red of maple. Fall is the time to see this forest at its best. But early spring also has its charms; before the hardwoods leaf out and shade the forest floor, you'll find it carpeted in wildflowers — milkworts, hepaticas, starflowers, wood lilies, trilliums, clematis, and violets.

Sadly, many creatures who once roamed these forests have moved north or disappeared altogether. Don't bother trying to find gray wolves, mountain lions, or woodland caribou. But you may see white-tailed deer and black bears and such smaller forest-dwellers as beavers, mink, fishers, opossums, squirrels, rabbits, raccoons, and porcupines. Woodland birds are abundant; look for cedar waxwings, kinglets, chickadees, nuthatches, scarlet tanagers, orioles, and ruffed grouse.

In the 19th and well into the 20th century, Appalachia was synonymous with rural poverty and backwardness; these were hardscrabble mountains, a poor place to farm. Today we know more about the sturdy Appalachian culture that produced American crafts of distinction— baskets, quilts, ironwork, pottery—and sweet mountain music. Climb an Appalachian summit today, or walk beside a stream as a puff of dogwood seems to drift among the trees, and you will see in these mountains the beauty that has been there all along. ■

Maryland's Panhandle

- 1,087 square miles ■ Western Maryland ■ Year-round. Oct. for foliage
- Camping, primitive camping, hiking, white-water rafting and kayaking, swimming, fishing, biking, mountain biking, cross-country skiing, snowshoeing ■ Contact Garrett County Chamber of Commerce, 15 Visitors Center Dr., McHenry, MD 21541, phone 301-387-4386. www.garrettchamber.com; or Allegany County Visitors Bureau, 13 Canal St., Cumberland, MD 21502, phone 800-508-4748 or 301-777-5132. www.mdmountainside.com; or www.dnr.state.md.us /publiclands/western (state forests and parks)

NATIONAL GEOGRAPHIC dubbed Maryland "a delightful geographic miniature of America" with good reason. One of the country's smallest states, the Free State ranks high in natural diversity, as anyone who drives across it will see. From east to west the landscape unfolds, changing shape and coloration like a documentary film in introductory geology: coastal plain, Piedmont, Ridge and Valley province, Appalachian Plateau.

In the panhandle that makes up the far western part of the state, comprising Garrett County and its neighbor to the east, Allegany County, the landscape takes on star quality. Here Maryland's tallest mountains rise

Savage River, western Maryland

above 3,000 feet—not much by western standards, but of surpassing grandeur all the same. The mountains are not steep and peaked; their slopes are gentle, their tops rounded off in long north-south ridges. Between the mountains lie deep valleys through which wild rivers run and sometimes pool, behind dams, into mirrored lakes.

The land is cloaked in forest, predominantly northern hardwoods: oak, maple, beech, hickory, and birch, with a few stands of eastern hemlock interspersed. In the understory, viburnum and hawthorn share space with blueberry, mountain laurel, Virginia creeper, and rhododendron. Forty-four percent of Maryland's land area is forested, and much of that woodland is here. These tree-clad mountains seem light years from the urban bluster of the nation's capital, only a few hours' drive away.

Allegany County is home to Green Ridge State Forest, the state's second largest. In Garrett County, one-fifth of the land is devoted to parks, lakes, forests, and wildlife management areas. Some of Garrett County's parks offer well-developed (e.g., hot showers) campgrounds, swimming beaches, and picnic areas within undeveloped state forests with primitive campsites; serious hiking, biking, and horseback riding trails; and whitewater rivers. This variety of recreational opportunities and the beauty of the land make Maryland's panhandle a prime outdoor destination.

What to See and Do

Maryland's Panhandle offers such a dazzling diversity of outdoor activities in so many striking locales and varied conditions that it is a challenge to decide what to do and where to go. Your best approach might be to pick your primary recreational activity first, then head for the spot that seems most conducive to it.

Garrett State Forest

Three miles of trout streams (*state fishing license required*) winding among stands of maple and oak mark the woodlands of 8,000-acre Garrett State Forest, which lies along the West Virginia border south of I-68. In winter Garrett County's public lands become a playground for cross-country skiers and snowshoers. All roads and trails in the state forest are open to them.

Within the forest are two state parks: 365-acre **Herrington Manor State Park** features 53-acre **Herrington Lake,** with a swimming beach, nonmotorized boats for rent, and fishing for stocked rainbow trout. It has 20 cabins (available year-round) and access to a hiking-biking trail system that winds through the state forest. Though the park's campgrounds close in winter, it offers not only the cabins but ski rentals as well.

Four miles away the Youghiogheny River cascades through 300-acre **Swallow Falls State Park,** near the 65-site Swallow Falls Campground on Maple Glade Road. To the south is 11,461-acre **Potomac State Forest,** where, for fly fishermen, the **North Branch Potomac River** near Lostland Run boasts the "Maryland Grand Slam": brook, brown, rainbow, and cutthroat trout.

(Contact sites c/o the State Forest and Park Service, 222 Herrington Lane, Oakland, MD 21550. 301-334-2038, state forests, or 301-334-9180, state parks.)

"The Yough"

The Youghiogheny River—say "Yock-ah-GAIN-ee," or "the Yock" for short—flows north through Western Maryland for only 38 miles, but it may be the state's best known river. This stretch is referred to as the **Upper Yough** to distinguish it from middle and lower sections in Pennsylvania (pp. 158-160). In 1968 the Upper Yough from Millers Run (near Herrington Manor State Park) to Friends-ville became the first Maryland waterway to be named a state Wild and Scenic River.

South of Oakland, it's a placid stream, meandering through farmlands. Then, excitement builds as it narrows, deepens, and steepens, rushing through towering stands of virgin hemlock. In Swallow Falls State Park, the river drops 280 feet in 4 miles. It levels out for about 6 miles; then, near Gap Falls, the Yough begins a long, dramatic descent of about 100 feet per mile until it levels out again and is stopped at Youghiogheny River Lake, which lies on the Maryland-Pennsylvania border.

This stretch of water is justifiably famous among river runners, who hail it as the best river east of the Mississippi for white-water

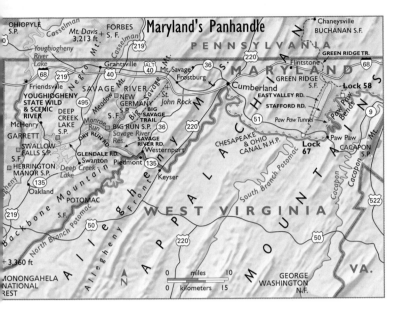

canoeing, kayaking, and rafting. With about 20 Class IV and Class V rapids between the usual put-in at Sang Run Road and the take-out at Friendsville, the Upper Yough is a river for kayakers and rafters who've been there and done that.

For list of licensed white-water outfitters, contact Deep Creek Lake Recreation Area, Youghiogheny River Management *(898 State Park Rd., Swanton, MD 21561. 301-387-4111.)*

The Upper Yough is also well known among fly fishermen. The 6-mile stretch of riffles and pools near **Hoyes Run** is prime dry-fly territory. Plentiful hatches of caddies and mayflies, coupled with regular releases of cold water from the hydroelectric plant at Deep Creek Lake, insure the presence of great numbers of voracious brown and rainbow trout. Another good spot on the Yough is off Sang Run Road near Oakland.

Deep Creek Lake State Park

Formed behind the hydroelectric dam that stands above the confluence of Deep Creek and the Youghiogheny River, **Deep Creek Lake** spreads out to an area of about 6 square miles and has 65 miles of shoreline. The lake is home to largemouth and smallmouth bass, pickerel, northern pike, walleye, crappie, yellow perch, bluegill, and brown, brook, and rainbow trout. For boating, flat-water canoeing, and fishing, Deep Creek Lake is an obvious choice.

On the lake's east side lies 1,818-acre Deep Creek Lake State Park *(898 State Park Rd., Swanton, MD 21561. 301-387-7067 or 301-387-5563)*, which offers a 700-foot swimming beach, canoe rentals, and a 112-site developed campground. Park rangers also conduct guided canoe trips on the lake.

Negotiating rapids on the Upper Youghiogheny

Savage River State Forest

Just beyond Deep Creek Lake State Park to the east is 54,000-acre Savage River State Forest, Maryland's largest. Within the forest are 455-acre **New Germany State Park** and 300-acre **Big Run State Park.**

New Germany State Park features a campground; the 13-acre **New Germany Lake** for swimming, fishing, and canoeing; and a trail system. From late spring through early fall, the park conducts guided canoe trips on the **Savage River Reservoir** *(Fee).*

Big Run State Park has some of the most beautiful streamside primitive campsites anywhere, as well as canoeing and good fishing on the reservoir for bluegill, walleye, and bass.

For an easy walk or bike ride with a fine view, follow the 1.5-mile-round-trip **Meadow Mountain Trail** in the state forest along an old woods road from Frank Brenneman Road to the Meadow Mountain Overlook.

Hikers can also trek the 4.4-mile (one way) **Monroe Run Trail** in the state forest. Drive along New Germany Road to a parking area at the trailhead, located just north of the Monroe Run Overlook at the top of Meadow Mountain, and hike down, meandering back and forth across **Monroe Run** some 18 times. There are no bridges, but you'll find plenty of tempting chances to cool off in this inviting mountain stream fringed with ferns. For an overnight, camp at Big Run, where the trail ends, and walk out the next day—if you don't mind climbing back up the 1,140 feet you descended from Meadow Mountain.

Serious backpackers should do the 17-mile **Big Savage Trail** *(no bikes allowed),* often voted the best hike in Maryland. The sometimes rugged trail, which follows the ridge line of **Big Savage Mountain** at about 2,500 feet, is more easily hiked from north to south, heading toward the Savage River Reservoir from St. John Rock *(Funzel Rd. off I-68, then S on Beall School Rd. to Old Beall School Rd., then 0.5 mile to St. Johns Rock Rd.).* The trail encompasses about a 1,500-foot change in elevation, most of it occurring in the few miles closest to the reservoir. It passes through dense forest, so the best views are to be had in early spring, when sight lines are not yet blocked by the leafed-out trees and there are plenty of colorful wildflowers. For more great trekking, check *Hikes in Western Maryland,* published by the Potomac Appalachian Trail Club *(703-242-0693. www.patc.org).*

For fine trout fishing, drop your line in the state forest's **Savage River** or, just beyond the forest boundary, in the **Casselman River,** north of I-68 via the Bittinger Road exit. In winter the forest also opens 23 miles of trails to cross-country skiers.

(Contact Savage River Complex, 349 Headquarters Lane, Grantsville, MD 21536, 301-895-5759, state forest, or 301-895-5453, state parks.)

Garrett County Scenic Drive

A 65-mile driving circuit through the backwoods beauty of Garrett County begins and ends at Grantsville. You can loop around the edges of Savage River State Forest on the basic route: Take Md. 495

Wild Trout

Many state parks now stock streams for trout fishing. Brook, brown, and rainbow trout are most commonly stocked. Streams that still support populations of wild brook and brown trout usually are not stocked for fear of unspecified "negative effects" on the wild trout from interactions with hatchery fish. But some anglers don't discriminate between streams, and wild trout are thus threatened by overfishing. Give the wild trout a break and fish only in stocked streams. If you must fish the wild ones, practice catch and release, use barbless hooks, and land your catch with a rubberized net to save the fish's protective slime from abrasion. Wild brook trout are more valuable in their habitat than on the dinner plate. Because they can live only in clean water, they are one of our best indicators of water quality and the state of the environment.

of you across the water will be Big Savage Mountain; to your right, near the end of the reservoir, will be Backbone Mountain. Turn right onto Savage River Road and proceed south to the dam at the southeastern end of the reservoir. Continue on Savage River Road, following the river through the mountains to Md. 135, where you rejoin the loop.

Variation 2: To visit Deep Creek Lake, take Glendale Road west off Md. 495, cross the lake, and turn right (north) on US 219. Just after you cross the lake again, turn right (east) onto Rock Lodge Road. Follow the shore until you meet Glendale Road again; turn left (east) and return to Md. 495.

Green Ridge State Forest

In Allegany County, about 22 miles east of Cumberland, lies 43,000-acre Green Ridge State Forest *(28700 Headquarters Dr. N.E., Flintstone, MD 21530. 301-478-3124. Take the M.V. Smith Rd. exit off I-68).* Part of the Ridge and Valley province of the Appalachians, Green Ridge sprawls from the Pennsylvania border southward over the mountains above the serpentine section of the Potomac River (and the C & O Canal) known as the **Paw Paw Bends.** An undeveloped forested maze of dirt and gravel roads, logging sites, primitive campsites, power-line cuts, private hunting camps, and rugged trails, Green Ridge is a rough retreat for the fit and experienced outdoors person.

Ambitious cyclists will find plenty of gratifying challenges here. The woods look scruffier than those to the west because the

south to Md. 135 east, then Md. 36 north to US 40A and return west to the starting point. By adding some mileage on secondary roads, you can make a deeper foray into the forest and get a look at its beautiful lakes.

Two alternative routes provide a different look:

Variation 1: To cut through the state forest, take Dry Run Road east off Md. 495 to the Savage River Reservoir. Directly in front

Fly-fishing on the Savage River

oak and hickory have been hit hard by gypsy moths, which have killed off about 30 percent of the oaks in recent years. But the trails, dirt roads, and off-road-vehicle tracks go on and on—mostly up and down, and mostly steep.

Green Ridge also features an 11.5-mile trail loop built expressly for mountain biking *(maps available at forest headquarters)*. Rated moderate for technical difficulty, the well-signposted trail offers four bailouts that allow cyclists to return on easy roads.

For a tough aerobic workout on a 9-mile loop of double track, park at the intersection of Stafford and East Valley Roads *(Fifteen Mile Creek Rd. exit off I-68)*, pedal straight up Stafford, then hang a right at Mertens Avenue and another at East Valley Road to complete the loop. The payoff: lots of heavy breathing and great views of the Potomac as it slides through the Paw Paw Bends.

Surprisingly, the best cycling time is June through October. Spring can be wet and muddy, while summer is cooler in the mountains than in the muggy cities to the east—and, as a big bonus, there are no mosquitoes

Headquarters overlook, Green Ridge State Forest

or ticks. The mountain laurel blooms in June, and fall foliage peaks in early October.

Green Ridge Trail/ C & O Canal Loop

The Green Ridge State Forest offers the chance for a wonderful 40-mile loop hike—working out to a 4- or 5-day trek for the average hiker (see map p. 111). It is based on the 24-mile Green Ridge Trail, whose northern end, at the Pennsylvania state line, connects with the **Pennsylvania Mid-State Trail** to Chaneysville.

After the first 6 miles south from the state line (known as the **Pine Lick Blue Trail**), the Green Ridge Trail splits. The 11-mile western branch continues south along the ridge and drops down to the Potomac at Lock 67 of the C & O Canal by following the **Deep Run-Big Run Green Trail** and the **Log Roll Orange Trail.** The eastern branch, called the

Long Pond Red Trail, heads east for 7 miles, crossing the slopes of Town Hill before it, too, reaches the canal and the Potomac at Lock 58. Connecting the dots between the two locks—a stroll of 18 miles along a particularly beautiful section of the canal towpath through the Paw Paw Bends—creates the heart of this long loop hike.

Start at forest headquarters and hike east across Town Hill to Lock 58. Then walk along the towpath to Lock 67 and climb back up and along Green Ridge to headquarters. You'll start and finish your loop in the oak-and-hickory second-growth forest of the Appalachian Mountains. There are primitive campsites along the way; get a permit at forest headquarters.

Truly hard-core hikers can take the northern spur of the Green Ridge Trail as well and—oh, why not?   cross into Pennsylvania and trek the 19 additional miles to Chaneysville. ■

Catoctin Mountain Parks

Cunningham Falls State Park ■ 4,946 acres ■ North-Central Maryland
■ Best months April and Oct. ■ Camping, hiking, boating, swimming, fishing
■ Day-use fee ■ Contact the park, 14039 Catoctin Hollow Rd., Thurmont, MD
21788; phone 301-271-7574. www.dnr.state.md.us/publiclands/western/
cunninghamfalls.html
Catoctin Mountain Park ■ 5,770 acres ■ Best months April and Oct.
■ Camping, hiking, fishing, hunting, horseback riding, cross-country skiing, bird-
watching, wildlife viewing ■ Contact the park, 6602 Foxville Rd., Thurmont, MD
21788; phone 301-663-9388. www.nps. gov/cato

ALTHOUGH PEOPLE OFTEN SPEAK of the Catoctin Mountains, there's really
only one: a 50-mile-long ridge, 2 to 4 miles wide, that stretches between
Leesburg, Virginia, and Emmitsburg, Maryland. This unusual mountain
is so long that people refer to Piney Mountain (1,724 feet), Round Top
(1,702 feet), Bobs Hill (1,760 feet), and other knobs atop it as if they were
individual mountains: thus, the Catoctins. In fact, Catoctin Mountain is
the easternmost edge of the Blue Ridge, which in turn is the east ridge of
the Ridge and Valley province of the Appalachians.

While you're in either of its two parks, you will see outcroppings of
the erosion-resistant rocks that kept this mountain from melting into the
foothills below. The characteristic greenstone—a grayish rock interlaced
with green flecks—of the western part of the parks and at Cunningham
Falls is Catoctin metabasalt, which originated 600 million years ago as
lava. At high places in the eastern part of the parks look for rock that
geologists call Weverton formation: sandstone metamorphosed to very
hard, weather-resistant quartzite.

Catoctin Mountain also displays another geological oddity: ribbons
or fields of small boulders, known as stone streams, on slopes and in low
places. During periods of extreme cold, water froze in rock fissures,
expanded, and fractured the rocks, which fell apart. Then, held within a
layer of supersaturated soil sliding over frozen ground, the broken rocks
flowed slowly downhill in a process that geologists call solifluction.

Lingering signs of human exploitation can be spotted on the mountain. When Europeans arrived about 1700, Native Americans had been
here for at least 12,000 years. A mere two centuries of timbering, tanning,
roadbuilding, and ironmaking left the mountain stripped bare. (It's estimated that an 18th-century ironworks consumed 800 bushels of charcoal
a day—the equivalent of an acre of 25-year-old hardwood trees.)

Under FDR's New Deal, Catoctin Mountain became one of 35 Recreational Demonstration Areas in the country. The plan: Put unemployed
men to work rehabilitating abused land as recreation areas, particularly
for the children of the urban poor. Of the structures built by the Works
Progress Administration (WPA), the Misty Mount cabins, used for
decades by school, church, charitable, and scouting groups, are now available for rent to park visitors. Another WPA camp, called Hi-Catoctin,

became FDR's presidential retreat in 1942; President Eisenhower re-named it Camp David, after his grandson. Today most of the area supports second-growth climax (and near-climax) hardwood forests of oak, hickory, and tulip poplar. You'll find chestnut oak and pitch pine on the dry ridges; sugar maple, hemlock, and birch in the moister ravines. Yet within the forest there are still traces of the work of woodcutters, timber haulers, and charcoal makers. The instructive half-mile **Charcoal Trail,** beginning at the Thurmont Vista parking area in **Catoctin Mountain Park (CMP),** will show you what to look for.

As you drive or hike through the parks, you may notice that the forest seems conspicuously devoid of understory vegetation. That's the work of browsing white-tailed deer, and a sure sign that the deer population is larger than the parks can support. **Cunningham Falls State Park** tries to cope with the problem by opening the park in season to hunters; the deer, no dummies, simply move across Md. 77 to CMP, where hunting is not allowed. To learn more about deer and probably see some, walk CMP's 1.5-mile **Deerfield Nature Trail**; it begins near campsite no. 30 in the Owens Creek Campground. Noncampers may park at the Sawmill parking area on Foxville-Deerfield Road and walk through the campground to the trailhead.

What to See and Do

Cunningham Falls State Park has two public campgrounds; Catoctin Mountain Park (CMP) provides a campground and the Misty Mount cabins. William Houck Campground (140 sites) in the state park *(S off Md. 77)* is the most popular, probably because it's near 44-acre **Hunting Creek Lake.**

Your first hike should be the easy 0.5-mile-loop **Hog Rock Nature Trail** in CMP. Pick up a trail leaflet first at the park's visitor center on Park Central Road, then continue north on that road for about a mile to park at the trailhead. The trail provides a chance to brush up on your botany with a detailed introduction. About halfway along you'll reach **Hog Rock** (1,610 feet), an outcrop of Catoctin greenstone, which offers a great view to the south over the Monocacy Valley.

To see Maryland's tallest waterfall, the 78-foot-high **Cunningham Falls,** as it cascades down a greenstone cliff face, take the **Lower Trail** from the Hunting Creek Lake beach area, off William Houck Road in the state park. The half-mile-long trail follows **Hunting Creek** through a hemlock forest to the falls. A small parking area on the south side of Md. 77 serves the short, accessible **Cunningham Falls Trail** for people with disabilities.

There are additional short trails in the **Owens Creek** area of CMP, and another 25 miles of trails throughout the two parks. Don't miss the 2-mile round-trip trek (sometimes steep) from CMP headquarters *(N of Md. 77)* to **Chimney Rock,** where you will find more stirring views of the Monocacy Valley.

Autumn in Catoctin Mountain Park

Hunting Creek Lake offers swimming, a boat launch, and canoe and boat rentals—and it's stocked for fishing. There's stream fishing on Owens Creek and **Little Hunting Creek** and catch-and-release fly-fishing (only) for trout on challenging **Big Hunting Creek,** along Md. 77. For visitors with horses (no local rentals), a 6 mile-loop horse trail in the Owens Creek area is open from mid-April through November. For bird-watchers, nature trails in the Owens Creek area provide opportunities to spot pileated wood-peckers, wild turkeys, great horned owls, chickadees, tufted titmice, and nuthatches.

Most people visit the two Catoctin Mountain parks in sum-mer, when the range of park activ-ities is greatest, or in fall, when the turning leaves add colorful brilliance to mountain views. But winter and spring have peculiar beauties of their own.

In winter, when the trails open for cross-country skiing, the CMP visitor center offers seminars introducing the sport. In spring the park holds wildflower walks. Or you can go looking yourself along Hunting Creek or **Browns Farm Trail,** in the Owens Creek picnic area, for rue anemones, wood anemones, dwarf ginseng, hepaticas, and yellow violets. ∎

Appalachian Trail

IT WAS BENTON MACKAYE, a forester and visionary from Shirley, Massachusetts, who first proposed an Appalachian Trail (AT). In 1921, in an article in the *Journal of the American Institute of Architects,* he set forth his novel idea for a linear park. Two years later MacKaye joined other hikers on the first 6 miles of the AT, built by the New York-New Jersey Trail Conference in Bear Mountain and Harriman State Parks in New York.

By 1928 the AT extended from the Hudson River to the Delaware River. Maryland's section was completed by the Potomac Appalachian Trail Club in 1932; Pennsylvania's AT was in place by 1933. With help from the Civilian Conservation Corps, the rest of the trail was ready by 1937.

The 2,167-mile AT was designated the first National Scenic Trail in 1968. It now lies within a 1,000-foot-wide corridor administered by the National Park Service and is maintained by volunteers from hiking clubs along the way. The AT lies between Springer Mountain, Georgia, and Mount Katahdin, Maine; 432 miles of it run through four middle Atlantic states. Hundreds of miles of regional and local trails link up with the AT, offering countless possibilities for short hikes.

The Appalachian Trail Conference reports that three to four million hikers use parts of the trail each year. Most through-hikers—a relatively small but growing number—start in spring and walk from south to north, advancing with the warm weather. To hike a short section, check trail and topographic maps to determine the easier direction of travel.

The southern starting point for the middle Atlantic section is the C & O Canal at the Goodloe Byron Footbridge, which carries the trail across the Potomac from historic Harpers Ferry, West Virginia. The trail follows the canal towpath along the river to Lock 31, then ascends South Mountain to provide a 38-mile walk along the ridge crest. East of Hagerstown the trail crosses the border into Pennsylvania, where it runs along the northernmost ridge of the Blue Ridge, then descends into the Cumberland Valley southwest of Harrisburg.

After crossing the Susquehanna River, the trail climbs again and follows Blue Mountain north to the Delaware Water Gap near Stroudsburg. There it passes into New Jersey and the Delaware Water Gap National Recreation Area (see pp. 134-39), following rugged Kittatinny Mountain.

At High Point State Park it turns east along the state line as far as Abram S. Hewitt State Forest, then north into New York and the least wild section of the entire route. Traversing Harriman and Bear Mountain State Parks (see pp. 94-100), it then crosses the Hudson River and goes east through the Hudson Highlands. Past Wingdale it enters Connecticut.

There's something for every hiker in the middle-Atlantic stretch—from the ambling towpath to rugged ridges such as Kittatinny. Elevations range from 1,880 feet on Quirauk Mountain, Maryland, to 124 feet just west of the Hudson; the scenery varies from the farmlands of the Cumberland Valley to the forests of Pennsylvania and New Jersey to the suburbs of New York.

The AT passes through history here: Native American rock shelters, routes of the Revolutionary Army, stagecoach stops, canals, Civil War battlefields,

Appalachian Trail near the Delaware Water Gap

ruins of the iron industry, old coal mines, disused railroads, once famous resorts, and three great historic and strategic rivers.

Where to hike is a matter of such personal taste that you will probably want to decide it yourself after studying maps and guides and talking with your local hiking club. Local ATC chapters have much to offer: courses in environmental education and essential skills such as orienteering, plus lots of guided hikes for every age group and level of experience.

Warning: The trail is addictive. About 375 hikers a year go the distance. Earl V. Shaffer, who made the first solo through-hike in 1948 and described the experience in his classic *Walking with Spring,* hiked through again in 1965 and yet again, at age 79, in 1998. But this is not a competition. As Benton MacKaye said, the purpose of hiking the Appalachian Trail is "to see, and to see what you see."

For backpacking books and publications, including official AT maps and trail guides, as well as a list of affiliated regional and local hiking clubs, contact the Appalachian Trail Conference *(P.O. Box 807, Harpers Ferry, WV 25425. 304-535-6331. www.appalachiantrail.org)* ■

Pocono Mountains

■ 2,000 square miles ■ Northeastern Pennsylvania ■ Year-round ■ Camping, hiking, rafting, canoeing, swimming, fishing, biking, horseback riding, downhill skiing, cross-country skiing, bird-watching ■ Contact Pocono Mountains Vacation Bureau, 1004 Main St., Stroudsburg, PA 18360; phone 570-421-5791 or 800-762-6667. www.800pocono.com

IN NORTHEASTERN PENNSYLVANIA the eastern edge of the Appalachians lies across the valley from **Kittatinny Mountain.** Along the crest of Blue and Kittatinny Mountains, the Appalachian Trail runs through the wind-scoured woodlands of scrubby chestnut oak. A hiker pausing on the AT to enjoy the expansive view to the north and west looks out on the rolling forests of the Pocono Mountains—known to generations of honeymooners as, simply, the Poconos.

Unlike so much of the surrounding land that was pushed up by tectonic collisions into the high Appalachians, the bedrock sandstones of the Pocono Mountains did not fold. Remaining horizontal and almost level, they also resisted subsequent erosion—much like the Allegheny Plateau (see pp. 152-157) beyond the Appalachians.

West of the Delaware River and north of Stroudsburg, the land sharply rises 1,500 feet in what is generally called the Pocono Front. In fact, this is the escarpment of the Pocono Plateau; it is also just about the only place where the escarpment is steep enough to make an easily detectable mark on the landscape. To the north the plateau gradually slopes away toward Honesdale.

The Pocono Mountains extend northwest from valleys bordering Kittatinny Mountain to another Appalachian ridge, the **Moosic Mountains.** The western border of the Poconos lies roughly along the **Lehigh River,** which flows southeast to breach Blue Mountain in the Lehigh Gap near Palmerton and joins the **Delaware River** at Easton. The Delaware, too, breaches Kittatinny

> **Pocono Views**
>
> For a scenic thrill, drive up **Camelback Mountain**—at 2,133 feet one of the highest spots in the Poconos. The mountain is the center of 1,306-acre **Big Pocono State Park** (P.O. Box 387, Tobyhanna, PA 18466. 570-894-8336. Closed in winter). Take Camelback Road to the summit—but not if you're pulling a trailer. There, drive the scenic circuit on 1.4-mile **Rim Road.** For a better look, hike the steep and rocky, half-mile-long, orange-blazed **Indian Trail** from the center of the Rim Road loop. **North Trail** begins at the same trailhead, permitting a 2-mile loop hike that includes a return on **South Trail.** To reach the park, take the Tannersville exit off I-80; then follow Pa. 715 north a quarter mile and turn left onto Camelback Road.

Azaleas, Pocono Mountains

Heavenly Hemlock

The eastern hemlock *(Tsuga canadensis)* is an evergreen. When young, it has a classic Christmas tree shape; but as it grows, it loses its lower branches. Its needles are about half an inch long—narrow, flat, and rounded at the tip; they are dark green with a lighter underside. Hemlocks flower in May—the male, or staminate, flowers being rounded and yellow and about a quarter-inch long. By October the fertilized female, or pistillate, flower has grown into a ripe, seed-filled cone that turns from green to brown as its thick scales open. The cones remain on the tree, gradually releasing seeds to be dispersed by the wind. Thus young hemlocks tend to grow close to the old.

As they grow, hemlocks shade the forest floor and carpet it thickly with needles, deterring the growth of other vegetation. A hemlock can reach a height of 130 feet and a diameter of 5 or 6 feet, though the average size is closer to 70 feet with a diameter of 2 to 3 feet. In early northern and middle-Atlantic forests, hemlock dominated, creating a dense canopy that discouraged the sun-loving hardwoods.

In the 19th century the leather industry consumed hemlock bark at a devastating rate. By the end of the century the industry had to close down for lack of hemlock. Luckily some trees survived, mostly in inaccessible places. Today hemlocks are thinly scattered in the transition forests of New York, Pennsylvania, and New Jersey. If you're lucky enough to see a stand, savor the feeling of the shady, open forest, the stately trunks soaring skyward, sunlight filtering like fine rain through the dark branches overhead. Poets have called these groves the cathedrals of the forest.

Mountain in the better-known **Delaware Water Gap,** which Pennsylvanians consider to be the gateway to the Poconos.

This area was a rich wilderness of hemlock and white pine forests inhabited by Native Americans until 1791, when President George Washington sent troops to conduct a brutal scorched-earth campaign from which the Iroquois Confederacy never recovered. The northern part, scoured eons ago by the Wisconsin glacier, was full of rocks and gravelly till, while the southern part had only poor, thin soils. The area was thus no good for farming, but loggers and settlers moved in.

In the 19th century, entrepreneurs caught canalbuilding fever—on the Delaware and the Lehigh. The canals were followed, and driven out of business, by railroads. After the Civil War, leather tanning became big business. The process required tannic acid, which was extracted from the bark of felled oaks and hemlocks, and by 1900 the forests of the Poconos were gone, save for a few pockets of hemlock still visible today in steep ravines. The land was fit only for sheep, and for a time the wool industry flourished. Some late 19th-century businessmen got rich by bottling another natural resource: pure mountain spring water.

In the 20th century, tourism came to the Poconos, bringing rustic lodges, resort hotels, tennis courts, walking trails, bridle paths, golf courses, downhill-ski venues, and private fishing and hunting lands. The glacier had dotted the northern Poconos with lakes; now dams were built to create lakes in the southern reaches as well. Three-quarters of all the resorts built in Pennsylvania were in the Poconos, and many of them began to specialize in romantic Pocono honeymoons. In the 1930s and again in the 1960s, the federal government acquired lands in the area for parks. The tourism industry produced one natural benefit: protecting the area's second-growth forest as it took hold.

Today the Poconos are partially forested again and thrive on year-round tourism. Summer is the biggest season; resorts and campgrounds fill with visitors who want to hike, bike, raft, canoe, ride horseback, fish, swim, view wildlife, or picnic. Autumn brings hawk-watchers to the nearby ridges and leaf-peepers to the brilliant forests of maple, birch, and beech. In winter, both downhill and cross-country skiers are out. Naturalists arrive with spring, in search of birds (migrating warblers, wood ducks, and turkeys) and wildflowers (trillium, moccasin flower, and jack-in-the-pulpit). Deep in the ravines, amid stands of virgin hemlock, you can still hear at dusk the liquid tones of the hermit thrush. ∎

Lehigh Gorge State Park

∎ 4,548 acres ∎ Northeastern Pennsylvania ∎ Year-round. White-water rafting mid-March–June ∎ Camping, hiking, white-water rafting and kayaking, canoeing, fishing, biking, cross-country skiing, bird-watching, wildlife viewing ∎ Contact Hickory Run State Park, R.R. 1, Box 81, White Haven, PA 18661; phone 570-443-0400. www.dcnr.state.pa.us/stateparks/parks/l-gor.htm

THE LEHIGH RIVER, running clear and swift between forested mountains at the edge of the Poconos, presents precisely the kind of beautiful natural setting that American industrialists of the 19th century just couldn't seem to leave alone. Between 1835 and 1838, the Lehigh Coal and Navigation Company, bent on shipping coal downstream to market, built 20 dams and 5.5 miles of canals with 29 locks along this 26-mile stretch of river. When floods wiped out the canals, the company laid down a railroad through the gorge.

Meanwhile loggers clear-cut the virgin hemlock forests, and entrepreneurs built the country's second largest tannery on the river. A great fire in 1875 wiped out those operations, along with the rest of the forest. A century later, the Bureau of State Parks took over and transformed the ruins of these abandoned industrial projects into a prime recreational—and once again beautiful—park.

The centerpiece is the **Lehigh River.** Most of the time the stream runs shallow, riffling over its rocky, boulder-strewn course, but in spring it rumbles with Class III white water. A great way to see the gorge is from a raft or kayak between mid-March and the end of June, or from a canoe

Lehigh Gorge State Park

when the flow is not quite so high. Conditions on the river can vary—flow is controlled by the U.S. Army Corps of Engineers at the Francis E. Walter Dam, just north of the park—so it's wise to call the park office at neighboring Hickory Run State Park for current river information. Camping is available at Hickory Run.

The park advises inexperienced boaters to travel with an outfitter (see Resources, p. 283). The possible river trips are 8.7 miles from White Haven to Rockport, 15.4 miles from Rockport to Jim Thorpe, and a combination of the two, running the river for 24.1 miles (10 to 11 hours) from White Haven to Jim Thorpe. Incidentally, the river is stocked with trout; the best luck is to be had at the northern end.

But the river is only one way to travel through the gorge. The abandoned railroad track bed has become the broad, smooth, riverside **Lehigh Gorge Trail** for hikers and cyclists, with many bike rental and shuttle services in the area. In winter the trail makes for great cross-country skiing. The rugged overlooks, ravines, and gorge are home to mixed oaks, maples, hemlocks, and rhododendrons.

You're likely to see kingfishers, mergansers, great blue herons, and, in spring, black-and-white warblers. Look for snakes and fence lizards, or even deer or black bear. You'll also spot mementos of the industrial revolution—ruins of the old dams and locks and traces of a canal towpath—as you hike or bike along the resurrected **Lehigh Gorge**. ■

Hickory Run State Park

■ 15,500 acres ■ Northeastern Pennsylvania ■ Year-round. Rhododendron and mountain laurel bloom mid-June–mid-July ■ Camping, hiking, swimming, fishing, cross-country skiing, ice-skating, sledding, tobogganing, bird-watching, wildlife viewing ■ Contact the park, R.R. 1, Box 81, White Haven, PA 18661; phone 570-443-0400. www.dcnr.state.pa.us/stateparks/parks/hickory.htm

THE WESTERN AREA OF THIS big park in the foothills of the Poconos slopes down toward the Lehigh River and touches upon **Lehigh Gorge State Park** (see pp. 125-27). It's the place to camp if you're planning to raft the gorge. As at Lehigh Gorge, Hickory Run's virgin forests were clear-cut for timber and tanning by 1880. An Allentown businessman, Harry C. Trexler, bought up the denuded land; after his death in 1933, the National Park Service purchased 12,900 acres. The Hickory Run area became a Recreational Demonstration Area, built by the Park Service and the WPA. In 1945 the Park Service turned it over to Pennsylvania to maintain as a state park. A two- or three-hour drive from Harrisburg, Philadelphia, or New York, Hickory Run today is a popular and beautiful park. Take the park exit off I-80 or the White Haven exit (N.Y. 940) off the northeast extension of the Pennsylvania Trunpike.

Your first stop, half a mile past the park office, off Pa. 534, should be the famous **Boulder Field,** the largest of its kind in the Appalachians and a designated National Natural Landmark. During the last ice age, repeated freezing and thawing fractured the sandstone and conglomerate

White-tailed fawn

ridges visible on both sides of the boulder field. Great chunks of rock fell off. As the rocks moved downhill over thousands of years, they ground against each other, acquiring smooth edges and producing the boulder field of today: 400 feet wide, 1,800 feet long, and at least 12 feet deep. Most of the boulders are small—less than 4 feet in diameter—but some are 25 feet across. They range from the angular red sandstones at the northern end of the field to the polished red-and-white conglomerates at the southern end. For the full effect of their red color, visit the rocks at sundown; for a sense of their mystery, visit in a fog.

In summer you can swim in **Sand Spring Lake** or fish the park's lakes and streams. **Fourth Run** and **Sand Spring Run** are stocked with brook and brown trout. But you'll want to get out into the forest, especially in June and July, when it is spectacularly adrift in flowering dogwood, laurel, and rhododendron.

The park offers 45 miles of hiking trails, and most are available in winter for cross-country skiing. Be sure to hike the first half mile of the 2.3-mile **Fireline Trail** from the trailhead just beyond the park entrance sign on Pa. 534. It's an easy walk to a vantage point with fine views over Lehigh Gorge—especially good for watching hawks and sunsets. (The rest of the trail is hilly and very rocky; you might want to skip it.)

For wildlife viewing, try the 1.3-mile-long (one way) **Deer Trail,** which starts by the fork of the Sand Spring day-use area road. It's an easy-walking old logging road that passes through beech-and-maple forest and a big hemlock thicket. Around forest edges look for white-tailed deer, screech owls, and great horned owls. The 3.5-mile **Boulder Field Trail** from Hawk Falls to the Boulder Field is also a fine place for spotting deer, bears, owls, turkeys, grouse, and snowshoe hare. Finally, take the road to the fire tower (2 miles E of park office) and climb up for a panoramic view of the forested hills of the Poconos. ∎

Tannersville Cranberry Bog Preserve

The Tannersville bog, covering 150 acres in the eastern Poconos near Stroudsburg, is a boreal bog, such as you might see in Canada. It originated in a kettle lake gouged out by a glacier and filled with rainwater. Having no inflow or outflow, the lake was low in oxygen and nutrients, but northern seeds left by the glacier managed to grow. For thousands of years sphagnum moss grew over the lake in a thick, dense mat. It supported the growth of other northern species, such as tamarack and black spruce; June-blooming bog flowers such as rose pogonia, wild calla, and pitcher plants; and wild cranberry vines. Access is by guided tour only (fee), held weekly in summer and several weekends a month in spring and fall. Contact the Monroe County Environmental Education Center (8050 Running Valley Rd., Stroudsburg, PA 18360. 570-629-3061).

Following pages: Boulder Field, Hickory Run State Park

Promised Land State Park

■ 3,000 acres ■ Northeastern Pennsylvania ■ Best seasons summer and early fall ■ Camping, hiking, canoeing, swimming, fishing, ice fishing, biking, mountain biking, horseback riding, cross-country skiing, snowshoeing, ice-skating, bird-watching, wildlife viewing, ■ Contact the park, R.R. 1, Box 96, Greentown, PA 18426; phone 570-676-3428. www.dcnr.state.pa.us/stateparks/parks/p-land.htm

THE NAME IS IRONIC. Shakers abandoned the thin-soiled area when their farms failed. Now, after a century of reforestation, Promised Land has become one of Pennsylvania's most popular parks. It's a great family park (487 campsites) with a full range of activities. A summertime environmental education program includes everything from fishing lessons (for adults and children) and canoe trips to "hug-a-tree" wilderness survival courses for kids.

Big draws are two large lakes (422-acre **Promised Land Lake** and 173-acre **Lower Lake**); two beaches; five boat launches; a rental facility for rowboats, canoes, kayaks, and paddleboats; and fishing for bass, pickerel, muskie, perch, and catfish.

In addition, the park is surrounded by a 12,350-acre segment of **Delaware State Forest,** and it adjoins the forest's 2,845-acre **Bruce Lake Natural Area** (570-895-4000), a formerly glaciated terrain that supports Bruce Lake, Egypt Meadow Lake, and significant upland wetlands. It all adds up to more than 30 miles of trails for hikers and winter sports enthusiasts. (Mountain bikers and equestrians can use the state forest roads and trails as marked.)

You'll find modern family camping at Lower Lake Campground (2 miles W of park office on Lower Lake Rd.). For the best tent camping, try the lakeside walk-in sites at Pickerel Point Campground (1 mile E of park office on Pickerel Point Road).

For a fine short hike, hit the instructive mile-long nature trail on tiny **Conservation Island** in Promised Land Lake; the trailhead is on Park Avenue, a scenic drive along the lake shore.

Hawk Mountain Sanctuary

Dedicated to the conservation of raptors, which were once hunted here relentlessly, 2,400-acre Hawk Mountain Sanctuary (off Pa. 895 at 1700 Hawk Mountain Rd., Kempton. 610-756-6961. www.hawkmountain.org) stands atop Blue Mountain (adm. fee). From its lookout stations you should be able to spot bald eagles, American kestrels, ospreys, and broadwinged hawks in September; Cooper's, sharp-shinned red-shouldered, and red-tailed hawks in October; and golden eagles, rough-legged hawks, and northern goshawks in November.

The South Lookout is only 300 yards from the parking lot; the North Lookout requires a mile-long hike but offers better views. Don't forget your binoculars.

Angling in Promised Land Lake

The Bruce Lake Natural Area offers a feel of the North Woods. The forest is predominantly oak and maple, but at this elevation (1,800 feet) you'll see northern bog forest—black spruce, balsam fir, and tamarack—and an understory of pink-blossomed sheep laurel. **Bruce Lake** has cliffs at its north end that were formed 21,000 years ago; at the south end lies a bog of floating sphagnum moss where pitcher plants and bog orchids bloom in July and August. You can make a 3-mile out-and-back hike by following the **Bruce Lake Trail** to the Egypt Meadow Bridge, or a 3-mile loop hike by taking the **Egypt Meadow** and **Panther Swamp Trails** near Egypt Meadow Lake. Better yet, make a 6-mile loop of the Bruce Lake, **Ridge,** and **Brown Trails** around Bruce Lake and a decidedly north-country upland balsam swamp. Along the way you'll see woodpeckers, flickers, towhees, catbirds, chipmunks, and perhaps deer and gray foxes. At the lake watch for kingfishers, ospreys, and bald eagles. ■

Delaware Water Gap
National Recreation Area

■ 70,000 acres ■ Eastern Pennsylvania-northern New Jersey border ■ Best months May-Oct. ■ Camping, primitive camping, hiking, boating, canoeing, fishing, biking, nature study ■ Day-use fee ■ Contact the recreation area, Bushkill, PA 18324; phone 570-588-2451. www.nps.gov/dewa

AS IF IT WEREN'T ENOUGH that the Delaware River bored a hole through erosion-resistant Kittatinny Mountain, geologists believe the river actually did it backward. Millions of years ago, they say, when the Delaware was a south-flowing river far to the east and south of its present location, the headwaters ate their way upriver toward Kittatinny Mountain. Finding a fracture, they cut through even the hardest conglomerates to form

Delaware Water Gap, viewed from Mount Tammany, New Jersey

a tight, S-curve gap through the ridge—a gap that is a mile wide today.

The railroad entered the gap in 1855, bringing tourists to savor the scenery and fresh air. Industrialists proposed damming the river in the 19th century but were stymied by fierce local opposition. When Congress in 1962 approved construction of the Tocks Island Dam, which would have inundated the area under a 28-mile-long reservoir, public outcry saved the river again.

In 1965 President Johnson authorized the Park Service to preserve this compelling place—a 40-mile stretch of land totaling 70,000 acres on both the Pennsylvania and New Jersey sides of the river. Today much of the gap is still dramatic and beautiful, though the southern end—the gap itself—has been marred by the intrusion of I-80. Still, a visit here is a lesson in the power of water. Stop first to pick up maps and information at Kittatinny Point Visitor Center *(908-496-4458)* off I-80 in New Jersey or the Bushkill Visitor Center *(570-588-7044)* on US 209 in Pennsylvania.

What to See and Do

For classic hilltop views, you must climb. You can reach the crest of 1,463-foot **Mount Minsi** (in Pennsylvania) by walking the white-blazed **Appalachian Trail** (see pp. 120-21) from the Lenape Lake parking area in the town of Delaware Water Gap. (The AT descends from Kittatinny Mountain here.) The trail climbs 1,060 feet in 2 miles and makes a 4-mile loop with the Mount Minsi Fire Road.

The True Romance of the Poconos

A former honeymoon hotel has been given a new life as the Pocono Environmental Education Center (PEEC) *(R.R. 2, Box 1010, Dingmans Ferry, PA 18328. 570-828-2319. www.peec.org)*. On its grounds are access to 13 miles of nature trails that lead into the recreation area, two canoeing ponds, an indoor pool, a craft center, a library, a darkroom, and classrooms.

PEEC conducts programs *(reservations required)* in nature study, environmental education, bird-watching, photography, and outdoor skills. Bird-watching weekends focus on warblers in spring, raptors in fall, and bald eagles in January.

There are weekends for all sorts of family groupings, and week-long summer programs for different age groups. PEEC is located 5 miles south of Dingmans Ferry on US 209 in the Delaware Gap NRA.

To reach the 1,545-foot summit of **Mount Tammany** in New Jersey by the shortest route, climb a rocky track on the 1.5-mile round-trip **Red Dot** (or Tammany) **Trail.** The trailhead is at the I-80 rest area east of the Kittatinny Point Visitor Center.

For a gentler climb, take the white-blazed AT from the Dunfield parking area; branch off on the **Blue Trail,** then turn right on the Mt. Tammany Fire Road to connect with the Red Dot Trail at the summit. That's a total climb of 1,250 feet in 2.5 miles. Using these two routes, you can make a loop in either direction.

New Jersey Side

Once you've got the lay of the land, start your tour of the area on the New Jersey side, taking the Old Mine Road *(under I-80)* north into 5,878-acre **Worthington State Forest.** Almost completely wooded, Worthington offers several trails that climb to the AT—which at this point runs along Kittatinny Mountain parallel to the river and follows the ridge as it diverges northeastward through **Stokes State Forest** and **High Point State Park.**

The big attraction on the ridge is **Sunfish Pond,** a glacially carved basin that is one of New Jersey's natural wonders and a popular swimming hole for AT through-hikers (though swimming is technically not permitted). A 1.5-mile trail follows its circumference. Take either the easy-to-moderate **Douglas Trail** or **Garvey Springs Trail** to reach Sunfish Pond. Both

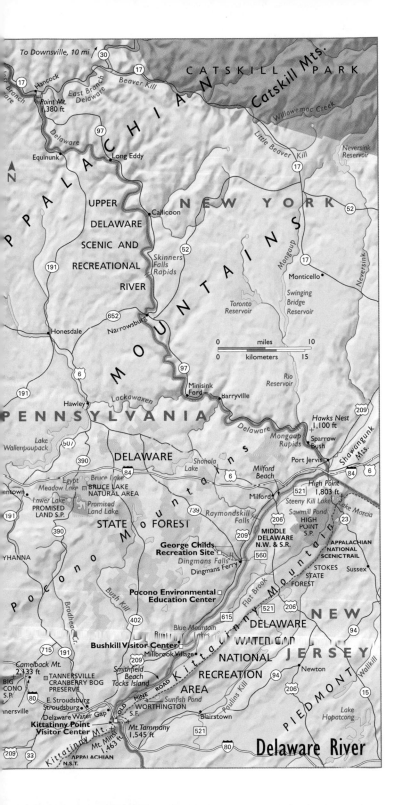

To Downsville, 10 mi · 30
17
CATSKILL MTS. PARK
East Branch · Beaver Kill
Delaware · Catskill Mts.
17
Hancock
Point Mt. 1,380 ft
Willowemoc Creek
Delaware
Little Beaver Kill
97
Neversink Reservoir
Equinunk
Long Eddy
52
NEW YORK
52
Callicoon
UPPER
DELAWARE
Mongaup
17
SCENIC AND
Skinners Falls Rapids
52
RECREATIONAL
191
Monticello
RIVER
Toronto Reservoir
Swinging Bridge Reservoir
Neversink
652
Honesdale
Narrowsburg
miles · 0 · 10
6
kilometers · 0 · 15
Rio Reservoir
191
97
Lackawaxen
Minisink Ford
Rio Reservoir
Hawley
Barryville
209
PENNSYLVANIA
Delaware
Hawks Nest 1,100 ft
Lake Wallenpaupack
507
Mongaup Rapids
Sparrow Bush
Shawangunk Mts.
390
DELAWARE
Shohola Lake
Milford Beach
Port Jervis
84
6
Egypt
Bruce Lake
84
6
Meadow Lake
BRUCE LAKE NATURAL AREA
Milford
High Point 1,803 ft
entown
Lower Lake
PROMISED LAND S.P.
Promised Land Lake
739
Raymondskill Falls
206
Steeny Kill Lake
Lake Marcia
191
STATE
o
FOREST
209
MIDDLE DELAWARE N.W. & S.R.
Sawmill Pond
HIGH POINT S.P.
23
APPALACHIAN NATIONAL SCENIC TRAIL
YHANNA
390
George Childs Recreation Site
Dingmans Falls
560
STOKES
Sussex
Dingmans Ferry
STATE FOREST
Bush Kill
Pocono Environmental Education Center
NEW
402
615
521
206
Blue Mountain
DELAWARE
94
Mountains
Brodhead Cr.
Bushkill Visitor Center
WATER GAP
JERSEY
715
191
209
Millbrook Village
Newton
Camelback Mt. 2,133 ft
TANNERSVILLE CRANBERRY BOG PRESERVE
Smithfield Beach
Tocks Island
NATIONAL
94
206
15
BIG POCONO S.P.
80
E. Stroudsburg
RECREATION
Sunfish Pond
Lake Hopatcong
nnersville
Stroudsburg
WORTHINGTON S.F.
AREA
PIEDMONT
Delaware Water Gap
Blairstown
Kittatinny Point Visitor Center
Mt. Tammany 1,545 ft
521
209
33
Mt. Minsi 1,463 ft
80
Delaware River
APPALACHIAN N.S.T.

Appalachian Trail, overlooking the Delaware Water Gap

start on Old Mine Road about 3 miles north of I-80 in the forest.

If you want to spend more time here or anywhere in the water gap, Worthington's gorgeous riverside grounds *(3 miles N of I-80 on Old Mine Rd.)* are the place to camp. Cyclists will enjoy Old Mine Road, too, and can continue north on County Road 615 to Port Jervis, New York, a distance of 43.2 miles. Steer clear of the heavy traffic on narrow US 209 on the Pennsylvania side. Mountain bikers

should head for the 7-mile-loop **Mountain Bike Trail** at Blue Mountain Lakes, New Jersey *(off Blue Mountain Lake Rd. past Millbrook Village)*.

Pennsylvania Side

Continue north to Dingmans Ferry and cross the river *(toll)* to **Dingmans Falls.** Here on the Pennsylvania side, where streams rush down from the Pocono Mountains to join the Delaware River, is the place to enjoy waterfalls; thanks to a series of board-walk trails through ravines of rhododendrons and ancient hemlocks, it's easy to do. The half-mile round-trip boardwalk route to Dingmans Falls takes you past exquisite **Silver Thread Falls** as well. At the George Childs Recreation Site nearby, a 1.8-mile loop trail with stairs and boardwalks descends 100 feet into a hemlock ravine, past three tumbling falls.

Farther north, off US 209, a quarter-mile trail leads to **Upper Raymondskill Falls**, and a half-mile trail with stairs leads to the **Middle Falls.** South of Dingmans Falls off US 209 is the **Pocono Environmental Education Center** (see sidebar p. 136).

For swimming, head north on US 209 to **Milford Beach** or south to **Smithfield Beach.** For fishing you'll find trout streams and ponds (with panfish, bass, and pickerel) throughout the area; the river has smallmouth bass, walleye, catfish, muskie, and American shad. A license from either Pennsylvania or New Jersey is valid in the recreation area.

Canoeing

Probably the best way to see and enjoy the water gap is to get out on the Delaware; this stretch is designated a National Scenic River. Alternating between shallow riffles and quiet pools, it provides even novice paddlers a peaceful passage. There are access points every 8 to 10 miles and primitive campsites. Best of all is the long string of islands where camping (first-come first-served) is permitted. Write the park for a list of outfitters and plan a canoe-camping trip for early October, when the oaks and maples are in full flame and hawks course through the skies. ■

High Point State Park

■ 14,880 acres ■ Northwestern New Jersey, south of Port Jervis, New York
■ Year-round activities ■ Camping, hiking, boating, swimming, fishing, mountain biking, horseback riding, cross-country skiing, snowshoeing ■ Adm. fee Mem. Day–Labor Day ■ Contact the park, 1480 State Route 23, Sussex, NJ 07461; phone 973-875-4800. www.state.nj.us/dep/forestry/parknj

A PRIVATE ESTATE BEFORE it became a park in 1923, High Point was spared some of the ravages of the industrial age. It was subjected instead to the romantic rustic "improvements" of the landscape-architect sons of park designer Frederick Law Olmsted. Luckily, lack of funds left many changes on the drawing board. Today **Lake Marcia,** a 20-acre spring-fed lake, is the jewel of High Point, while the man-made **Sawmill Pond** and **Steeny Kill Lake** provide boating and good bass and trout fishing. Tent camping in the trees beside Sawmill Lake is as good as it gets.

High Point's old red oak and eastern hemlock forests—home to black bears, deer, and raccoons—and its location high on Kittatinny Mountain make the park prime hiking country. More than 50 miles of trails, including 11 marked trails ranging from half a mile to 4.5 miles long, can be

combined in endless looping variations; a 10.1-mile stretch of the
Appalachian Trail traverses the park. All but the AT and the Monument
Trail are open to mountain bikes; some are open to horses. In winter,
trails south of N.J. 23 allow dogsledding, while those north of N.J. 23 are
reserved for cross-country skiing and snowshoeing.

One trail not to miss is the 3.7-mile circular **Monument Trail,**
which passes an old and stunningly beautiful Atlantic white cedar
swamp—at 1,500 feet the highest in the world. That's a great consola-
tion prize if you have to miss the real high point of High Point (the
monument), unfortunately closed for repairs until at least 2002. An
obelisk modeled on the Bunker Hill Monument and located at New
Jersey's highest point—1,803 feet—the 220-foot-tall structure affords
views of the Poconos to the west, the Catskills to the north, and the
Wallkill River Valley to the southeast. When it reopens, there will be
no better place to survey the lay of the land. Meanwhile, go hiking.
With its clear-running streams, craggy rock outcrops, and stately old
hardwoods, High Point has a peculiar beauty that should be taken in
slowly, step by step, and savored. ■

Upper Delaware Scenic and Recreational River

■ 73 miles long ■ Northeastern Pennsylvania-southeastern New York ■ Best
months May-Oct. ■ White-water rafting and kayaking, canoeing, tubing, fishing,
bird-watching ■ Contact the Park Service, R.R. 2, Box 2428, Beach Lake, PA
18405; phone 570-729-8251. www.nps.gov/upde

THE DELAWARE RIVER originates in two streams in New York's Catskill
Mountains: the 77-mile-long East Branch and the 91-mile-long West
Branch. The two converge at the base of Point Mountain near Hancock,
New York, to form the 330-mile-long Delaware. The 73-mile stretch from
Hancock to Sparrow Bush (near the northern end of the Delaware Water
Gap National Recreation Area; see pp. 134-39) is known as the Upper
Delaware. Designated a Scenic and Recreational River, the Upper
Delaware is part of the National Wild and Scenic Rivers System.

River runners know that the **Upper Delaware** was made to be canoed.
The busiest canoeing river in New York State, it carries hundreds of craft
during Memorial Day weekend. With guides and outfitters located the
length of the river and an estimated 2,500 canoes available to rent, you
can easily make a run yourself (see Resources, p. 283). The first stretch—
27 miles from Hancock to Callicoon, with a gradient of only 6 feet per
mile— should be negotiable at medium water levels by anyone with a
few hours' paddling experience. After that, however, real skill is required.
The next stretch, 26 miles to Minisink Ford, has the greatest variety of

Upper Delaware Scenic and Recreational River

river conditions, including some rough rapids. The final 19-mile stretch to Sparrow Bush has additional Class II rapids, including the **Mongaup Rapids** and more rough water as the river passes the cliffs of the **Hawks Nest** area. Below Port Jervis, the river flattens out to make the 41-mile stretch of striking scenery in the Delaware Water Gap National Recreation Area easy paddling for novices.

Simply choose a stretch to match your paddling skills. No experience at all? Sign up for a raft or tube trip, offered daily all summer long. You can get a list of outfitters from the Park Service. Alternatively, take a few lessons and practice on the perfect beginner's stream, the 33-mile stretch of the **East Branch** from Downsville to Hancock. You'll paddle through pristine countryside, and in June and July the banks are radiant with laurel and rhododendron.

Anglers will find the Upper Delaware challenging. The stretch above Callicoon boasts the best brown trout fishing on the river. The American shad run peaks in early May below Callicoon, in late May above. Fish for largemouth and smallmouth bass in eddies between Narrowsburg and Barryville. In spring and fall, striped bass strike south of Narrowsburg from cold, deep pools; you'll find walleye there, too, at night. ■

Northern Shawangunks

■ 90 square miles ■ Southeastern New York, west of I-87 ■ Year-round
■ Hiking, rock climbing, boating, canoeing, swimming, scuba diving, fishing, mountain biking, horseback riding, cross-country skiing, bird-watching, carriage rides
■ Adm. fee ■ Contact Minnewaska State Park Preserve, P.O. Box 893, New Paltz, NY 12561, phone 845-255-0752; or Mohonk Preserve, P.O. Box 715, New Paltz, NY 12561, phone 845-255-0919. www.mohonkpreserve.org

THE EASTERNMOST RIDGE of the Appalachians, which we encountered as Blue Mountain in Pennsylvania and Kittatinny Mountain in New Jersey, becomes the Shawangunk (say SHON-gum) Mountains of southeastern New York State (see map p. 99). But the Shawangunks are quite different from their fellow peaks to the south, especially along their northernmost 20 miles, between Ellenville and Rosendale, where 25,000 acres have been preserved in a near-natural state. The combination of extraordinary rocks, cliffs, sky lakes, vegetation, and plentiful wildlife have captured for the Northern Shawangunks the Nature Conservancy's designation as one of "the Last Great Places."

The ridge-making rock of the Shawangunks is a hard conglomerate of white quartz pebbles, deposited in braided rivers more than 400 million years ago and uplifted by the tectonic collision that raised the Appalachians. This rock—called Shawangunk Conglomerate—is extremely hard and wear resistant. Only the mile-thick glaciers that passed over the mountain during the last ice age carried any of it off.

But ice age freezing and thawing fractured the rocks, uplift forces tilted them, and erosional forces carved away the softer underlying shale to produce dramatic white cliffs that seem to lean over the valley below. The cliffs are highest at Sams Point (2,255 feet) near Ellenville; from there the ridge slopes gradually into the valley of Rondout Creek at Rosendale. Here and there this sloping has caused the conglomerate to split into crevasses or spread apart to create slim canyons known locally as ice caves because they sometimes contain ice year-round.

Atop the mountain are five beautiful lakes that are nothing at all like ordinary lakes. They get their water from the sky. Contained in straight-sided rock basins carved by glaciers, they are replenished now by rainwater. A rare underwater sphagnum moss lives in the lakes, as do fish in Lake Mohonk and amphibians in Lake Minnewaska. High on the ridge, stunted pitch pines cling to the rocks. Above them, resident and migratory raptors, such as red-tailed and broad-winged hawks, kestrels, ospreys, and bald eagles, ride the rising air.

In the late 19th century twin brothers Albert and Alfred Smiley built grand resort hotels beside the most spectacular sky lakes—Minnewaska (1,650 feet) and Mohonk (1,245 feet)—and laced them together with 50 miles of carriage roads and countless foot trails. Many are still in use, and after more than a hundred years they seem part of the landscape.

Rock climbing in the Mohonk Preserve

The Shawangunk Mountains are now protected by several cooperating entities. The Open Space Institute owns , and the Nature Conservancy manages, the 5,000-acre **Sams Point Dwarf Pine Ridge Preserve** (*400 Sams Point Rd., Cragsmoor. 845-647-7989. Day use only. Parking fee*), which includes Lake Maratanza (2,242 feet), several ice caves, and ridge-top dwarf pine barrens. The private Awosting Reserve manages 3,000 acres along the southern escarpment. The midsection of the ridge lies within the 12,000-acre **Minnewaska State Park Preserve,** administered as part of the Palisades Interstate Park Commission. The **Mohonk Preserve** manages 6,000 acres to the north, including "the Gunks," one of the most popular rock climbing sites in the east.

Adjacent to the Mohonk Preserve is the private 2,200-acre Mohonk Mountain House, still operated by the Smiley family (*845-255-1000*). Tremendously popular with tourists, it's the Smiley brothers' original, immense resort hotel, built in sections between 1879 and 1910 on the cliffs of Mohonk Lake, surrounded by a golf course, tennis courts, stables, and that maze of carriageways and scenic trails.

....

What to See and Do

Minnewaska State Park Preserve

This is the most accessible part of the mountains, off US 44/N.Y. 55, just west of the village of Gardiner. With its steep cliffs, caves, and carriageways, Minnewaska is perfect for the full range of hikers, from those who love a rugged climb to those who prefer an easy walk on a smooth surface.

Head first for the jewel of the preserve—**Lake Minnewaska,** three quarters of a mile up the main entrance road. You can swim in its waters, launch your own (nonmotorized) roof-top boat, or (if you're certified) scuba dive to see its rare underwater sphagnum mosses. Follow the **Minnewaska Carriageway** around the lake (1.9 miles), or simply find a quiet spot by the water for contemplation.

The shortest walk to some of the Shawangunks' sweeping views is the 2-mile loop to **Beacon Hill.** From the Wildmere parking lot,

walk a short distance back down the paved entrance road; turn right onto the orange-blazed **Beacon Hill Carriageway** and follow it to Beacon Hill. The panoramic view takes in the Catskill Mountains to the north and, on a clear day, the Taconic Range of Massachusetts and Connecticut to the east. From there the Beacon footpath leads along a rock ledge before climbing through dwarf pines to more great views eastward and southward toward the Hudson Highlands. Continue along the footpath to the Minnewaska Carriageway and then return.

It's a long walk to **Lake Awosting** (1,865 feet elevation), largest of the sky lakes, but an easy one along the **Upper Awosting Carriageway** from the Wildmere parking lot (3.2 miles). You can then stroll around the lake (3.4 miles) and return by the **Hamilton Point Carriageway** (about 4 miles) or the **Castle Point Carriageway** (about 5 miles), both with fine viewpoints. If you're equipped, you can make these circuits by mountain bike, horse, or carriage. (It's a fine sight to see visitors in carriages behind a matched pair.) In winter, do it on cross-country skis. If these hikes merely whet your appetite, don't miss the more strenuous 8-mile loop to the crag called **Gertrude's Nose,** reached via the Minnewaska and **Mill-brook Mountain Carriageways** and the **Gertrude's Nose Path.**

Mohonk Preserve

There's more prime hiking country here: For 25 miles of carriage roads and 40 miles of foot trails, obtain detailed maps at the Trapps Gateway Visitors Center *(3197 US 44/N.Y. 55 in Gardiner)*. To enjoy an easy carriageway walk with views of the Hudson Valley and up-close looks at the cliff face, take the 5.4-mile loop on the **Overcliff** and **Undercliff Roads.** (Note: Although carriageways are called "roads" in this preserve, they are not open to motor vehicles.)

There's rock climbing in Minnewaska State Park Preserve on the lower **Peters Kill** escarpment, but the 7-mile-long band of cliffs—the **Trapps,** the **Near Trapps, Lost City, Bonticou Crag**—here in the Mohonk Preserve is the hot ticket for aspiring world-class climbers. At least 2,000 established climbing routes are described in various Gunks climber guidebooks *(available at visitor center)*, and some climbers still feel impelled to blaze their own routes. Climbs range in technical difficulty from novice to spiderwoman. The preserve strongly encourages beginners to get instruction and recommends four licensed outfitters. Outfitters are on hand *(by prearrangement)* almost every day for group and private lessons for those who want to reach the ridgetop the hard way.

A note for equestrians and carriage drivers: There's trailer parking at both Minnewaska State Park Preserve and Mohonk Preserve *(Spring Farm trailhead off Mountain Rest Rd.);* horses can be boarded in the stables at Mohonk Mountain House *(845-255-1000)*. Both preserves are very popular, and on summer weekends the carriageways can be crowded with backpackers, mountain bikers, families with baby strollers and dogs, fishermen with poles, and boaters portaging canoes or kayaks to the lakes. Many of the carriageways are on the cliff edge. For the safety of yourself and others, make sure you have a placid horse. ■

Carriage road, Minnewaska SP Preserve

Catskill Mountains

■ 705,500 acres ■ Southeastern New York ■ Year-round ■ Camping, primitive camping, hiking, tubing, fishing, biking, horseback riding, downhill skiing ■ Contact New York State Department of Environmental Conservation, Region 3 Headquarters, 21 South Putt Corners Rd., New Paltz, NY 12561; phone 845-256-3083. www.dec.state.ny.us/website/dlf/publands/cats/index.html

NEW YORK'S CATSKILL MOUNTAINS (see map p. 99) were immortalized in fiction by Washington Irving as the land of Rip Van Winkle. In the 19th century they were celebrated in poetry by William Cullen Bryant, popularized in paintings by Thomas Cole and other members of the Hudson

Catskill Mountains near Edgewood, New York

River school of American art, and blanketed with resorts. Today the Catskills are just as popular, with a community of resident artists centered on the town of Woodstock and thousands of visitors each year.

The Catskills reach much higher elevations than the other Appalachians. Almost 100 peaks stand 3,000 feet high, and 35 of them soar to 3,500 feet or more. The tallest, Slide Mountain, reaches 4,180 feet. They stand out prominently because the Catskills are actually the eroded edge of the Allegheny Plateau, and the softer rock around them has been so deeply cut away by streams that they tower over their surroundings. Despite their steep sides, however, the mountains are mostly plateau-like on top—as the names Sugarloaf, Table, and Round Top suggest. You can see the bedrock—mostly sandstones and shales—in the horizontal layers in which they were laid down as sediments in an inland sea millions of years ago. The Catskills are heavily forested; you'll find no polished rock ledges or exposed conglomerate outcrops as in the Shawangunks (see pp. 142-45) just down the road. The short drive from the Gunks to the Catskills is a giant leap from one geophysical province to another.

The Catskills have been preserved by historic flukes. In 1708 Queen Anne granted ownership of 1.5 million acres in the area to a group led by one Maj. Johannis Hardenburgh. Squabbling and legal battles among the members of that group and their heirs kept settlers out until well into the 19th century. Then the tanning industry rose, and in a pattern now familiar, the hemlocks fell. In their place grew the hardwood forests—maple, birch, oak—that predominate today. Tanning collapsed when the hemlocks were gone. Farms failed on the poor soil. Mountain resorts hosted summering families and a variety of tourists, including the wealthy and the notable, among them President Ulysses S. Grant and Gen. William Tecumseh Sherman.

Then environmentalists launched a campaign to save the Adirondack Mountains to the north from logging. When the state legislature passed a bill in 1885 to create a forest preserve, the Catskills piggybacked on the Adirondacks. The extraordinary constitutional provision stipulates that the state cannot sell, give away, exchange, or lease lands of the preserve, nor can any corporation, public or private, touch them.

Today Catskill Park encompasses 705,500 acres—1,100 square miles. Forty-one percent is state land that must remain "forever wild." You'll see houses, businesses, resorts—whole villages—along roads, but the forests beyond the backyards are as wild as can be.

What to See and Do

Catskill Park is not the sort of outdoor spot where you simply plug in your RV and take a stroll along the guided nature trail. It's just there, and you're on your own. Many visitors are content to take a driving tour (see p. 151) of this beautiful region, making stops at art galleries in Woodstock and the ice-cream store in Phoenicia.

But if you want truly to experience the wilderness, explore it on foot. Hundreds of miles of trails wind through the Catskills, and a 94-mile stretch of the **Long Path** (see p. 99) passes through. Trails are blazed with blue, red, or yellow Department of Environmental Conservation (DEC) markers. Primitive camping is permitted 150 feet from trails, roads, and water sources.

Slide Mountain Wilderness

One of the most popular areas for backcountry hiking and camping is the Slide Mountain Wilderness in the northwest corner of Ulster County, the site of **Slide Mountain** and nine other peaks over 3,500 feet. The popular (and shortest, at 2.7 miles) trek to the top of Slide Mountain begins at the Slide Mountain trailhead just south of Winnisook Lake on County Road 47. Take the yellow-

Kaaterskill Falls

blazed **Woodland Valley-Denning Trail** and turn left onto the red-blazed **Burroughs Range Trail.** The elevation gain is 1,780 feet.

The difficult, steep Burroughs Range Trail continues onto the summits of **Cornell** and **Wittenburg Mountains.** The trail reaches its northern terminus at the Woodland Valley Campground, making a 9.75-mile one-way hike.

The trackless summits of four tall peaks here—**Lone, Rocky, Friday,** and **Balsam Cap Mountains**—require bushwhacking, as do 13 peaks in other areas of the preserve *(access the four via Denning trailhead parking area).* The Slide Mountain Wilderness is the place for experienced hikers to start. But you must bring good maps, good orienteering skills, good equipment, and good sense.

Haines Falls

If bushwhacking is not your idea of fun, head north to Haines Falls on N.Y. 23A. Just east of the village, the road crosses Lake Creek, and you'll see **Bastion Falls.** A moderate trail starts at the east end of the bridge and follows Lake Creek upstream to the much taller **Kaaterskill Falls,** the favorite spot of Natty Bumppo, the fictional hero of James Fenimore Cooper's Leatherstocking tales.

From Haines Falls, turn north on N.Y. 18 to the parking lot at North Lake. (You can camp nearby at the DEC's North-South Lake Campground.) An easy uphill path will bring you in five minutes to the site where the Catskill Mountain House catered to the rich and famous from 1824 to 1942—on the edge of a 2,000-foot cliff. The hotel is gone, but the once famous view of the Hudson Valley and the Berkshires is still matchless.

Catskill Streams

The Catskills are equally famed for their clear streams. Fly-fishing

Hiking path near North-South Lake Campground

was "invented" here, so there's no better place to do it. Many streams are stocked with brook, brown, and rainbow trout. Among the best: **Schoharie Creek** near Jewett Center, **Willowemoc Creek** near Livingston Manor, **Bushkill** between Arkville and Covesville, and **Esopus Creek** between Phoenicia and Mount Tremper.

Another popular way to enjoy the Catskills on a hot summer day is to venture down shallow, swift Esopus Creek by inner tube. You can float 2.5 miles in about two hours, then return from Mount Pleasant to Phoenicia by train.

Other Activities

For cyclists there are possibilities from easy to killer on the winding routes through the Catskills. You can ride the relatively flat country of Greene County; the steep roads of Slide Mountain Wilderness; or long circuits around **Pepacton Reservoir** (a 50-mile loop) or **Ashokan Reservoir** (a 40-mile loop). Both reservoirs are bisected, so shorter loops are also possible.

The 11-mile-long **Sleepy Hollow Horse Trail** system at Palenville offers some great views, and some steep, gravelly descents as well. For an experienced rider with a fit horse, it's a fine ride. The trailhead is on Schutt Road, off N.Y. 18 north of Haines Falls. (Be sure to get a copy of DEC's "Horse Trails in New York State.")

For winter sports enthusiasts, the Catskills offer three major downhill ski areas: Belleayre Mountain Ski Center *(914-254-5600. www.belleayre.com)* in Highmount, Hunter Mountain *(800-367-7669 or 518-263-4223. www.huntermtn.com)* in Hunter, and Ski Windham *(518-734-4300 or 800-754-9463. www.skiwindham .com)* in Windham. In summer both Belleayre and Hunter offer chairlift skyrides—an easy way to see a lot of wilderness without wearing out your hiking boots.

Although summer is the most popular Catskills season, many say the best time to visit is October, when the foliage is at its most dramatic. Others prefer late fall or early spring, when bare trees afford better views. A surprising number of wilderness hikers climb in winter, entranced by the changing seasonal faces of the landscape.

Scenic Drive

Driving the Catskills can be a big undertaking. This route, a loop that begins and ends in Kingston, takes you to some of the highlights of the eastern Catskills. Take N.Y. 28 northwest 3 miles; at Stony Hollow turn west on N.Y. 28A and follow the south side of the Ashokan Reservoir. Before the dam, cross over the water; on the north side of the reservoir, turn west on N.Y. 28. At Mount Tremper turn right onto N.Y. 212, then immediately turn left on N.Y. 40 and follow Esopus Creek to Phoenicia.

At Phoenicia turn north on N.Y. 214 and drive through Stony Clove (between Plateau and Hunter Mountains) to N.Y. 23A. (Turn west to Hunter and stop for a skyride at Hunter Mountain if the lift is running.) Turn east on N.Y. 23A to Haines Falls.

Take a diversion here by going north on N.Y. 18 to see the view from the site of the famed Catskill Mountain House (see p. 150). Return to Haines Falls and turn east to the falls of **Kaaterskill Creek.** (Look for them on your left, and stop to hike up to the second, more spectacular falls.)

Continue east on N.Y. 23A, following Kaaterskill Creek to Palenville. From there you may proceed on N.Y. 23A to I-87 north or south. Or, to continue your tour, turn south, taking N.Y. 32 and N.Y. 35 to Woodstock. After visiting the town, backtrack a mile to the east to pick up N.Y. 375 south to West Hurley; turn southeast on N.Y. 28 to return to Kingston or I-87. ■

Catskill flora

Allegheny
High Plateau

Mountain laurel, Hyner View State Park

SUCH DRAMATIC EVENTS took place at the eastern edge of North America between 500 million and 450 million years ago that landscapes farther inland were bound to feel the effects. In the east, the Earth's surface was rising as mountains formed during a period of geological upheaval known as the Taconic orogeny; lands to the west sank, creating a huge basin that filled with seawater. Over time, erosion removed tons of material from the mountains and deposited it as sediment on the basin floor. The process

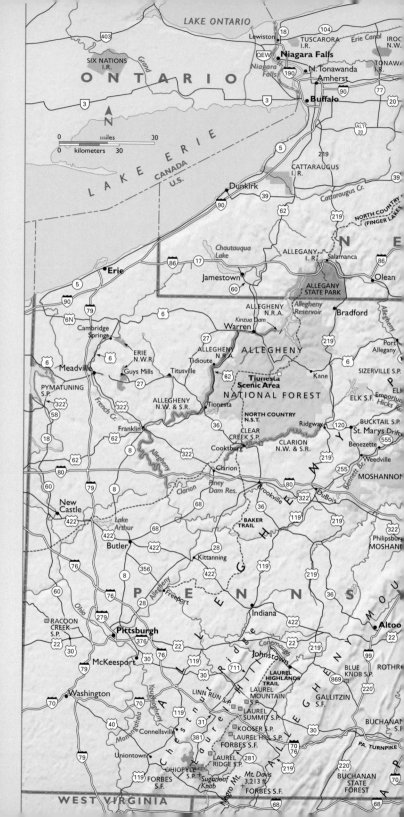

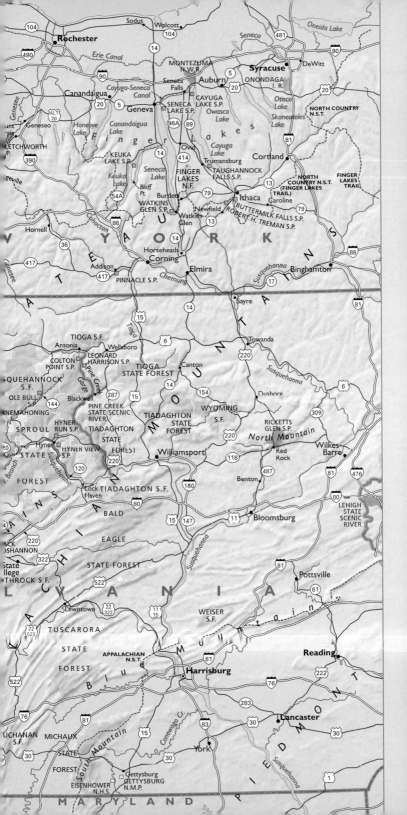

continued during a second stage of mountain building (the Acadian orogeny) between 405 million and 365 million years ago.

As the basin filled, plants grew in swamps along the shores of the new sea and were later trapped between layers of sediment eroded from highlands to the east. Subjected to extreme pressure, the remains of this vegetation eventually became coal. By 350 million years ago, when the last and greatest period of mountain building (the Alleghanian orogeny) began, the sea was gone, but erosion of the mountains continued to deposit sediment farther west, creating a vast alluvial plain that sloped westward across Pennsylvania and New York into Ohio. From about 250 million years ago, the landscape was primarily shaped by water.

Streams and rivers cut paths across the Allegheny Plateau and then slowly deepened those paths to form V-shaped valleys. What remained between the streams were fragments of plateau looking just like hills or mountains. Some two million years ago, thick ice crept out of the north to leave its mark upon the landscape. During the two million years of the Ice Age, a series of glaciers—perhaps four or more—descended from Canada to cover New York and the northeast and northwest corners of Pennsylvania. The ice scraped the tops off high places, carried away soil and rocks, and scoured out valleys, and deposited the eroded material in other places. It brought with it a nasty climate of alternate freezing and thawing that shattered rocks. The ice gouged and deepened stream valleys that ran parallel to the direction of the ice flow. Finally, as the last in the series of glaciers began to melt and retreat, it dumped tons of rock and gravel in New York, damming the southern ends of long valleys that filled with meltwater and became the 11 dramatic Finger Lakes.

Elsewhere, big blocks of ice from the receding glacier became embedded in the land. Each block eventually melted, and the hole left by the melted ice filled with water to become a kettle pond. Between the Finger Lakes and Lake Ontario, the glacier strewed drumlins across the landscape, now one of the largest drumlin fields in the world. What's a drumlin? It's a streamlined hill of glacier-dropped debris that is usually elongated in the same direction as the ice that once flowed over it. The ice also formed eskers—long, low ridges of sand and gravel that snake across the land.

At many side streams, where smaller rivers of ice had flowed into the main glacier, the retreating ice left hanging valleys as it eroded upstream, carving glens and gorges that were soon awash in waterfalls. The ice backed off a high scarp near Lewiston, New York, leaving a waterfall (Niagara Falls) that migrated upstream to form a 7-mile-long gorge. Bogs, swamps, upland marshes, and field after field of scattered boulders are also memorabilia of the Ice Age.

The Appalachian Plateau encompasses a number of physiographic areas. Moving west in Pennsylvania from the Valley and Ridge province, one encounters what seems to be a ridge that originates midway along the state's southern border and sweeps to the northeast corner. In fact, this is the Allegheny Front, a steep escarpment where elevations average 2,500 feet or more; it marks the line where the Valley and Ridge province of the Appalachian Mountains ends and the Appalachian Plateau begins. In southern Pennsylvania, the area west of the front is known as the plateau's Allegheny Mountain section; it is made up of three ridges running parallel to the escarpment. The ridge closest to the front is called Negro Mountain. It reaches 3,213 feet at Mount Davis, the state's highest point, and extends southward into the panhandle of western Maryland. Farthest west is Chestnut Ridge, which climbs to 2,779 feet and stretches south into Maryland and West Virginia. The ridge in the middle, reaching 2,799 feet, is Laurel Ridge—the backbone of Pennsylvania's Laurel Highlands.

In north-central Pennsylvania and from New York's western border to the Hudson Highlands, the area west of the front is called the Allegheny High Plateau. It tilts slightly to the south, marching down from New York toward Pennsylvania in a series of stairsteps, but this gigantic "staircase" is so subtle that you probably won't even notice it. To the north in New York are lowland regions of the Appalachian Plateau and a small tilted mesa known as the Tug Plateau, abutting the Adirondacks. To the west in Pennsylvania are lower areas known as the Pittsburgh and Glaciated Plateaus. This chapter focuses mainly on the Allegheny High Plateau. Not only is it the biggest part of the Appalachian Plateau, it also has the richest geological heritage.

Both the Allegheny High Plateau and the Allegheny Mountain region were covered with forests of immense white pines and hemlocks when William Penn and other Europeans first came upon them. (Pennsylvania means "Penn's woods.") But before the end of the 19th century, the forests had been cut down. Stumps and discarded tree limbs, which had piled up in the ruined forests, caught fire and burned with such intensity that plants still will not grow in some of the soils there. As lumber magnates who had made their fortunes sold off their worthless property, the states began to buy up the land. Pennsylvania has made a particular effort to live up to its name: Today, 60 percent of the state is forested again, and all of those forests are open to the public.

The modern forests, of course, are nothing like the woodlands of old. They are transition forests of hardwoods—maples, beeches, birches, and oaks—with only a smattering of hemlocks and white pines. The wood bison, gray wolves, wolverines, moose, and mountain lions that once lived here have gone the way of the hemlock forests; now you'll find white-tailed deer, black bears, coyotes, bobcats, and reintroduced elk. Many smaller critters are here, too: beavers, opossums, rabbits, hare, otters, fishers, and a wide array of snakes, lizards, turtles, skinks, salamanders, frogs, and toads. Fish are plentiful, and hundreds of species of birds nest in the plateau region while hundreds more pass through it.

As you travel through these wonderfully scenic hills, valleys, and reforested mountains of Pennsylvania and New York, remember that you are on a vast plateau that has been eroding for hundreds of millions of years. That will help you understand—when you reach a high vantage point in your journey—why the "mountains" here are all about the same height: Technically, they are all parts of the same ancient plateau. ■

Laurel Highlands

■ Southwest Pennsylvania, off I-79, I-70, and Pennsylvania Turnpike ■ Best months April-Oct. ■ Camping, hiking, white-water rafting, kayaking, swimming, fishing, biking, horseback riding, cross-country skiing, bird-watching, wildlife viewing ■ Contact Laurel Highlands Visitors Bureau, 120 E. Main St., Ligonier, PA 15658; phone 724-238-5661 or 800-925-7669. www.laurelhighlands.org

NAMED FOR ITS PROFUSION of mountain laurel, the Laurel Highlands region is one of the most popular outdoor playgrounds in Pennsylvania. Along the backbone of the highlands—Laurel Ridge—are seven state parks, whose presence can be explained not only by the closeness of Pittsburgh but also by the diversity of the ridge itself. Laurel Ridge falls geographically on the four corners of the eastern deciduous forests: northern hardwood and hemlock to the north, beech and maple to the west, Appalachian oak forest to the east, and mixed mesophytic forest to the south. It gets ample rain and presents a range of elevations, slopes, and exposures to persnickety trees. The result is an extraordinarily rich and interesting mix in Forbes State Forest. The diversity of trees makes for variety in the understory as well, inviting a great many birds and other animals to set up housekeeping. Botanists and bird-watchers will find surprises in the Laurel Highlands, and everyday hikers will find much to admire.

What to See and Do

Ohiopyle State Park

Southernmost in the parade of parks along Laurel Ridge is Ohiopyle State Park (P.O. Box 105, Ohiopyle, PA 15470. 724-329-8591. www.dcnr.state.pa.us/ohio.htm). To get there from the Pennsylvania Turnpike, go east on Pa. 31 and take Pa. 381 south through Forbes State Forest (see pp. 164-65).

The park's name is said to come from ohiopehle, a Native American word that means "frothy white water." In this case, the white water is in the **Youghiogheny River,** continuing its northward journey from western Maryland to the Monongahela River just above Pittsburgh. (The Monongahela meets the Allegheny River at Pittsburgh to form the Ohio.)

At Ohiopyle State Park, the "Yough" shows off its power in more than 14 miles of a deep river gorge carved from sandstone and shale. In the middle of the village of Ohiopyle—in the center of the park—the river cascades in impassable falls; it then makes a spectacular, nearly perfect S-turn 1,000 feet down in the gorge. Here, someone may tell you a story about young George Washington: Assigned to capture Fort Duquesne (later Pittsburgh) during the French and Indian War, the future U.S. President gave up plans to transport his troops by water when he came upon Ohiopyle Falls.

Today's white-water rafters and kayakers—at least 100,000 each April-to-October season—put in

Forbes State Forest

Laurel Highlands

below the falls on the **Lower Yough** for a 7.5-mile whoosh through Class III and IV rapids, or they start well above the falls on the **Middle Yough** for a gentler 9-mile float with Class I and II rapids. (For the Upper Yough, see p. 114.) After 3 p.m., the park lets hard-core kayakers put in at the S-curve, take-out around the loop, walk 600 yards, and do it all again. The obliging Yough at Ohiopyle offers a stretch to suit almost anyone's preferred rate of speed or level of difficulty.

Outfitters authorized by Ohiopyle State Park operate from the village, and they have just about everything you will need for pursuing white-water activities and more, including rental bikes for visitors who would rather pedal than paddle.

For those who prefer terra firma, maps are available at the visitor center in the old railroad depot *(Main St., at village center. 724-329-0986. April-Oct.).* Pick one up and head out on the **Youghiogheny River Trail,** which starts at the center and parallels the river through the park. This 28-mile rail-trail of crushed limestone is quite level and easy for bikers, joggers, walkers, and cross-country skiers. (At Connellsville, it joins the **Yough River Trail North,** 43 miles to McKeesport; both trails are part of the Pittsburgh-to-Washington, D.C., trail project.) Another access point for the Youghiogheny River Trail is from the high bridge just off Main Street (Pa. 381) at the edge of the village. Take along a fishing pole and stop for a while to catch trout in the stocked river *(license required).* Mountain bikers will want to try the more challenging 9.5-mile **Mountain Bike Trail** at the southern end of the park on Sugarloaf Knob; it's also open to horseback riders.

Don't miss the 100-acre **Ferncliff Peninsula Natural Area**, a national natural landmark on the peninsula where the Youghiogheny makes the big S-curve. Flowing north, the river transports seeds from farther south and drops them on the bank when it turns. In the microclimate of the south-facing peninsula deep in the gorge, southern plants flourish as they do in only a few other places at this latitude in North America. Here, find umbrella magnolia, Carolina tassel-rue, blue iris, autumn willow, and—rarest of all—the large-flowered marshallia, its lavender and pink blooms rising improbably from the rocks in June. From the natural area's parking lot, take the 1.7-mile **Ferncliff Trail** (it connects to four other loop trails) or join one of the interpretive

Mountain Laurel

An evergreen shrub or sometimes a small tree, mountain laurel *(Kalmia latifolia)* grows in the understory of mixed forests on upland mountain slopes and valleys. It likes acidic soils—dry or moist—and often grows in dense thickets to the exclusion of other plants, forming "heath balds" or "laurel slicks" that shelter wildlife. Mountain laurel appears from southeastern Maine to northern Florida and as far west as Indiana. It is Pennsylvania's state flower, blooming in great profusion in June. With a compact, rounded crown and large clusters of pink flowers, mountain laurel is one of the most beautiful native flowering shrubs. The leaves are poisonous to livestock, but they are good grub for ruffed grouse.

hikes frequently conducted by park naturalists.

To explore other parts of the sprawling park, follow any of the 41 miles of hiking trails. From early spring through July, hike the **Cucumber Falls Trail** and the **Cucumber Run Ravine** *(Pa. 381 N to Kentuck Rd. for parking and access),* carpeted with wildflowers and abloom with rhododendron in June and July. In spring you're sure to see some of the 36 species of warblers that visit the park, including the golden-winged, yellow, and cerulean varieties. For

Following pages: Fly-fishing on Youghiogheny River

A Rock with a View

Blue Knob peak is the second highest point in Pennsylvania, rising 3,146 feet in 5,614-acre **Blue Knob State Park** (E of Johnstown on Pa. 869). Its location on a projecting spur of the Allegheny Front ensures some of the best views in the state—along the front, eastward to the Valley and Ridge province, and westward across rolling mountains. Hike the 5-mile **Mountain View Trail** (access from Park Rd., near park office) for great lookout points. The trail descends along Beaverdam Creek and then follows the peak's eastern slope to the Willow Springs picnic area. The rest of the trail is steeper and more difficult, so you may want to stop here and go back the way you came. For information, contact the park (124 Park Rd., Imler, PA 16655. 814-276-3576. www.dcnr.state.pa.us/b-knob.htm).

a spectacular view of the gorge, hike to the scenic overlook on the **Kentuck Trail,** a 1-mile loop with access from Tharp Knob picnic area on Kentuck Road.

Ready for the long haul? At the Youghiogheny River, you can pick up the 70-mile-long **Laurel Highlands Trail,** which runs north along Laurel Ridge to the Conemaugh River at Johnstown, with lean-tos every 8 to 10 miles. The trail's most scenic part is the 11.5-mile leg through Ohiopyle State Park.

Forbes State Forest

Home to deer, black bears, ruffed grouse, and turkeys, the 58,000-acre Forbes State Forest (724-238-1200. www.dcnr.state.pa.us/forests/forbes .htm) surrounds Ohiopyle and six other parks located along Laurel Ridge, as well as the Laurel Highlands Trail.

This multiple-use forest also offers facilities of its own: about 100 miles of hiking trails; 92 miles of snowmobile, mountain bike, and equestrian trails; 60 miles of cross-country ski trails; and several wild natural areas.

Among its great diversity of tree species—55 different kinds—Forbes State Forest counts many familiar trees. Go exploring along miles of woodland trails and you can't help noticing sugar maples, red and white oaks, birches, tulip poplars, cherries, and hemlocks. Look closely and you may get to see birds, deer, and other creatures that make their homes here.

One of the popular areas in the forest is 3,935-acre **Laurel Hill State Park** (814-445-7725. www.dcnr.state.pa.us/l-hill.htm). Just north of Ohiopyle, this park features 65-acre **Laurel Hill Lake,** which has a 1,200-foot swimming beach, a boat launch, and enough bass, catfish, trout, bluegill, crappie, and perch to please any angler. When winter comes, you can try ice fishing and ice-skating on the lake, or head out on the 10 miles of snowmobile trails.

At Laurel Hill you will also find seasonal camping and picnic grounds centered around the lake, as well as 12 miles of hiking trails. For a short hike, don't miss the park's 1.2 mile interpretive

Hemlock Trail; it follows Laurel Hill Creek to a small stand of old-growth hemlock.

For a quiet, more rustic time in Forbes State Forest, camp at either of two parks located just north of Laurel Hill. The 250-acre **Kooser State Park** *(814-445-8673)* offers primitive camping and a 4-acre lake for swimming and fishing. At 612-acre **Linn Run State Park** *(724-238-6623),* simple cabins stand beside a waterfall and a stream full of trout.

Continue north through the forest and you'll come to **Laurel Summit State Park** *(contact Laurel Hill State Park),* a picnic area at 2,739 feet. It's a good place to have lunch while feasting on views of the ridge.

If you're looking for a good place to go mountain biking, visit 493-acre **Laurel Mountain State Park** *(contact Linn Run State Park);* it's also great for hiking and for downhill and cross-country skiing *(contact Laurel Mountain Ski Resort 714-238-9860).*

All of these parks are tied together like bangles on a bracelet by the linear **Laurel Ridge State Park** *(724-455-3744),* corridor for the 70-mile Laurel Highlands Trail (see p. 164) running along the ridge crest.

If possible, plan your visit to Forbes State Forest and the parks so that you will arrive in time to see an amazing sight: the blooming of the heaths that give the Laurel Highlands region its name. Mountain laurel blooms during the first or second week of June and continues for three weeks; rhododendron follows, blooming for three weeks. If you're familiar with these blossoms only as occasional sprigs in a florist's bouquet, prepare to be astonished. ∎

Black Moshannon State Park

■ 3,394 acres, including 1,592-acre Black Moshannon Bog Natural Area
■ Central Pennsylvania, off Pa. 504, 9 miles east of Philipsburg ■ Best months April-Dec. ■ Camping, hiking, swimming, boating, canoeing, fishing, biking, cross-country skiing, ice-skating ■ Contact the park, R.R. 1, Box 183, Philipsburg, PA 16866; phone 814-342-5960. www.dcnr.state.pa.us/b-mo.htm

BLACK MOSHANNON'S LOCATION high atop the Allegheny Front makes it both a cool summer getaway and a popular winter sports venue. The park offers tent and trailer camping, cabins, a 250-acre spring-fed lake with swimming beach, boat launches (no powerboats), boat rentals, and good fishing for sunfish, catfish, bass, perch, and pickerel. (Fish for trout in **Black Moshannon Creek.**) It maintains a 16-mile trail system, including the 1.7-mile Dry Hollow Trail and 1.1-mile **Snowmobile Trail,** both of which lead mountain bikers and snowmobilers to miles of roads and trails in the surrounding 43,000-acre Moshannon State Forest.

But the must-see attraction is the **Black Moshannon Bog Natural Area** *(Beaver Rd., 10 miles E of Philipsburg),* assuredly the most interesting bog on the Allegheny Plateau. Most bogs formed when retreating glaciers

Flowering water lily in Black Moshannon State Park

marooned huge hunks of melting ice in bowl-shaped depressions, or kettles, that lacked proper drainage. Black Moshannon is different because it stands on unglaciated land, resting in a dishlike depression in impermeable sandstone. Like most bogs, it's full of spongy sphagnum moss that slowly accumulates and decomposes, forming layers of peat moss under the living sphagnum. Tannin in the peat moss turns crystal-clear bog water to the color of iced tea.

Short of a canoe, the best way to see the bog is on foot. For a brief jaunt, walk a half-mile loop on the **Bog Trail** (*1 mile N of park office*). From the elevated boardwalk you'll see sphagnum moss, sedges, rushes, leatherleaf shrubs, water lilies, and perhaps carnivorous pitcher plants, bladderworts, and sundews. Watch for pickerel frogs, salamanders, king-fishers, wood ducks, and ospreys. For a better look, make a 10.7-mile loop on the **Moss-Hanne Trail** (*access next to trailhead for Bog Trail*). The trail leads through hemlock and spruce groves, pine plantations, and hardwood forests; boardwalk sections traverse a marsh and an alder swamp. Along the way are beaver ponds and—in August—ripe blueberries. ■

Allegheny National Forest

■ 513,000 acres ■ Northwest Pennsylvania, in Elk, McKean, Forest, and Warren Counties ■ Year-round ■ Camping, primitive camping, hiking, boating, canoeing, swimming, fishing, biking, mountain biking, horseback riding, cross-country skiing, bird-watching, wildlife viewing ■ Contact the national forest, P.O. Box 847, Warren, PA 16365; phone 814-723-5150. www.penn.com/forests/anf

NATIVE AMERICANS BEGAN HUNTING in these woods perhaps thousands of years ago. They also lived here: Burial mounds of the Hopewell culture date from about A.D. 300 and can still be seen in the Buckaloons area in the forest's northwest corner. By the time of the American Revolution, the forest was home to the Seneca Nation of the Iroquois Confederacy, who sided with the British. When peace was made, the Seneca were consigned to a reservation in New York State, and new Americans moved in.

From 1800 until mid-century, white pines and hemlocks were cut and rafted down the Allegheny River. Then, in 1864, railroads came to the high plateau, and forests farther from the river could be felled. Railroad logging was practiced intensively until President Coolidge established the national forest in 1923. The forest of today holds more than 20,000 acres of pine plantations created in the 1930s by the Civilian Conservation Corps to slow soil erosion and save the Allegheny watershed, but it's dominated by northern hardwoods such as red and sugar maples, black cherries, yellow poplars, and white ash. A few pockets of old-growth pines and hemlocks still stand and should be high on any visitor's list.

Like most other national forests, Allegheny is a multiple-use area, and one of the uses here is oil drilling. This part of Pennsylvania is oil country; private owners of mineral rights operate about 6,000 oil- and gas-producing wells occupying 5,000 acres of forestland. Between 80 and 150 new wells are drilled every year, each having a life expectancy of 20 to 25 years. Logging, or "timber harvesting," is another use; about a third of the world's commercial black cherry timber comes from the Allegheny High Plateau, much of it from the national forest.

If you can ignore the oil wells and logging operations, Allegheny offers recreational facilities for great outdoor holidays. There are 16 campgrounds and more than 700 miles of trails, ranging in length from the 0.8-mile **Buckaloons/Seneca Interpretive Trail** to the 87.3-mile section of the North Country National Scenic Trail (NCNST), which runs from Freeport, Pennsylvania, to the Willow Bay Recreation Area at the New York border (see pp. 168, 191-92, and 195). Seven hundred miles of fishing streams are here as well, plus the Allegheny River and Allegheny Reservoir.

Nine thousand acres are designated wilderness areas, and 23,000 acres make up the Allegheny National Recreation Area, established in 1984. In three segments, the recreation area includes lands on both sides of the Allegheny Reservoir above Kinzua Dam, and along the east side of the Allegheny River in the western part of the forest. Each section offers different opportunities for outdoor activities.

What to See and Do

Kinzua Dam Area

If water sports and fishing are your favorite outdoor activities, head for the Kinzua Dam Area *(Bradford Ranger District 814-362-4613)* in the northeast corner of Allegheny National Forest. Just north of US 6, this area is the most developed and most popular part of the forest.

Built on the Allegheny River in 1965 by the U.S. Army Corps of Engineers, Kinzua Dam created the **Allegheny Reservoir,** whose 12,000 acres stretch north into New York and include inundated lands that belonged mostly to the Seneca Nation. Ten of the forest's campgrounds are located in the national recreation area along both sides of the reservoir; five are primitive and accessible only by foot or boat.

Most popular of the developed camps is **Kiasutha Recreation Area** *(10 miles N of Kane)*. Among the primitive campgrounds, tiny **Hopewell's** eight sites and **Handsome Lake's** ten sites are popular with hikers on the North Country National Scenic Trail, while many boaters like the **Pine Grove** campground, close to Kinzua-Wolf Run Marina *(E of Kinzua Dam. Late May–Oct.)*. The marina is the main boating access to the reservoir; additional access is via seven more boat launches located at various points around the reservoir. The marina rents boats, canoes, pontoon boats, and houseboats.

For a good all-day, 6.3-mile hike through oak forests laced with beech, black cherry, and hickory,

take the **Tracy Ridge Trail** from the Tracy Ridge Recreation Area south along the east shore of the reservoir and turn northeast on the **Johnnycake Trail** to return to the ridge. For a more ambitious walk, pick up the **North Country National Scenic Trail** off Tracy Ridge Trail.

Clarion River Area

There are two kinds of outdoor people: the silent and the motorized. Allegheny National Forest is big enough to have set aside a section for the noisy ones—the Clarion River Area *(Marienville Ranger District 814 927-6628)*, south and east of Pa. 66, in the southeast corner of the forest. Here you can buzz along the 38-mile **Timberline** and 37-mile **Marienville ATV trails** or zip onto the 362-mile **Allegheny Snowmobile Loop Trail System;** mountain bikers also use the trails.

The **Marienville Trail** is divided into a 16-mile recommended ATV loop and a 20-mile recommended bike loop. The bike loop—rated most difficult—has all the mud, rocks, twists, and inclines you could want (experienced riders only, please). The two most popular and scenic snowmobile trails are **Mead Run Loop** and **Longhouse Loop,** both north of Kane.

Some of the forest's best opportunities for wildlife viewing occur in the **Buzzard Swamp Wildlife Management Area** *(off FR 157)*, which is off-limits to motors. Fifteen impoundments on more than 3,000 acres make this a welcome spring and fall stop for

Allegheny National Forest

waterfowl on the Atlantic flyway; you might also see bears, deer, coyotes, beavers, snapping turtles, turkeys, ospreys, and bald eagles. Visitors can walk, bike, or ski 9.6 miles of interconnecting trails, or try fishing the ponds for bass, bluegill, crappie, perch, and catfish. Within the swamp is the 1.5-mile **Songbird Sojourn Interpretive Trail** *(off FR 157)*, a good place to bone up on trees.

The great treat is to canoe the **Clarion River.** A 32-mile stretch of the river from Ridgway to Clear Creek State Park, called the **Irwin Run Recreation Area** *(easy canoe access at Ridgway),*

marks the southern boundary of the forest; you can continue 28 miles beyond that, as far as Piney Dam Reservoir. The Clarion River is smaller and faster than the Allegheny, but it has just four classified rapids. Only paddlers with at least intermediate skills should make the fastest run—19 miles from Ridgway to Hallston— during high-water periods.

Tionesta Area

Lying in a wedge in the central and western part of the Allegheny National Forest is the Tionesta Area *(Marienville Ranger District 814-927-6628);* it is located south and west of US 6, and north and west of Pa. 66. Along its western border is the broad, slow-moving Allegheny River, dotted with wilderness islands. Here in the least developed part of the forest, experienced backcountry hikers can enjoy quiet treks and camping in a wilderness that encompasses beautiful Hickory Creek, the Allegheny River Islands, and the last vestiges of an old-growth hemlock forest.

Two areas accessible by car should not be missed during a visit to Tionesta. The **Hearts Content National Scenic Area** (see pp. 172-73) holds a 120-acre section of old-growth hemlock forest traversed by a 1.3-mile interpretive trail; pick up the trailhead off Pa. 2002. Walking through this soaring forest, where even the fallen giants are impressive, you may gain a new appreciation for trees and get a sense of what a forest might be. From the parking area at Hearts Content, there is access to an 11.1-mile, yellow-blazed loop

---

Conifer Cathedral

On the Clarion River south of Allegheny National Forest is **Cook Forest State Park** *(P.O. Box 120, Cooksburg, PA 16217. 814-744-8407).* What sets the 6,668-acre park apart is its old-growth forest, which is most accessible in the 555-acre **Forest Cathedral Natural Area** behind the Log Cabin Visitor Center *(off Pa. 36).* The 1.2-mile **Longfellow Trail** leads to 200-foot-tall white pines and hemlocks with diameters up to 4 feet; it also connects to trails that go deeper into the forest. Take the **Joyce Kilmer Trail** to pass through 1.5 miles of old-growth pine and hemlock. The 246-acre **Swamp Forest Natural Area,** in the park's northeast corner, can be reached only by the NCNST (locally the Baker Trail).

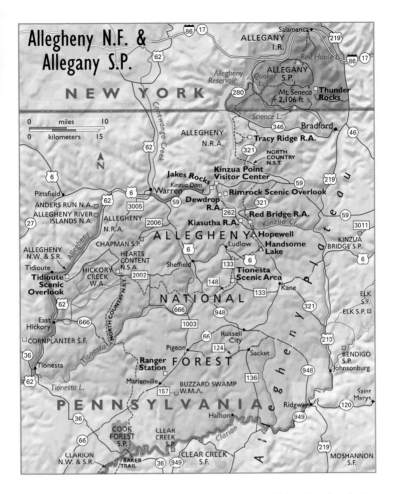

trail that goes through upland oak, beech, birch, and hemlock forest in the 8,663-acre **Hickory Creek Wilderness Area.** (Only low-impact camping is permitted.) If you are a quiet backpacker, you will have a good chance of seeing black bears or hearing pileated woodpeckers; at night, listen for the curious barred owl: *who-cooks-for-you, who-cooks-for-you-all.*

The 2,018-acre **Tionesta Scenic Area** *(8 miles W of Kane on FR 133),* though blasted by a 1985 tornado, contains remnants of 400-year-old beeches, hemlocks, and sugar maples. The 1.5-mile **Tionesta Scenic Area Trail Loop** proceeds through the best old beech and hemlock stands and connects to the **North Country National Scenic Trail,** which runs for 53.3 miles through the Tionesta section of the national forest. Walk a few hundred yards south (left) along the NCNST, and pass through the area still recovering from tornado damage.

Finally, use the canoe launch at Buckaloons and take to the

Allegheny River for a float trip to the seven wilderness islands between Buckaloons Recreation Area and the town of Tionesta. Unlike the rest of the forest, this is river-bottom land and therefore rich in willows, sycamores, and silver maples; on some islands the old trees reach 50 inches in diameter. Together, the seven islands make up the 368-acre **Allegheny River Islands Natural Area,** which has no marked trails or facilities. Only skilled wilderness campers should undertake a stopover on the islands, but little experience is required for the timeless experience of floating the slow, flat water of the Allegheny.

Scenic Drives

Kinzua Area: The main east-west highway crossing the national forest is US 6. East of Warren, where US 6 bears southeast through the forest to Kane, stay on Pa. 59 and proceed due east to **Kinzua Dam.** Continue east along the rim of the beautiful Allegheny Reservoir and stop at the **Kinzua Point Visitor Center** for the view, plus information and maps.

Just short of the bridge over Allegheny Arm, turn south on Forest Road 262—the **Longhouse National Scenic Byway**—which follows the wooded western shore of Kinzua Arm. After 1.2 miles, stop at **Jakes Rocks Scenic Overlook** for long views of the reservoir and forest, especially lovely when graced by mountain laurel in June or fall foliage in October. (The rocks, by the way, are Olean conglomerate boulders deposited on this spot hundreds of millions of years ago.)

At the south end of Kinzua Arm, turn north on Pa. 321 to cross Kinzua Creek and drive up the eastern shore of the arm. When you hit Pa. 59 again, turn west and travel 5.1 miles to **Rimrock Scenic Overlook,** offering more perspectives on the reservoir and yet another formation of Olean conglomerate boulders.

The 29-mile loop from Kinzua Point gives access to **Kiasutha, Dewdrop,** and **Red Bridge Recreation Areas;** the Elijah Run Boat Launch; the popular **Red Bridge Bank** fishing area; and **Kinzua Beach.** For a geological close-up, stop at the road cut on Pa. 59 near the dam, where the deposition of ancient sedimentary layers is plain to see.

Tionesta Area: From Warren, drive west on US 6 and turn south on US 62, following the Allegheny River. You will see the string of Allegheny River Islands while driving south toward the village of **Tidioute.** Cross the river to visit the rustic old community; then return and just opposite the village, take Pa. 3005 uphill. Be sure to stop at the **Tidioute Scenic Overlook** for a memorable panorama of the river and the village, now far below.

Continue on Pa. 3005—it makes a sharp left and heads north—to Pa. 2002 (Hearts Road). Turn right (southeast) and drive to Hearts Content National Scenic Area, where you'll want to hike the interpretive trail through the old-growth forest. To return, go back the way you came on Pa. 2002; then turn north (right) on Pa. 3005 to Warren. ■

Old-growth hemlock forest, Hearts Content Scenic Area

Orienteering

Wish you could just strike off into the forest and explore on your own? That's where orienteering—finding your way through unfamiliar terrain by using a topographical map and a compass—can help you out. Ardent wilderness walkers have turned orienteering into a sport, with courses that let you test yourself, compete with others, or perhaps cooperate with your family or friends to achieve a goal together. That goal is to take the best possible route in the shortest time to a number of established markers, called controls. (The best route is not necessarily the shortest, of course; you can't hike as the crow flies when a cliff lies in your path.) At each control, you copy down a code symbol or number as proof that you found it.

A good place for testing your orienteering skills is the Hearts Content Recreation Area of Allegheny National Forest. The test involves three courses of increasing difficulty. The introductory course sets three controls over 1.6 miles and uses established trails all the way for easy hiking and easy navigation. The intermediate course, 80 percent on trails, is easy hiking but harder navigation. The advanced course, with six controls over 2.1 miles, poses very difficult navigational problems involving off-trail hiking half the time.

At the Bradford Ranger Station (814-362-4613) in Hearts Content, pick up a leaflet including a topographical map of the area and a description of the controls. If you finish all the courses—it should take one or two hours for each one—you can present your course record at the ranger station. In return, you'll receive a certificate of completion.

Allegany State Park

■ 65,000 acres ■ Southwest New York, off N.Y. 17 in Cattaraugus County
■ Year-round ■ Camping, hiking, boating, swimming, fishing, biking, horseback
riding, cross-country skiing, bird-watching, wildlife viewing ■ Contact the
park, 2373 ASP Route 1, Suite 3, Salamanca, NY 14779; phone 716-354-9101.
www.nysparks.com

WHEN WESTERN NEW YORKERS complained that established parks served
only the eastern part of the state, the legislature of New York authorized
Allegany State Park in 1921. Built on deforested and damaged lands in
an era well aware of the need for conservation, the park opened with the
Allegany School of Natural History—a summer camp for serious nature
study, where students swam in newly dug Science Lake.

Today, the emphasis in public use here is on recreation. Open year-
round, with winterized cabins and a first-rate, 35-mile system of cross-
country ski trails, Allegany State Park has much to offer visitors in any
season. The park adjoins Allegheny National Forest (see pp. 167-172) at
the Pennsylvania state line, while on the east, north, and west it abuts
lands of the Seneca Nation, including the Allegheny Reservoir (see p. 168)
on its western boundary. This makes the park part of a wild and forested
area covering three-quarters of a million acres.

In summer Allegany State Park offers three campgrounds, cabins,
and lifeguarded beaches and boating (with rentals) on two lakes. Visitors
have access to the reservoir and can make use of ball fields, tennis courts,
picnic areas, playgrounds—even miniature golf areas. Be sure to pick up
information and maps at the enormous pseudo-Tudor administration
building in the Red House area at the north end of the park; some of
the first accounts of the park describe the architecture of the building
as "Early American." There are 6 miles of paved bikeways (with rentals),
18 hiking trails, and an 18-mile stretch of the North Country National
Scenic Trail. The cross-country ski-trail system is open to summer
hiking and biking, and the snowmobile and dogsledding trails are open
to horseback riding. In addition, the park has a full program of nature
study and walks, including hunting for fossil corals, clams, crinoids, and
brachiopods; nocturnal owl prowls; and basic bird-watching among
common and conspicuous belted kingfishers, redstarts, and orioles.

What to See and Do

Start at the lovely **Quaker Lake**
area adjoining the Allegheny
Reservoir. (Across the reservoir,
which is narrow here, you'll see
another good camping alternative:
the Seneca Highbanks Campground, owned and operated by
the Seneca Nation.) Just down
Park Route 3 to the east of Quaker
Lake is the popular 4-mile **Bear
Caves Trail,** which scrambles
up Mount Seneca to two caves
ascribed by legend to resident
bears. Take this hike with a ranger

Park denizen

to learn about the many black bears still living in the park.

Turn north on Park Route 2 and you'll come to 5-mile **Ridge Run Road**, which you can walk or drive to **Thunder Rocks,** a hilltop scattering of Olean conglomerate boulders studded with round, white quartzite pebbles. Although the rocks look like glacial erratics, they are not; in fact, the Allegany State Park area was just about the only part of New York to escape the last period of glaciation. These rocks were deposited millions of years ago, probably by an ancient river later drowned by the inland sea, and buried under sediments.

Now, after eons of erosion, softer sand and siltstones have worn away and left the more resistant boulders high and dry.

For another instructive hike, take the steep three-quarter-mile **Mount Onondaga Tornado Blowdown Trail** from the trailhead on Park Route 1 *(2 miles N of the intersection with PR 3).* Following the track of a tornado in 1990, observe the shrubby succession of raspberry, blackberry, young black cherry, white ash, hazelnut, and basswood—and perhaps spot some of the porcupines, foxes, turkeys, grouse, and deer that find this new growth appealing. ■

Elk County

■ North-central Pennsylvania ■ Best months Sept.-Dec. ■ Camping, hiking, fishing, cross-country skiing, bird-watching, wildlife viewing ■ Contact Elk County Visitors Bureau, P.O. Box 838, St. Mary's PA 15857, phone 814-834-3723, www.pavisnet.com/elk; or Bureau of Forestry, Forest District 13, P.O. Box 212, Emporium, PA 15834, 814-486-3365

ONCE THE AUTUMN FORESTS of Pennsylvania echoed with the clarion of bugling elk, but settlers and loggers destroyed the animals' habitat and shot them down. In 1867, a hunter killed the last Eastern elk (*Cervus elaphus canadensis*). Between 1913 and 1926, the Pennsylvania Game Commission introduced 177 Rocky Mountain elk (*Cervus elaphus nelsoni*), mostly from Yellowstone National Park. But in 1923, even before the reintroduction effort was complete, hunters happily started killing them again during Pennsylvania's first elk-hunting season. As hunters prepared to exterminate the last elk for the second time in history, Pennsylvania called off elk hunting in 1932. Seventy years later, the herd has grown to between 300 and 500.

The animals live mainly in Elk and Cameron Counties, in an area of about 200 square miles bounded roughly by St. Marys, Weedville, Driftwood, and Emporium. Much of this range lies within **Elk** and **Moshannon State Forests.** Many visitors are drawn to the area by the desire to see these beautiful creatures in the wild, and they usually do spot them—if they know when and where to look. Elk tend to disappear into the forest in summer; that's when the cows tend new calves (born in May) and the bulls grow new antlers to replace those lost in March. By August, the calves are about as big as deer. Soon after, the cows and calves begin to appear in herds, preparing for the breeding season.

In September—prime viewing time—the dramatic bugling and rut take place. The season begins slowly, builds to a peak in about three weeks, and begins to fade in October. During this period, cow elk gather in small groups with a breeding bull; the bull has a busy month

Cow elk nuzzling spring calf

breeding, keeping the cows in the herd, and driving off competing bulls. You'll hear the trumpeting calls, screams, roars, and whistles of the males, and you may see groups in the open, where it's easier for the herd bull to monitor things. Dawn and dusk are likely times to spot elk; under a bright moon, look for them in meadows at night. Toward the end of November, when elk regroup for the winter, you may see herds of 50 or more elk. They stay in large groups through December and into January. As winter deepens, look for cows along lowland streams; when snows disappear, you may see them kicking up their heels in spring meadows.

Elk-watching Drive

From Pa. 255 in Weedville go east on Pa. 555, following the deep stream cut of the Bennett Branch of Sinnemahoning Creek 10 miles to the little town of **Benezette.** You're apt to find elk on the main street, nibbling at somebody's garden. If not, take Winslow Hill Road 3.5 miles to the viewing area atop **Winslow Hill,** which affords long vistas over meadow and forest. Continue east across Winslow Hill on Wilmer Road, and descend Grant Hill Road to rejoin Pa. 555. Go east to gravel Hicks Run Road and turn north, entering **Elk State Forest.** (Pick up maps at the ranger station; there's primitive camping 2 miles farther—left at the fork—and access to 276-acre **Pine Tree Natural Area** via **Pine Tree Trail.**) Take East Hicks Road (right fork) and turn north on Pa. 3001 to Emporium. You'll see lovely rolling country along this route—and, with luck, some elk, too. ■

Bucktail State Park

■ 16,433 acres ■ North-central Pennsylvania, along Pa. 120 ■ Best months April-Oct. ■ Scenic drive ■ Contact State Park Region 1, R.R. 4, Box 212, Emporium, PA 15834; phone 814-486-3365

BUCKTAIL IS A 75-MILE scenic drive wrapped in a 16,433-acre linear park stretching through Pennsylvania's Big Woods Country. From Emporium, on the Allegheny High Plateau, Pa. 120 follows **Sinnemahoning Creek** until it flows into the **West Branch** of the **Susquehanna;** the road then follows the river to Lock Haven, at the plateau's edge. The track that the creek and river have carved into the sandstones of the plateau is so deep that locals call the valley a canyon—Bucktail Canyon. Native Americans called it the Sinnemahoning Trail and used it to cross the divide between the Allegheny and Susquehanna watersheds. Still forested with maples, poplars, and oaks, the riverine corridor is largely contained within the 500,000-plus acres of **Elk** and **Sproul State Forests.** The forest office in Emporium *(on Pa.155)* has maps that show access to significant trails and natural areas off Pa. 120, such as the 75-mile **Quehanna Trail** through the 48,186-acre **Quehanna Wild Area** in Sproul State Forest; it's the state's first wild area dedicated to peace and quiet. Lovely in any season, Bucktail is at its best when the forested canyon walls flame with fall colors. ■

Hyner Run and Hyner View State Parks

■ 180 acres (Hyner Run); 6 acres (Hyner View) ■ Central Pennsylvania, 20 miles northwest of Lock Haven, just off Pa. 120 ■ Best months April-Oct. ■ Primitive camping, hiking, swimming, fishing, hang gliding, wildlife viewing ■ Contact Hyner Run State Park, Box 46, Hyner, PA 17738; phone 570-923-6000

LIKE SEQUINS ON THE GREAT shaggy sleeve of **Sproul State Forest,** the two Hyner parks are small gems. The entrance road to both parks runs east off Pa. 120, 3 miles north of the village of Hyner. After almost 2 miles, the road forks. The left fork will take you to Hyner Run, a peaceful, primitive camping area *(April-Dec.)* nestled in a 60-year-old plantation of red and white pines beside a creek of the same name. Stocked with brown and brook trout, **Hyner Run** creek joins the West Branch of the

Hang gliding over Susquehanna River, Hyner View State Park

Susquehanna River just downstream. Lots of wildlife live here: Look for raccoons, coyotes, red foxes, gray foxes, and bobcats. This cozy spot is the eastern trailhead for the 50-mile **Donut Hole Trail** system and for the 64-mile **Hyner Mountain Snowmobile Trail.** But most people who come to Hyner Run are resting up between trips to Hyner View.

Back to that fork in the road. For 2.5 miles the right fork winds steeply up the mountain to Hyner View State Park, which consists of a woodsy picnic area offering spectacular views over the forested canyon and the Susquehanna West Branch 1,300 feet below. On the precipitous bank just below the stone wall of the viewing area (built by the Civilian Conservation Corps) is a makeshift wooden ramp. Resembling a stray barn door dumped here by a passing tornado, it's actually a takeoff ramp for hang gliders; in fair weather, you'll usually find a bunch of bright fliers, eagerly taking turns. The sight of them descending into the valley is a fine spectacle from the roadway below. Even better, of course, is the view the fliers have from their soaring hang gliders. ■

Return of the Black Bear

THE MID-ATLANTIC STATES are gradually restoring forests and wetlands that were destroyed in the 19th century. As a result, the black bear *(Euarctos americanus)* is returning to these areas, raising the chances of bear-human encounters. Even so, reports of black bears attacking people are extremely rare, and such incidents never occur without human provocation. Black bears are nocturnal and mostly afraid of people. They're also very unlikely to go looking for trouble, but the temptation of food left lying around can lead them to it. Wildlife and park managers therefore continue to ask property owners and campers to store and dispose of food and garbage properly.

Young black bear

In Maryland, where bears were wiped out in the 1950s, black bear conservation stamps ($5) are being sold to the public; the proceeds are used to reimburse property owners for any damage caused by new bears coming into the state.

Black bears are not the enormous grizzlies seen in the movies or in

Yellowstone and Alaska. Males are about 60 to 70 inches long, stand 3 feet tall at the shoulder, and average 300 pounds in weight. (Some rare giants reach 600 pounds.) Females are a little smaller, standing about 2.5 feet tall and weighing only 150 to 200 pounds. They like a mix of thick forest, with lots of undergrowth for cover, and somewhat open areas with berry bushes, a favorite food. Primarily vegetarian, bears eat fruit, nuts, acorns, grubs, beetles, ants, bees, honey, fish, small critters, and carrion.

Black bears are most active in the summer and fall, when they are mating (June-July) and eating, eating, and eating to prepare for hibernation. In winter they sleep for four months in dens—caves, rock crevices, hollow logs, or dense thickets—although the black bear's sleep is not the true hibernation of its bigger, more northerly cousins. (Because its body temperature falls only about 10 degrees, a black bear can be roused easily.) Tiny cubs, each weighing about half a pound, are born in the den in January. In March, bears emerge from their dens to begin teaching the youngsters and scouting for food.

Black bears are normally solitary creatures. Out of mating season, if you happen to see two or more bears together, you can bet they are probably a female and her cubs.

Hikers should bear in mind that these creatures have strong senses of smell and hearing, but their vision is not very good. This explains why a quiet hiker can sometimes surprise an unsuspecting bear, necessitating a discreet retreat. Never get between a mother and her cubs—or between any bear and its berry bush. ∎

Pine Creek Gorge from Colton Point

Pine Creek Gorge

Colton Point State Park ■ 368 acres ■ North-central Pennsylvania, 5 miles south of Ansonia ■ Best months April-Oct. ■ Camping, hiking
Leonard Harrison State Park ■ 585 acres ■ 10 miles southwest of Wellsboro ■ Best months April-Oct. ■ Camping, hiking, biking, cross-country skiing ■ For both parks, contact Leonard Harrison State Park, R.R. 6, Box 199, Wellsboro, PA 16901; phone 570-724-3061. www.dcnr.state.pa.us/leon.htm

IN 1900, IN A BID TO PROTECT the headwaters of beautiful Pine Creek, Pennsylvania bought the first tract of deforested, strip-mined land for today's 159,466-acre **Tioga State Forest.** Within the forest, at Ansonia, **Pine Creek** runs south in a deep gorge of red and gray sandstone—the "Grand Canyon of the East" (see p. 184). Crowning the rims of the canyon, at a point south of Ansonia where it's 800 feet deep, are two state parks: On the east is **Leonard Harrison;** on the west is smaller, quieter **Colton Point.**

Both parks offer great views, rustic campgrounds, picnic areas, and a scenic trail called **Turkey Path.** From the visitor center parking lot at Leonard Harrison, the trail descends 833 feet in 1 mile to Pine Creek and ascends another challenging mile to Colton Point. There's no bridge, so ask at the visitor center how much water is in the creek. For a quicker hike, descend half a mile from Leonard Harrison to a viewpoint; go about a quarter mile farther to see a waterfall on **Little Four Mile Run,** and return.

If you prefer flat-earth walking, take in views of the gorge from the 0.6-mile-loop **Overlook Trail** at Leonard Harrison, then drive to Ansonia *(Pa. 362)* or Blackwell *(Pa. 414)* to enter the **Pine Creek Trail,** an 18-mile rail-trail open to hikers, bikers, and cross-country skiers. In April or May, you can raft the Class II/III Pine Creek. For a two- to three-day hike along the gorge, walk the 30.5-mile **West Rim Trail** *(4 miles S of Colton Point State Park on Colton Rd.)* from Ansonia to Blackwell. After an initial climb, it levels off for spectacular walking 300 feet above the creek. ■

Ricketts Glen State Park

■ 13,050 acres ■ North-central Pennsylvania, 30 miles north of Bloomsburg via Pa. 487 ■ Year-round ■ Camping, hiking, climbing, swimming, fishing, horseback riding, cross-country skiing, picnicking ■ Pa. 487 is steep. Vehicles with heavy trailers should use Pa. 487 south from Dushore ■ Contact the park, 695 State Route 487, Benton, PA 17814; 570-477-5675. www.dcnr.state.pa.us/ricketts.htm

RICKETTS GLEN OCCUPIES a gorgeous location atop Red Rock and North Mountains on the Allegheny Front, the high escarpment of the Allegheny High Plateau, just where it rises from the Valley and Ridge province to the east. To get the lay of the land, hike the 1.9-mile **Grand View Trail** *(0.7 mile N of park, off Pa. 487)* to the highest point of **Red Rock Mountain** (2,449 feet). To the east and west, you'll see the great wall of the Allegheny Front looming 1,200 feet over the hills below; indentations at intervals along the front mark where streams have cut paths to the valley below. In the distance, the ridges of the Valley and Ridge province rise in the southeast. Looking to the north, you'll see the forests of the high plateau rolling away to the horizon. This terrain explains the jewel of Ricketts Glen State Park: the **Glens Natural Area.**

A national natural landmark, the Glens area is deep in old-growth forest. The moist microclimate here fosters lush vegetation, including a profusion of wildflowers and 500-year-old pines, hemlocks, and oaks—many 5 feet in diameter—that soar to 100 feet. In the forest above this natural amphitheater, two branches of **Kitchen Creek** begin their descent to the floor of the valley. They cut two deep gorges, **Ganoga Glen** and **Glen Leigh,** before coming together at **Waters Meet** to flow through the old-growth forest of Ricketts Glen. In 2.25 miles, Kitchen Creek drops 1,000 feet, cascading over 25 waterfalls.

For some reason, waterfalls evoke romance; they are classified by type as "wedding cake" and "bridal veil." The wedding cake version tumbles in small steps over thin sandstone layers, looking like white water on a steep incline. The bridal veil type pours over hard caprock overhangs and plunges straight to a scoured-out pool below.

You'll see many wedding cake falls in Ganoga Glen and, just below Waters Meet, the bridal veil of **Harrison Wright Falls.** Start at **Falls Trail** *(off Pa. 118)* and hike upstream along Kitchen Creek, facing the waterfalls for the best view. At Waters Meet, take Falls Trail up Ganoga Glen (where you'll find the highest falls, 94-foot Ganoga). Beyond **Mohawk Falls,** turn right onto the **Highland Trail** through the forest to the top of Glen Leigh; walk southwesterly along the stream to Waters Meet and return to the trailhead down Kitchen Creek. That's a 7-mile hike. The 3.5-mile Waters Meet loop is steep, rugged, rocky, and sometimes slippery, so wear good boots. For a shorter hike, go out and back along Kitchen Creek, or enter at the upper end of Ganoga Glen or Glen Leigh. The trailhead and a parking area are located about three-quarters of a mile behind the park office, which distributes a good map of the area. ■

Letchworth State Park

■ 14,350 acres ■ Western New York, 5 miles south of Rochester via I-390 and N.Y. 408 to Mount Morris ■ Year-round; camping (May-Oct.) ■ Camping, hiking, white-water rafting, kayaking, canoeing, swimming (pools), fishing, biking, horseback riding, cross-country skiing, snow tubing, ice-skating ■ Adm. fee ■ Contact Genesee State Park and Recreation Region, 1 Letchworth State Park, Castile, NY 14427; phone 716-493-3600. www.nysparks.com

FOR MOST OF ITS 163-MILE COURSE from northern Pennsylvania to Lake Ontario, the **Genesee River** is a mild-mannered stream meandering through broad valleys. But the 21.5-mile stretch from Portageville, New York, north to Mount Morris is spectacularly different. Here, a glacier dumped tons of rocky debris during the Ice Age and changed the river's course. A glacial moraine that was deposited near Portageville forced the Genesee to cut a new path across the plateau, a course that caused the river to drop more rapidly than before—from 1,100 feet at Portageville to 600 feet at Mount Morris, an average gradient of 23.2 feet per mile. For at least 10,000 years, the Genesee has excavated this new route through Devonian sandstone and shales. The result is the "Grand Canyon of the East" (see p. 182), a river gorge of near-vertical rock walls reaching 300 to 550 feet, and three big, beautiful waterfalls plunging 71 feet, 107 feet, and 70 feet. While there's no end of things to do in Letchworth State Park—Trailside Lodge is open year-round to accommodate winter sports enthusiasts—the center of activity (and contemplation) is the river gorge.

On a hot summer day, get out on the river below the falls for a raft trip through Class II rapids. The 5.5-mile paddle takes about two and a half hours. Or bring a kayak and register at the park office; you can also rent a duckie or a canoe from the rafting concessionaire in the park *(Adventure Calls 888-270-2410)*. Swimming in the river isn't allowed, but floating along in a kayak or canoe is an excellent way to take advantage of the water's cooling power.

For a different vantage point, pick up a trail map at the visitor center and walk the 7-mile **Gorge Trail** on the canyon's western rim. The trail runs from just north of the St. Helena picnic area southward to Erie High Bridge near the Upper Falls; it's accessible at many points in the park, so a shorter walk is possible along any stretch you choose. The scenic **Great Bend Overlook** *(Park Rd., 1.5 miles N of visitor center)* is a good place to start. Here the gorge is at its deepest—550 feet.

Feeling a bit lazy? Have a drink or enjoy a meal on the riverside terrace of Glen Iris Inn, former home of philanthropist William Pryor Letchworth, and contemplate the waterfalls he gave the state. Or on some calm, clear morning or early evening, join a park concessionaire on a hot-air balloon excursion *(716-493-3340)*. You launch from the Middle/Upper Falls picnic area and sail in perfect silence over the gorge, watching the river and forest open below you like gifts. ■

Finger Lakes Region

■ West-central New York ■ Year-round ■ Camping, hiking, boating, rafting, kayaking, swimming, windsurfing, fishing, biking, horseback riding, snowmobiling, cross-country skiing, ice-skating ■ Contact Finger Lakes State Park Region, P.O. Box 1055, Trumansburg, NY 14886; phone 607-387-7041.www.nysparks.com

NATIVE AMERICANS HELD THAT the Great Spirit once touched central New York with fingers outspread; geologists say the state's long, slender Finger Lakes are the handiwork of an enormous Ice Age glacier. Moving southward, the ice entered north-south stream valleys and carved them to great depths. As it receded, it deposited the Valley-Head Moraine at the south end, damming the valleys. Inflowing streams and glacial meltwater filled the valleys to the height of the moraine, forming the lakes we now call Canandaigua, Keuka, Seneca, Cayuga, Owasco, Skaneateles, Otisco, Conesus, Hemlock, Honeoye, and Candice.

But that's not the whole story. Because the side valleys of tributaries flowing into the lakes ran in an east-west plane, the north-south running glacier didn't cut into them as deeply as it did the main north-south channels. When the ice melted, the floors of these side valleys were left

Picnic area at Cayuga Lake State Park

hanging, a situation streams addressed by eroding the floors, working backward toward their headwaters. In this way, deep glens were carved into the bedrock of lakeside mountains, and streams continue to rush through them, often plunging in fierce, rock-rending waterfalls. (Many of these gorges are no longer at lakeside; as streams erode toward their headwaters and lake levels fall, streams and lakes "move" farther apart.)

While exploring the Finger Lakes, you may notice that a hardworking erosional side stream commonly deposits a delta of sand, silt, and gravel where it enters a lake. Examine the mountainside above, looking for gravelly outcrops higher up. These, too, are deltas—much older ones that were deposited by the stream when the lake level was higher. Over time, the lake repeatedly punches an outflow channel through its southern end; each time, the lake level drops and remains fairly constant until another outflow opens farther down. As a result, all the Finger Lakes have become lower and smaller. Presumably they still have a long future; thanks to the glacier, they are very deep.

North of the lakes, glaciation left a legacy of extensive wetlands—now mostly gone—and a drumlin field (see p. 156) about 20 miles wide. The huge field begins on a rough line about 30 miles north of the Valley-Head Moraine and ends on a parallel line 30 miles farther north.

What to See and Do

Camping

Eleven state parks are located on the shores of the Finger Lakes, and there are several others in the region. The most popular water-front parks include **Taughannock Falls State Park** (see p. 197) and **Cayuga Lake State Park** (*2678 Lower Lake Rd., Seneca Falls, NY 13148. 315-568-5163*). Both offer tent and trailer sites, rental cabins, swimming beaches, boat launches, and good fishing.

Boating

Six of the lakeside state parks are dedicated marine facilities. **Seneca Lake State Park** (*P.O. Box 665, Geneva, NY 14456. 315-789-2331*), at the north end of Seneca Lake, offers boat-launching ramps and transient boat slips. **Allan H. Treman State Marine Park** (*1 mile N of Ithaca on N.Y. 89. 607-272-1460*), at the south end of Cayuga Lake, is one of the largest inland marinas in New York; it has 399 slips.

The other state marine parks are **Canandaigua Lake** (*S of US 20, at N end of lake. 716-394-9420*); **Honeoye Lake** (*East Lake Rd., SE side of lake. 716-335-8111*); **Lodi Point** (*2 miles W of Lodi on N.Y. 414, E side of Seneca Lake. 607-272-1460*); and **Long Point** (*just off N.Y. 90, E side of Cayuga Lake. 607-272-1460*).

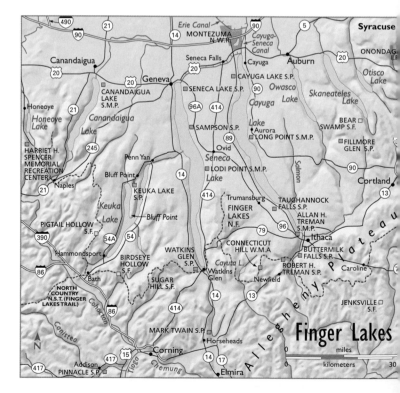

Cayuga Lake State Park

Boaters can explore the big lakes and travel on through an extraordinary system of waterways. From the Finger Lakes, you can reach the New York State Canal System (see pp. 220-21), the Great Lakes, the St. Lawrence Seaway, the Hudson River, and the Atlantic Ocean. The boatless will find a full array of rental craft—motorboats, canoes, single and tandem kayaks, paddleboats, windsurfers, sailboards, and day sailers—at many lakeside state and local parks. If you just want to be a passenger, call Seneca Daysails *(607-546-5812. www.hazlitt1852.com).* Try to get out early, when the water's smooth as glass and the loons, cormorants, ducks, and geese are out in force.

Biking

Road bikers will find scenic back roads in the Seneca/Cayuga area and throughout the Finger Lakes region. Try the **Bluff Drive** around Bluff Point, the long southward-pointing peninsula between the main body of Keuka Lake and the West Branch. **Keuka Lake State Park** (315-536-3666) on the West Branch makes a good stopover. Mountain bikers enjoy similarly rich pickings. Legendary hot spots in the vicinity of Ithaca include single-track-oval **Shindagin Hollow** (N.Y. 79 E from Ithaca, Boiceville Rd. to the end, and left to the fork); **Yellow Barn Forest** (N.Y. 13 N to Yellow Barn Rd.); and **Connecticut Hill Wildlife Management Area** (N.Y. 13 S to Newfield, right on Millard Hill Rd.), with 20 miles of roads and trails.

Hiking

There's plenty of hiking to be done up, down, and around the area's gorges. For a good long hike, walk a segment of the **Finger Lakes Trail** (716-288-7191 for maps, tips, conditions), traversing endlessly varied glacier-shaped terrain. This wilderness trail extends 544 miles from **Allegany State Park** (see pp. 174-75) on the Pennsylvania border to the Long Path (see pp. 98-99) in the Catskills. That's 544 as-the-crow-flies miles; the actual trail meanders to 800.

Try the 41-mile stretch of the Finger Lakes Trail from Watkins Glen to Ithaca (access is near the main entrance of Watkins Glen State Park; see opposite), a four-day hike that entails backcrountry camping; if you get a second wind, continue to the town of Caroline for a total of 87 miles. The trail is marked with rectangular white paint blazes and white and green plastic disks.

After a long uphill climb from Watkins Glen, you'll pass through the **Finger Lakes National Forest** (lean-tos, group camping grounds, and blueberries) and walk down through pine and aspen groves to little Cayuta Lake. You'll enjoy lengthy stretches of pine and spruce forest, traverse the quiet Connecticut Hill Wildlife Management Area, and descend through magnificent Enfield Glen to Robert H. Treman State Park (see pp. 194-95), a few miles south of Ithaca.

Golfing

Here's a little bonus: The New York parks system runs state golf courses, and three of them are in the Finger Lakes. (Urban New Yorkers apparently consider golf a wilderness sport.) There's 9-hole **Pinnacle State Park** (607-359-2767) in Addison, 9-hole **Bonavista State Golf Course** (607-869-5482) in Ovid, and the popular 18-hole Soaring Eagles Golf Course at **Mark Twain State Park** (607-739-0034) in Horseheads.

The Gorges

Six state parks protect Finger Lakes glens, or gorges. The best known gorge is **Watkins Glen** at Seneca Lake's south end. Three other beauties are near Ithaca: **Enfield Glen** in Robert H. Treman State Park and the gorges at Buttermilk Falls State Park (pp. 196-97) and Taughannock Falls State Park. ■

Watkins Glen State Park

■ 1,000 acres ■ West-central New York, off N.Y. 14 in village of Watkins Glen ■ Best months May-Oct.; Gorge Trail closed mid-Nov.–mid-May ■ Camping, hiking, swimming (pool) ■ Adm. fee ■ Contact the park, P.O. Box 304, Watkins Glen, NY 14891; phone 607-535-4511. www.nysparks.com

THE DEEP GORGE OF Glen Creek (**Watkins Glen**) is a fantastic monument to the power of water and the permutations of stone. Since it first opened to the public in 1863, under private ownership, it has drawn flocks of visitors. For a time it was the centerpiece of a resort, with a tourist hotel teetering on the rim of the gorge. Then, in 1906, New York bought the property; with the addition of a modern campground and swimming pool, the state park serves today's glen gawkers very well. Almost every summer evening, the park stages a full-bore sound-and-light show on the history of the gorge and its first inhabitants, the Seneca people.

To appreciate the glen, you must walk through it. Pick up a map at the park's main entrance and set out on the nearby **Gorge Trail,** which clings to the creek in the bottom of the glen, ascending 520 feet in 1.5 miles. (Along the way are 800 steps.) At the end of the gorge, don't climb the flight of stairs leading to the upper entrance; instead, retrace your steps (about a quarter mile) to Mile Point Bridge and cross over to the **South Rim Trail**—part of the **Finger Lakes Trail (FLT)** and the **North**

Hibernal Habitat

The Audubon Society has identified Cayuga Lake as an important migration and wintering site for at least 37 species of ducks and geese. The lake supports an average of 28,000 wintering Canada geese—57 percent of the state's winter population. Also wintering over in an average year are 2,100 redheads, 1,600 mallard, 1,400 black ducks, 550 canvasbacks, 125 goldeneyes, and 450 scaup. In addition, about 10,000 common loons use the lake on their migration from Lake Ontario to Delaware Bay. Tens of thousands of gulls and a lesser number of terns also stop by. Ornithologists worry about the impact of boating pollution on this important waterfowl habitat.

Country National Scenic Trail (NCNST). South Rim Trail will take you back to the entrance. To see more of the glen, bear left on the FLT and NCNST when they diverge from South Rim; cross the suspension bridge and go back upstream on the **Indian Trail** to the park's upper entrance. For an easier hike, take the shuttle bus *(fee)* from the main entrance to the upper entrance and walk down the Gorge Trail. The trail can be wet and slippery, and in summer the deep gorge can be very hot, so be prepared with sturdy footgear and plenty of water.

Whichever way you go, the experience of being deep in the glen is extraordinary. You'll pass over waterfalls and behind them. You'll hike through narrow places where strange lush plants spring from rock walls in the moist rain forest micro-climate of the glen. You'll find quiet spots to sit, too, and contemplate the rock-solid, ever changing beauty of this marvelous place.

Scenic Drive from Watkins Glen

For a taste of the Finger Lakes region, try this up-and-back, 85-mile drive from Watkins Glen village, at the south end of Seneca Lake, to the north end of Cayuga Lake and then back south to the city of Ithaca. Along the way are small towns and villages—tucked under hills along lakeshores—and broad, round remnants of high plateau that stand between the lakes and afford long, sweeping vistas.

Start by taking N.Y. 414 north out of Watkins Glen. Just 3 miles from town, an easy loop drive leads through the mixed woods and grasslands of the **Finger Lakes National Forest:** Go east on N.Y. 79 through Burdett, north on N.Y. 4, and then west on N.Y. 1 to return to N.Y. 414. Crossing the high watershed between Seneca and Cayuga Lakes, the two largest finger lakes, you'll see vineyards that have largely replaced the marginal farms of this scoured, thin-soiled land.

Continue driving north to Seneca Falls, then turn east on US 20 for the entrance to the Montezuma National Wildlife Refuge (see pp. 198-99). Return south along the western shore of Cayuga Lake on N.Y. 89. Eight miles short of Ithaca, stop for a while and explore Taughannock Falls State Park (see p. 197). ■

Bald Eagle Success Story

Over the last half century, a national symbol—the bald eagle (*Haliaeetus leucocephalus*)—came very close to extinction in the United States. Illegal hunting claimed many members of this species. In addition, habitats shrank drastically, and accumulations of pesticides in eagle bodies resulted in thin-shelled eggs that failed to hatch or broke too easily. The Endangered Species Act, passed by the U.S. Congress in 1973, gave notice of the species' precarious existence.

In 1976, New York began efforts to reestablish bald eagles in every part of the state where habitat still existed. That year, Montezuma National Wildlife Refuge (see p. 198) and New York's Department of Environmental Conservation undertook the first program to release young bald eagles, raised in captivity, into the wild. Between 1976 and 1980, the refuge released 23 eagles. The first two birds, set free in 1976, nested in northern New York in 1980; in 1987, three Montezuma eagles came home to roost, producing an average of two young each year. Similar programs have succeeded at other national wildlife refuges. Today, bald eagles have been removed from the list of endangered species—they're now merely "threatened"—and wildlife managers are optimistic about the birds' future.

Unique to North America, bald eagles are large birds of prey. A male measures 3 feet from head to tail, weighs 8 to 10 pounds, and has a wingspan of 6.5 feet. A female is 3.5 feet from head to tail, weighs 10 to 14 pounds, and has a wingspan of 8 feet. Immature eagles are a motley chocolate brown; they gain the white head and tail feathers at maturity (4 to 5 years old). Bald eagles live 25 to 35 years, generally mate for life, and occupy huge, high nests in big trees near water. They mate once a year, lay one to three eggs, and incubate the eggs for 35 days. Young birds leave the nest for the first time (fledge) at 10 to 12 weeks; like older eagles, they eat fish, carrion, small mammals, and snakes. They also eat other birds or steal food from them.

Scientific revelations about the greediness and bullying bad manners of bald eagles led some social commentators to lament the choice of this species as a national symbol; others said its members would fit right in on Wall Street.

Robert H. Treman State Park

■ 1,070 acres ■ West-central New York, 5 miles south of Ithaca off N.Y. 327 ■ Best months May-Oct. ■ Camping, hiking, swimming ■ Adm. fee ■ Contact the park, R.D. 10, Ithaca, NY 14850; phone 607-273-5761 (summer) or 607-273-3440 (winter). www.nysparks.com

THE HIDDEN JEWEL OF THE Finger Lakes gorges is **Enfield Glen** in Robert H. Treman State Park. Smaller than Watkins Glen (see pp. 191-92) and the gorge at Taughannock Falls (see p. 197), the upper glen is so aesthetically pleasing in its intimate scale and its bold, rectilinear forms that it might have been fabricated by designers for a movie set.

Enfield Creek lazes through hemlock forest, then narrows and dashes through chutes incised in shale to plunge over **Lucifer Falls,** cascading

Falls along Gorge Trail, Robert H. Treman State Park

115 feet to a grotto below. Geologists believe that the wider lower gorge below the falls, set deep between forested hills, was eroded by the creek in an earlier period between glacial advances, while the rocky, rugged upper section was carved after the last glacier receded. Together, the two sections of the glen make for some stunning hikes.

You can see the most dramatic part of the upper glen in a half-mile round-trip hike. From the parking lot at the park's upper entrance, follow the **Gorge Trail** a quarter mile to Lucifer Falls and return (an easy walk thanks to a walkway and steps). But to do the glen justice, hike the 2.25-mile **Rim Trail** from the upper park to the lower park. Swim in the deep pool under the falls, and return upstream along the creek on the 2.25-mile Gorge Trail. Look for a peaceful campground beside the creek in the lower park. A 3-mile stretch of the **Finger Lakes/North Country National Scenic Trail** parallels the Rim Trail along the park's southern edge. ■

Swimming area at Buttermilk Falls State Park

Buttermilk Falls State Park

■ 751 acres ■ West-central New York, off N.Y. 13 on southern outskirts of Ithaca ■ Best months May-Oct.; all trails closed Nov. 10 ■ Camping, hiking, swimming, bird-watching ■ Adm. fee ■ Contact Robert H. Treman State Park, R.D. 10, Ithaca, NY 14850; phone 607-273-5761 (summer) or 607-273-3440 (winter). www.nysparks.com

OVER THOUSANDS OF YEARS, **Buttermilk Creek** has wandered far from Cayuga Lake, carving out a deep, peaceful glen as it drops from 1,000 feet at Lake Treman—in the upper end of Buttermilk Falls State Park—to 400 feet at the lower end of the park. The creek obligingly displays its biggest and best waterfall in full view of the park entrance, but don't be tempted to stop there. That's merely the gateway to the rocky glen where the single spire of **Pinnacle Rock** rises 40 feet above the stream. Here the water swirls through rapids and a series of cascades and waterfalls, creating a cool and verdant corridor luxuriant with ferns, mosses, and wildflowers.

From the park entrance, hike up the glen on the gentler three-quarter-mile **Rim Trail,** then return by the three-quarter-mile **Gorge Trail.** The upper part of the park, beyond the gorge, is a lovely expanse of open woods and lawns with an inviting picnic area. You can drive around to it *(5 miles via W. King Rd.)* or include it in your hike. When you reach the top of the Rim Trail, cross West King Road and continue walking north along the creek on **Bear Trail** for about a quarter of a mile. At the upper end of the park, take the 1.5-mile trail around little **Treman Lake;** it's about the size of a big pond. Be on the lookout for birds near the lake, a popular resting place for herons and geese. You might see beavers as well—or at least tell-teeth signs of them in the lakeside brush.

When you return to the lower park near the main entrance, look for birds anywhere along the **Larch Meadows Nature Trail.** This interpretive trail runs for about a mile, encircling a wetland thought to have survived since glacial times. After all your explorations, don't miss the swimming hole under the big falls; it's just the ticket on a hot summer day. ■

Taughannock Falls State Park

■ 783 acres ■ West-central New York, 8 miles north of Ithaca off N.Y. 89
■ Best months May–Oct. Camping (late March–mid-Oct.) ■ Camping, hiking, boating, swimming, fishing, ice-skating, sledding ■ Adm. fee ■ Contact the park, Box 1055, Trumansburg, NY 14886; phone 607-387-6739. www.nysparks.com

DURING THE HEYDAY OF country resorts in the late 19th century, fancy hotels stood on both rims of a gorge cut by a small stream. They overlooked 215-foot **Taughannock Falls,** the tallest vertical drop falls in the Northeast. The hotels and their fashionable guests are gone now, but this geologic marvel remains, protected by Taughannock Falls State Park.

Today you can go swimming or boating in **Cayuga Lake,** largest of the Finger Lakes, but the park's center of attention is still the waterfall. The **Gorge Trail** begins directly across from the park entrance and winds through a quiet glen for three-quarters of a mile. When it emerges from woods at the bottom of the gorge, hikers find themselves standing in a great stone bowl at the base of the falls. The stream—in spring a grand rush of meltwater—drops straight down to churn a deep plunge pool below. You can see the falls from a drive-in overlook on the rim *(off Park Rd.),* but the walk in on the Gorge Trail is infinitely more rewarding.

For more dizzying views, hike the rim trails, too. The 1.2-mile **South Rim Trail** *(trailhead next to Gorge Trail)* and the 1.5-mile **North Rim Trail** *(1 mile N of main entrance)* connect above the falls to make a loop trail. The rim trails close in winter, but the Gorge Trail is open year-round. In winter, the falls freeze upward from the base to form a column of ice—a dazzling sight for hikers deep in the gorge. ■

Montezuma National Wildlife Refuge

■ 7,000 acres ■ West-central New York, south of I-90, on N.Y. 5 and US 20
■ Year-round. Wildlife drive closed to vehicles in winter ■ Hiking, cross-country
skiing, bird-watching, wildlife viewing ■ Contact the refuge, 3395 Routes 5 & 20
East, Seneca Falls, NY 13148; phone 315-568-5987. www.fws.gov/r5mnwr

RETREATING GLACIERS LEFT LOW and watery lands at the foot of the Finger
Lakes. These vast wetlands, replenished by Cayuga Lake outflow spilling
over the banks of the Seneca River, were surely among the most important
waterfowl habitats in North America. In the 19th century, some areas
were drained for farming, but most wetlands remained intact until 1910.
Then those busy builders, the 20th-century entrepreneurs, raised a dam at
the end of Cayuga Lake and converted the Seneca to a barge canal. Water
levels dropped, and marshes 12 miles long and 8 miles wide dried up.

A quarter of a century later, the U.S. government purchased 7,000
acres and dispatched members of the Civilian Conservation Corps
to reclaim the former marshland. The CCC built 6 miles of dikes and
Montezuma refuge's two largest impoundments: 1,200-acre **Main Pool**
and 1,100-acre **Tschache Pool.** Today, the lands are again an important
bird habitat and part of a larger wetlands complex that includes the
Northern Montezuma Wildlife Management Area, properties of the
Nature Conservancy, and other agency and private lands in the area.
The National Audubon Society has recognized Montezuma as its first
Important Bird Area in New York.

Within the refuge are small grasslands, maintained for songbirds, and
woodlands of red maple, oak, and cottonwood. The heart of the refuge
is the marsh. Oddly enough, this wild little tract is hemmed in on the east
by the Cayuga-Seneca Canal and bisected by I-90, yet it still feels like
wilderness. A 3.5-mile wildlife drive starts at the visitor center, passes
between the Main Pool and the barge canal, and ends at Tschache Pool. A
2-mile path, the **Esker Brook Trail** (next to visitor center), links to **Ridge,
Brook,** and **Orchard Trails**—short walkways that lead you through their
namesake habitats. Take a close look at the low ridges you see here and
there, rising about 100 feet above the marsh. Often said to resemble
"beached whales," they're drumlins.

Spring and fall are peak bird seasons, with fall taking the lead on this
refuge. The numbers include more than 25,000 black ducks, 12,000 snow
geese, 100,000 Canada geese, and a million mallard. You'll find wigeon,
goldeneyes, redheads, pintail, and teal as well. Spring is the time for
warblers and for shorebirds such as sandpipers, killdeer, and yellowlegs.
Several threatened or endangered species do well on the refuge. Ospreys
and black terns breed, and it was here in 1976 that the first captive-reared
bald eaglets were released—an experiment that succeeded (see p. 193).
Tschache Pool is closed to walkers for the sake of nesting eagles, but with
binoculars you can see them from the observation tower near the pool. ■

Inland Coast

Lake Ontario shore, Southwick Beach State Park, New York

THE EXTENT AND VARIETY of New York's waterways often surprise visitors to the state. Among them are the Hudson River, New York Harbor, and Long Island Sound in the east and southeast; the New York State Barge Canal, which is part of a major system of artificial waterways stretching across the level lowlands beyond the northern fringes of the Allegheny Plateau; and Lake Erie, Lake Ontario, and the St. Lawrence River, whose shores lie just north of the lowlands, forming an "inland coast" long

favored by outdoor enthusiasts. That "coast" includes Pennsylvania's northwest corner, which borders Lake Erie. Hugging the lake's southern shore is a narrow band of lowlands that runs from Pennsylvania into New York, where it extends along the entire northern border and loops around the rugged Adirondack Mountains in the state's northeast triangle.

Geologists differentiate four lowland provinces—Erie-Ontario, Hudson-Mohawk, Champlain, and St. Lawrence Lowlands—but these provinces are in fact about as different as four brands of vanilla ice cream. According to the geologists, the provinces are built upon layers of flat-lying sedimentary rock, and anyone can see the topographic result: They are all quite flat and

low, as the name says. But their geologic history is more dramatic than their surface features reveal; if you know that history, you'll find more in the appearance of the lowlands than first meets the eye.

As the Ice Age came to an end and the continental glacier covering this area began to melt, volumes of meltwater filled low-lying basins between the toe of the receding glacier and the high ground to the south, forming several big lakes. These lakes were only temporary; their waters found new spillways, and each time lake levels fell, the shape of the shorelines changed. Geologists have many names for the lakes of the late Pleistocene epoch, including Lake Iroquois (in what is now the Lake Ontario basin) and Lake Vermont (in the current Lake Champlain basin). The shores of these ancestral lakes were marked by all the geologic structures you might see on any lakeshore today: beaches, dunes, rocky cliffs undercut by waves, and gravelly deltas built up where streams entered the lakes. As the glacier retreated farther into Canada, leaving the St. Lawrence Valley open to the sea, water rushed in and covered the St. Lawrence and Champlain Lowlands. The resulting Champlain Sea was only temporary: The land rose because it was no longer depressed by the weight of the glacier, and the sea diminished. As the land rebounded, the Lake Iroquois-Ontario basin tilted southward, drowning the mouths of rivers entering the lake from the south and forming lagoons behind offshore bars, a pattern that still characterizes Lake Ontario's south-shore harbors. The departing glacier also left a great field of drumlins in the lowlands, and it dropped erratics everywhere. (Drumlins are hills of rock and soil debris deposited and shaped by glaciers; erratics are rocks picked up by glaciers and moved elsewhere, often quite far from original locations.)

One of the most dramatic episodes in the glacier's retreat took place at what is now the city of Lewiston, in the northwest corner of New York. Here the land is mostly flat, but it takes three big steps up from the Lake Iroquois-Ontario shore. The first step up from the lakeshore plain is called the Niagara scarp; the second is the Onondaga scarp; the more gradual third step rises to the Allegheny Plateau. (The Niagara scarp is not a local feature but continues around Lakes Huron and Michigan into Illinois.) About 12,000 years ago, as the melting glacier backed off the 250-foot-high Niagara scarp, water from the newly forming upper Great Lakes began to spill over the scarp into Lake Iroquois. It also filled another temporary ancestral lake, known to geologists as Lake Tonawanda, which lay slightly inland (and upland) between the Niagara scarp and the Onondaga.

Lake Tonawanda was an intermediate basin, one step down from Lake Erie and one step above Lake Ontario. It stretched east all the way to present-day Rochester, and it poured water over the Niagara scarp into Lake Iroquois at several other points along the shore. The floor of Lake Tonawanda, however, tilted west just enough to spill the greatest volume of water over the scarp at Lewiston, New York. Soon that spillway captured all the overflow, drained Lake Tonawanda, and began its 12,000-year career as Niagara Falls, steadily cutting a 7-mile-long gorge southward toward its source in Lake Erie. Today the city of Lewiston stands adjacent to the plunge pool of the original Niagara Falls, 7 miles north of the present falls. The lake has moved, too, for present-day Lake Ontario is much smaller than ancestral Lake Iroquois. Thus, the Niagara River has another 7 miles to run north from Lewiston to reach Lake Ontario.

To the east of Lewiston and the Niagara frontier, the lowland plain stretches away along the southern shore of Lake Ontario. This plain, exposed by the shrinkage of the lake, once lay in the bed of glacial Lake Iroquois. The ancient beach of Lake Iroquois is not hard to find, for New York conveniently built N.Y. 104 (Ridge Road) on top of the beach ridge all the way to Rochester. It's hard to recognize the roadway as a former beach, thanks to 12,000 intervening years and the highway department, but the ridge shows up in the local architecture. The fantastically detailed stonework of local homes was done between 1825 and 1860 by a superfluity of stonemasons unemployed after building the Erie Canal. The building material consists of well-worn cobblestones cast up on the beach of the great inland Lake Iroquois.

American coots

In Rochester, N.Y. 104 crosses the Genesee River, which carves a gorge here just as it does in Letchworth State Park (see p. 184). (Interestingly, the rock strata through which the Rochester Gorge is carved are almost identical to those of the Niagara Gorge.) At Rochester, N.Y. 104 leaves the beach ridge and runs north of it to Sodus; the ancient ridge also goes on to Sodus, merging with the northern edge of the great drumlin field. Western New York's drumlin field– perhaps the largest in the world—is a landscape of gentle hills extending from Rochester to Syracuse. Here the land takes on a decided and regular roll, displaying the typical ups and downs of what geologists call "drumlinoid" topography. Many of these drumlins are cut off at the beach ridge where, more than 12,000 years ago, they were eroded by the waves of Lake Iroquois. (You can see the same thing happening to drumlins today on the lakeshore between Sodus and Oswego.) Somewhere between Sodus and Oswego, where the land rolls along in the heart of the drumlin field, the ancient beach fades away.

East of Oswego, the lowlands curve around the southeastern shore of Lake Ontario to Cape Vincent, which marks the entrance to the St. Lawrence River on the border between the United States and Canada. Driving northeast on the route called the Seaway Trail, you have the lakeshore and then the river on your left, though they are usually not visible from the roads; on your right, the land begins to rise toward the Adirondacks. Near Alexandria Bay another peculiar geologic feature intrudes. Called the Frontenac Arch, it is an uplifted northwest-trending arch of rock from which the upper strata have been worn away, revealing a somewhat bumpy dome beneath. This dramatic arching occurs under ground, but the bumpy dome surfaces as the Thousand Islands of the St. Lawrence. They are composed mostly of pink granitic rock called Alexandria Bay gneiss—a visible link to the rock of both the Adirondack Mountains and the Canadian Shield. Then the lowland band narrows, following the river northeast as far as Massena. There the New York border and the lowlands swing east, circling the northern rim of the Adirondacks, and the St. Lawrence continues northeastward to the sea. ■

Pymatuning State Park

- 21,122 acres ■ Northwest Pennsylvania, 1.5 miles north of Jamestown
- Best season summer ■ Camping, boating, canoeing, swimming, windsurfing, fishing, cross-country skiing, ice-skating ■ No boats above ten horsepower allowed ■ Contact the park, 2660 Williamsfield Rd., Jamestown, PA 16134; phone 724-932-3141. www.dcnr.state.pa.us/stateparks/parks/pyma.htm

ONCE THE PYMATUNING AREA was a great swamp where moundbuilding Native Americans made their homes. Then the Erie Nation lived here, and later the Seneca used the great swamp as their hunting grounds. In 1784 the U.S. Army defeated the Seneca and drove them from Pennsylvania.

Today, park publications say the name of this area derives "probably from the Seneca," means "the Crooked-mouthed Man's Dwelling Place," and "refers to deceit rather than facial disfigurement." But the writings of early missionaries report that a Delaware chief named Pihmtomink lived nearby, and this chief had a jaw that was badly deformed. In any case, when white settlers moved in at the end of the 18th century, they found the swamp to be poor farmland and immediately set out to change it. Over the decades, proposals were made to drain the swamp, but each

Anglers returning to dock, Pymatuning State Park

one of them eventually failed. Then, in 1934, a dam was built on the site; as a result, the swamp was flooded—not drained—and a lake 17 miles long with 70 miles of shoreline was created.

Now Pymatuning is a park for people: More than three million visit each year. It is the largest park in Pennsylvania, offering the state's biggest reservoir (17,088 acres) as the center of fun. There are 657 Class A campsites in three areas; 25 lakeside cabins; countless picnic areas; five life-guarded swimming beaches *(Mem. Day–Labor Day);* three marinas with pontoon boats, motorboats, rowboats, and canoes for rent; and one of the world's largest warm-water fish hatcheries. The well-stocked reservoir is especially popular with anglers, who catch tons of walleye, as well as a variety of panfish, bass, carp, and muskellunge. Two small natural areas, fragments of the original wetlands, can be visited by boat: 725-acre **Black Jack Swamp** and 161-acre **Clark Island,** with its forest of mature hardwoods and white pines.

Although it violates universal park rules against feeding wildlife, one of the most popular attractions in the park attracts nearly 300,000 visitors each year. At the **Pymatuning Spillway**—"where the ducks walk on the fishes' backs"—the ducks and geese compete with the carp for the bread that people throw their way. Resist the temptation. ■

Erie National Wildlife Refuge

■ 5,206 acres (Sugar Lake Division), 3,571 acres (Seneca Division) ■ Northwest Pennsylvania, 10 miles east of Meadville ■ Best seasons spring-fall ■ Hiking, fishing, snowshoeing, bird-watching, wildlife viewing ■ Contact the refuge, 11296 Wood Duck Lane, Guys Mills, PA 16327; phone 814-789-3585. erie.fws.gov

ESTABLISHED IN 1959 to provide habitat for migratory birds, the Erie National Wildlife Refuge includes more than 2,500 acres of swamps, marshes, impoundments, wet meadows, creeks, and beaver ponds. There are mixed woodlands, too, and stands of old-growth hemlock. The refuge's several creeks, given such inglorious names as "Muddy" and "Dead," are tributaries of **French Creek,** a small river of uncommon clarity that flows to the Allegheny. The Erie refuge has developed upland meadows of native prairie grasses—important nesting habitat for woodcocks, turkeys, mallard, teal, meadowlarks, and bobolinks. It has also set up a cooperative farming program, turning over several acres to farmers who leave portions of corn, oats, and winter wheat unharvested for birds and other wildlife. The grains not only help geese and dabbler ducks get through the winter but also sustain deer, squirrels, turkeys, pheasants, raccoons, and songbirds.

Erie does not draw the great masses of waterfowl that flock to some other refuges, though on any given day in spring or fall you might see 2,500 ducks and 4,500 geese. What sets Erie apart is its great diversity of habitat and residential species. Of 237 bird species sighted, 113 nest on the refuge; among them are abundant wood ducks, hooded mergansers, blue-winged teal, Canada geese, mallard, great blue herons, red-tailed hawks, kestrels, and bald eagles.

There is no refuge drive, but several local roads enable you to pass through the refuge. From Refuge Headquarters (*just E of Guys Mills*), take Pa. 198 east; turn right on McFadden Road, right again on Shaffer Road, and left on wooded New Road, which is a good place to see white-tailed deer and other wildlife. Farther south on New Road, turn right on Pa. 27 and left on Boland Road to continue through the heart of the **Sugar Lake Division.** Look for the photo-observation blind on **Reitz's Pond** just before Pa. 173. **Deer Run Overlook** on Allen Road, high above 130-acre Pool 9, is a good perch for spotting eagles on the wing. The most interesting walking path is **Tsuga Nature Trail** (opposite), a self-guided two-loop walk of 1.2 or 1.6 miles through a variety of habitats including a beautiful beaver pond and a stand of *Tsuga canadensis* (hemlock). From May into September, wildflowers vividly punctuate the pathway.

Ten miles away in the dense woods of the **Seneca Division,** you won't want to stray from the 1-mile **Muddy Creek Holly Trail.** This long boardwalk runs deep into murky terrain thick with black alder, ferns, skunk cabbage, and black mud, giving new resonance to the word "swamped." ■

Tsuga Nature Trail, Erie National Wildlife Refuge

Presque Isle State Park

■ 3,200 acres ■ Northwest Pennsylvania, on Lake Erie ■ Year-round ■ Hiking, boating, kayaking, canoeing, waterskiing, swimming, fishing, biking, in-line skating, cross-country skiing, bird-watching, boat tours ■ Contact the park, P.O. Box 8510, Erie, PA 16505; phone 814-833-7424. www.dcnr.state.pa.us/stateparks/parks/presqueisle.htm

PRESQUE ISLE IS A WORK in progress—a restless sandspit that is constantly migrating eastward. This 7-mile-long, gracefully curved peninsula is shaped like an old-fashioned feather pen with the point stuck in the southern shore of Lake Erie; about 300 years ago, that "pen" was probably 3 miles west of its present location.

Presque Isle moves because it is always being worked on by erosional processes: The prevailing strong westerly winds and waves of Lake Erie sweep sand from the western shore of the peninsula and pile it up to the north and east. Over time, erosion and accretion have built a series of dune ridges running east to west; ponds and lagoons have formed behind the ridges. Although Presque Isle—named by French explorers—means "almost an island," it has, in fact, been an actual island at least four times in the last 200 years (once for 30 years), when erosion severed the thin ribbon of sand that ties Presque Isle to shore.

A series of 55 offshore breakwaters slows erosion while preserving the natural processes that continually re-create this extraordinary place.

Today, as you walk across the skinny sandspit, you can pass through six distinct successional zones: the bay and shoreline; sand plains and new ponds; dunes and ridges; old ponds and marshes; thickets and subclimax forest; and climax forest. In doing so, you might see dozens of rare and fragile species of plants and birds.

Start your visit by picking up maps and information at the Stull Interpretive Center, opposite Barracks Beach and not far from the park entrance *(off Pa. 832)*. From Memorial Day to Labor Day, **Presque Isle** is a paradise for swimmers, with the longest beach—and the only sand-and-surf beach—in Pennsylvania. Hikers, bikers, joggers, in-line skaters, and wheelchair jockeys make good use of the 9.6-mile, paved multipurpose trail located near the water. An additional 11 miles of trails, for hikers only, wind through beautiful pond and marsh areas in the interior of the peninsula. Using a park map, you can easily connect a number of short trails for a long, leisurely amble.

> **Cattaraugus Creek**
> Known as western New York's most interesting stream for canoeing, Cattaraugus Creek is a beautiful challenge. Its source is Java Lake, elevation 1,651 feet, in Wyoming County, not far west of Letchworth State Park (see p. 184). Twisting like an itchy snake, the creek flows south, then west, then northwest; it shinnies down from the Allegheny Plateau to the Erie lowlands and slithers into Lake Erie, elevation 572 feet. That's a 65-mile rush and a drop of 1,079 feet. The most popular section is a 38-mile stretch from Arcade to Gowanda, a drop of 710 feet through the Zoar Valley, a gorge with steep shale cliffs. That takes expertise, but from Gowanda, you'll have an easy paddle of 18 miles across the lowlands to the beach at Lake Erie.

For a special walk through the ecological kaleidoscope, follow the 2-mile **Dead Pond Trail** through sand plains, pines, and oak forest. The youngest part of the peninsula, 319-acre **Gull Point Natural Area,** is also especially interesting. Take the 1.5-mile loop **Gull Point Trail** from the east end of Budny Beach (Beach 10); at the southeast end of the loop, pick up the trail to the observation platform at the edge of the **Special Management Area** on the point. This is a great spot for viewing shorebirds and waterfowl in the SMA, which is off-limits from April through November, when migratory birds are resting and feeding. Located on the Atlantic flyway, Presque Isle is a hot spot for birders: Watch for waterfowl migrations in March and in late November through December; shorebirds in April and September; and warblers in May and September.

The park also has a 500-slip marina, four boat-launch areas, and a rental concession *(814-838-3938)* for watercraft at **Grave Yard Pond.** Get a kayak, paddleboat, or canoe to explore the interior lagoons by water. Or register at the boat dock for the free four-times-daily tour of the interior by 20-passenger pontoon boat, with a park naturalist as your guide. ■

Niagara Falls

■ Western New York ■ Most attractions open Mem. Day–early Oct. ■ Hiking, walking, wildflower viewing, scenic views ■ Adm. fee ■ Contact Niagara County Tourism Department, 139 Niagara St., Lockport, NY 14094, phone 800-338-7890; or Niagara Reservation State Park, P.O. Box 1132, Niagara Falls, NY 14303, phone 716-278-1796. www.nysparks.state.ny.us/parks/

ONLY ABOUT 30 MILES LONG, the Niagara River carries the outflow of four Great Lakes—Superior, Michigan, Huron, and Erie—northward from Lake Erie to Lake Ontario. Along the way, it drops 326 feet in elevation, including 170 feet at the famous falls. The river pours over a 72-foot-thick layer of Lockport dolostone at Niagara Falls State Park. This hard, 400-million-year-old sedimentary rock caps an underlayer of fossil-rich shale that wears away, causing the unsupported, fractured dolostone to fall of its own weight. In the 12,000 years since the falls began as runoff from a melting Ice Age glacier, they have receded about 7 miles, forming the scenic Niagara Gorge.

Niagara Falls divides into two main parts—the Canadian Horseshoe Falls and the American Falls—at Goat Island, which is accessible by foot and car at the state park. Close-up views of Horseshoe Falls, 2,500 feet

Niagara Falls from U.S. observation tower

across, are available from the island's Terrapin Point. The 1,100-foot-wide American Falls can be viewed from Luna Island (off Goat Island) and from Prospect Point on the mainland.

People have long been drawn to this area along the Niagara River. On the swift-moving waters above the falls, early settlers built water-driven mills that, in turn, led to the region's development as a manufacturing center. As rail travel increased, visitors and tourists flocked here in ever greater numbers to view the falls. It wasn't long before the area immediately surrounding the falls became a tourist trap and an industrial slum.

Something had to be done, and in 1857 a growing "Free Niagara" movement found a much needed rallying point in Frederick Church's "Niagara," a magnificent painting that captured the grandeur of the falls. Recognizing the need to restore and preserve the area around this natural wonder, members of the New York State Legislature eventually authorized the Niagara Reservation State Park, which opened in 1885. Across the river, Canada began similar efforts.

Famed landscape designer Frederick Law Olmsted and his partner Calvert Vaux devised a plan for the New York park including scenic walkways and carriage trails that would not interfere with the area's natural beauty. Olmsted was particularly interested in preserving the native plants

Maid of the Mist

and aesthetic views found on Goat Island. His plan called for grassy areas planted with trees, an arrangement that allows visitors to enjoy magnificent views of the rapids without being distracted by the hustle and bustle of the surrounding city.

Olmsted's vision is evident even at the visitor center. Built to celebrate the park's centennial in 1985, the center belatedly fulfills a recommendation that Olmsted made to park commissioners in 1887.

What to See and Do

Visitor Center

Maps, information, and discounted Master Pass tickets for in-season attractions are available at the **Niagara Reservation State Park Visitor Center** *(off Robert Moses Pkwy. inside park entrance)*, along with a film on the history of the falls.

Outside, in front of the center, is a living map of the upper Great Lakes. Walkways and planted areas represent land; grassy areas are shaped like the lakes; metal tablets mark major population centers. Follow the main path to a terrazzo map of the city of Niagara Falls circa 1885, when the park was es-

tablished. Also near the center is a stop for the viewmobile *(fare)*, a tram that serves all the scenic areas.

Maid of the Mist

The *Maid of the Mist* boat ride *(fare)* began in 1846 as a ferry across the Niagara River; today it is one of the most famous tourist attractions. Take the observation tower elevator down to the dock, don a plastic poncho, and board the boat for a ride full of thrills. You'll cruise past the **American Falls** and **Bridal Veil Falls,** then head into the churning waters and drenching mist at **Horseshoe Falls.**

Goat Island

Half-mile-long, quarter-mile-wide Goat Island is reached by either a vehicular bridge or a pedestrian bridge (across tiny Green Island). To make the most of the experience, leave your car on the mainland and stroll the pedestrian bridge over the ever increasing rapids. Walking downstream along the riverside trail, you'll come to **Terrapin Point,** directly overlooking Horseshoe Falls; it's the closest view of the falls from land, and a memorable one. From Goat Island, you can take footbridges to the picturesque **Three Sisters Islands,** each one farther out in the rapids, where the power of the water is almost overwhelming.

If you don't mind getting wet, visit Goat Island's **Cave of the Winds** *(fee)*. First, put on a slicker and nonskid felt booties; then descend 180 feet in an elevator and walk along a path to a boardwalk that takes you within 25 feet of Bridal Veil Falls. On the boardwalk's "hurricane deck," windborne mist and spray will truly douse you—a classic encounter with the falls. You can also visit the cave after dark, when colored lights illuminate the falls.

Schoellkopf Geological Museum

Built on the site of a hydropower plant destroyed by a 1956 rockfall—not far north of the falls—the Schoellkopf Geological Museum *(716-278-1780)* offers an interesting multiscreen slide show on the geological history of Niagara. The interpretive staff conduct periodic walks and nature programs along the gorge rim and more strenuous hikes into the spectacular gorge.

Rainbow Bridge and Canada

After you explore the American side, walk or drive across the International Rainbow Bridge into Canada for another look around. Just past customs, you can enter **Queen Victoria Park** and enjoy a panoramic view of Horseshoe Falls. Half a mile south of the falls are the 11 **Dufferin Islands,** worth a stop for a picnic and perhaps a hike. North of the falls is **Niagara Glen,** affording good views of the gorge and the river's lower rapids.

A 35-mile recreation trail for hikers and cyclists runs along the river from Fort Erie to Niagara-on-the-Lake, in Ontario. ■

Niagara Birds

The Niagara River corridor, recognized by both Canada and the United States as an Important Bird Area, has the largest and most diverse population of gulls in the world. More than 100,000 gulls of 19 different species have been seen on the river in late November. The one-day record for Bonaparte's gull, which uses the river for a migration stop, is 40,000 birds—about 8 percent of the world population. Many species of ducks and Canada geese also frequent the river, and in recent years peregrine falcons have nested on a narrow ledge of the gorge near Horseshoe Falls.

Following pages: Niagara Falls

Iroquois National Wildlife Refuge

■ 10,818 acres ■ Western New York, 30 miles northeast of Buffalo ■ Best seasons spring-fall ■ Hiking, walking, kayaking, canoeing, fishing, biking, cross-country skiing, snowshoeing, bird-watching, wildlife viewing, wildflower viewing ■ Contact the refuge, 1101 Casey Rd., Basom, NY 14013; phone 716-948-5445

IROQUOIS NATIONAL WILDLIFE REFUGE *(off I-90 via Pembroke exit, N.Y. 77 N to Alabama, N.Y.)* and the nearby **Oak Orchard** (2,500 acres) and **Tona-wanda** (5,684 acres) **Wildlife Management Areas** are the remnants of ancestral Lake Tonawanda, which filled the slight basin atop the Niagara scarp thousands of years ago. When the young Niagara Falls captured the waters of the lake, only wetlands remained, with deciduous forests in the bordering uplands. All this was Seneca Nation domain, but then the Iroquois Confederacy was defeated and settlers poured in to cut the forests and drain the wetlands. Fortunately, much of this area has now been restored: Today's refuge holds 16 impoundments, and incipient marshes are gradually being enhanced by careful management of water levels. The refuge and the two state wildlife management areas are known collectively as the **Alabama Swamps**—a name that is said to derive from an Iroquois word for "here we rest."

Public roads let you see a good deal and give access to four observation overlooks. You can also walk or bike the 3-mile section of **Feeder Road** that passes the four largest impoundments. There are three 1- to 2-mile walking trails—**Kanyoo, Onondaga,** and **Swallow Hollow**—each with unique features. If you don't mind muddy portages, you can launch a canoe in **Oak Orchard Creek.**

The emphasis at the refuge is on waterfowl such as tundra swans and Canada geese, which number up to 100,000 from March to May, and 24 species of ducks, including mallard, teal, pintail, gadwalls, wood ducks, redheads, shovelers, wigeon, and hooded mergansers. But with 266 recorded bird species, Iroquois holds surprises, too. Bald eagles may nest from February to June. Uncommon black terns and bitterns often nest here, as do elusive prothonotary warblers. Also keep an eye out for other wetland critters—especially leopard frogs and snapping turtles—or one of the 42 species of mammals found in the forests and fields. ■

War on the Waters

France and its Algonquin allies dominated the St. Lawrence River and the eastern Great Lakes until the French and Indian War ended in 1763. Following the American Revolution, these waterways took on strategic importance as Native Americans, British, and Americans struggled for control of western lands. Battles raged, on water and land, in the War of 1812. Along New York's 454-mile Seaway Trail (see p. 222), historical markers identify 42 sites important to that war.

Queen Anne's lace and other wildflowers, Iroquois NWR

New York State Canal System

WHEN GOVERNOR DeWitt Clinton proposed building a shipping canal across central New York in the early 19th century, the idea was derided as folly. Nevertheless, the governor persuaded the state to spend seven million dollars, and construction got under way in 1817, using manpower and horsepower, but not a single professional engineer. The 40-foot-wide, 4-foot-deep canal cut through 363 miles of wilderness, climbing the 568-foot rise from the Hudson River to Lake Erie in 83 locks.

Clinton thought the Erie Canal would open the frontier beyond the Allegheny Plateau—Michigan, Indiana, Illinois—and make New York City the country's leading seaport. He was right. In 1825, aboard a mule-drawn boat named the *Seneca Chief,* the governor made a triumphant first journey through the completed canal. Within nine years, the canal had more than paid for itself. Other feeder canals were soon added to the system, connecting Lake Champlain (60 miles); the two large Finger Lakes, Cayuga and Seneca (12 miles); and Lake Ontario (via 24-mile Oswego Canal).

The whole system—now 524 miles long—was enlarged twice in the 1800s and expanded again between 1905 and 1918 as the New York State Barge Canal. You can judge its importance by the fact that nearly every major city in New York lies along the route, with 75 percent of New Yorkers still living along the Erie Canal-Hudson River corridor.

Although boat traffic dwindled to a trickle as the canal was supplanted by interstate highways and the St. Lawrence Seaway (completed in 1959), things picked up again when pleasure boaters discovered it. Today, this former commercial waterway has been transformed into a recreational playground that is easily accessible from I-90 (New York State Thruway), which parallels the canal to the south.

From early May to mid-November, the modern canal system (with its 57 locks) is used by tens of thousands of boaters in canoes, kayaks, fishing boats, powerboats, refurbished canal boats, pontoon boats, houseboats, and yachts. With seven main harbors at Tonawanda, Rochester, Seneca Falls, Oswego, Little Falls, Waterford, and Whitehall, the system links hundreds of miles of lakes and rivers to the Great Lakes, the Atlantic Ocean, and five principal waterways in Canada.

Boatless visitors will find all kinds of watercraft that they can rent, as well as charters they can take (with or without crews) for an hour or a week or more. There are tours, too—from hour-long cruises or mule-drawn barge trips to multiday journeys that offer accommodations on board or at inns along the way. For complete listings, contact the canal office or check the website *(New York State Canal Corporation, P.O. Box 189, Albany, NY 12201. 800-422-6254. www.canals .state.ny.us).*

Old towpaths have been converted to the **Canalway Trail,** which contains more than 220 miles of trails that are used by hikers, bicyclists, cross-country skiers, and, in some sections, horseback riders. The longest section is the 70-mile gravel **Erie Canal Heritage Trail** (a national recreation trail) between Lockport and Fairport in western New York.

Lockport canal locks

Parts of it are open to horses. An especially lovely stretch (also a national recreation trail) runs 36 miles from DeWitt *(just E of Syracuse)* to Rome through linear **Old Erie Canal State Historic Park** *(R.D. 2, Andrus Rd., Kirkville, NY 13082. 315-687-7821).* A stone-dust-and-gravel path, it's open to horses throughout. Access is through the Cedar Bay and Poolsbrook picnic areas in the park.

A 25-mile, mostly paved section runs along the Mohawk and Hudson Rivers from Rotterdam *(W of Schenectady)* to Cohoes, north of Albany (no horses). An 8-mile stone-dust segment follows the historic feeder canal's towpath to Lake Champlain between Glens Falls and Fort Edward. Long distance bikers can string some of these sections together by adding New York bike routes no. 5 and no. 9. Call the canal at 800-422-6225 to request a trail map; call 888-245-3697 or 888-925-5697 for the latest information on trail conditions. ■

Eastern Lake Ontario

■ West-central New York, off I-81 ■ Best season summer ■ Camping, hiking, boating, swimming, fishing, cross-country skiing, snowshoeing, bird-watching, wildlife viewing ■ Contact Seaway Trail, Inc., P.O. Box 660, Sackets Harbor, NY 13685; phone 315-646-1000 or 800-732-9298. www.seawaytrail.com

FOR 454 MILES—from Ripley to Rooseveltown—the New York State Seaway Trail parallels the shores of Lake Erie, the Niagara River, Lake Ontario, and the St. Lawrence River. It's a national scenic byway with green-and-white signs that will guide you through a region blessed with a rich natural, cultural, and historical heritage. As you pass beaches, parks, boat launches, harbors, and small towns, look for outdoor visitor information centers, which have local and regional maps that identify recreational, historical, and cultural sites. When you reach the thinly populated eastern end of Lake Ontario, stop for a while, head for the beach, and walk; here you'll find dunes and swales that still speak of the wild. Better yet, get a canoe and go for a paddle.

Lake Ontario beach at Selkirk Shores State Park

What to See and Do

Selkirk Shores State Park

Established in 1925 and developed
in the 1930s by the Civilian Conservation Corps, 983-acre Selkirk
Shores State Park *(7101 S.R. 3,
Pulaski, NY 13142. 315-298-6921.
Adm. fee)* is a good base camp for
first-rate fishing. The swimming
and the sunsets are fine, too, but
the trout and the salmon are what
bring campers back each year. Both
Atlantic and Pacific (chinook,
coho, and pink) salmon are abundant, thanks to a fish hatchery just
upstream on the **Salmon River.**
There are brook, brown, rainbow,

and lake trout as well—so many
that nearby Pulaski bills itself as
the "Salmon Fishing Capital of
the Northeast." Upstream from the
hatchery, most of the river is catch
and release. Several small brooks
and lakes are nearby, and, of course,
Lake Ontario is well stocked. You
can launch small boats into the
Salmon River at Pine Grove, larger
boats at nearby Mexico Point.

Southwick Beach State Park

Take N.Y. 193 west from I-81 and
you'll come to Southwick Beach
State Park *(8119 Southwick Pl.,*

Dramatic Drumlins
Chimney Bluffs State Park
*(contact Fair Haven Beach SP
315-947-5205)*, on the shore
of Lake Ontario, is the setting
for glacial drumlins beaten by
waves and wind into fantastic
shapes—chimneys, peaks,
pyramids, and curves as sinu-
ous as sculptures. You won't
see such strange beauty anywhere else. Two miles east
of Sodus on the Seaway
Trail (N.Y. 104A), take Lake
Bluff Road to the park; the
lakeshore parking lot is about
6 miles past the campground.

*Woodville, NY 13650. 315-846-
5338).* Once the site of a 1920s
dance hall, a carnival midway,
and a roller coaster, the "Coney
Island of Northern New York" is
now a quiet state park with campgrounds, picnic grounds, and a
3,500-foot beach. It stands near the
northern end of a 17-mile-long
swath of Lake Ontario sand dunes.

The dunes form a barrier ridge
(usually a double one) between the
landward edge of the beach and
the inland wetlands. Sustaining the
dunes are beach grass, poison ivy,
and dune grape; the high dunes
support red oak and red maple
forests. Dense alder thickets mark
the edge between the dune barrier
and the inshore wetlands. Thousands of years old, many of these
dunes tower 70 feet or more above
the beach, making them the second
highest dunes (after Cape Cod,
Massachusetts) in the Northeast.

Southwick Beach State Park is a
good place to camp while exploring

this complex and unique environment. Start by walking the 1.1-
mile **Dune Trail** within the park
for a quick introduction to various
lakeshore habitats. From the trailhead at the park entrance booth,
you amble through sugar maples
and cherry trees, shrubby edge
forest, a meadow dotted with gold-
enrods and asters, a forest of
maple and red cedar, a beaver-dam
wetland, the sand-dune ridge, and
the beach where Caspian terns,
yellowlegs, and herring gulls dart
at the waves. Walk the beach and
then very carefully—always using
a boat or keeping to the trails—
explore some of the neighboring
natural areas behind those fragile,
irreplaceable dunes. Swimming or
picnicking is not permitted in the
natural areas.

Lakeview Marsh Wildlife Management Area

Adjoining Southwick Beach
State Park's south side is 3,461-
acre Lakeview Marsh Wildlife
Management Area *(315-785-2263)*.
To fully explore the inland ponds
and creeks of **Lakeview Marsh,**
you'll need a small boat; launch
areas off N.Y. 3, Pierrepont Place,
or Montario Point Road will put
you in the midst of meandering
streams and muskrat lodges. If
you come upon a colony of bank
swallows—a cluster of little nesting holes in the bank at waterside—keep your distance, because
these birds will abandon their
nests if disturbed. Other residents
to watch for are bitterns, wood
ducks, black terns, and great blue
herons. Make your way up dead-
end **Mud Brook,** deep in the
marsh, for great birding.

Campground at Southwick Beach State Park

If you're exploring on foot, a spur of the Dune Trail will take you into the wildlife management area for a 2-mile-loop hike; it leads through wetlands and across the dunes (on a walkover) to the beach. Walk south along the beach to the next walkover for a view of inland **Lakeview Pond.** Returning to the beach, continue south to the observation platform, which gives you a good view of the dunes and the wetlands behind. There's another observation tower at the management area's south end, on Montario Point Road. To get back to Southwick Beach State Park, simply walk north along the beach.

Sailboats at sunset, Southwick Beach State Park

Sandy Pond Beach Natural Area

South of Lakeview Marsh is a stretch of private property that contains **North Sandy Pond.** Two long peninsulas on the lakeshore embrace the pond like enfolding arms; at the place where the hands should meet, a channel intrudes, connecting lake and pond. If you have a boat, head for the tip of the southernmost peninsula: the Sandy Pond Beach Natural Area, a property of the Nature Conservancy *(716-546-8030)*. If not, you will have to drive around the pond; take N.Y. 3 south, then N.Y. 15 to the lakeshore, and walk 2 miles north.

Among the beach grass and cottonwoods, you'll see dune willow, a rare shrub that helps to trap sand and form dunes. Watch for shorebirds, too: sandpipers, yellowlegs, and killdeer—the latter recognizable by its piercing call of *kill-dee* or *dee-dee-dee.* Avoid the very tip of the peninsula, a roped-off sanctuary for plover. Before you come to the end of the beach, you will spot a walkover leading through the dunes and wetlands to North Sandy Pond. Return the way you came.

Deer Creek Wildlife Management Area

A couple of miles south of Sandy Pond Beach lies 1,195-acre Deer Creek Wildlife Management Area *(607-753-3095)*. By car, take N.Y. 3 south. To put a small boat in Deer Creek, continue on N.Y. 3 for 1 mile past Rainbow Shores Road to the launch.

To hike, go west on Rainbow Shores Road until it ends at the lakeshore; turn left on a dirt road and eventually follow the left fork to the parking area. The trailhead is beyond the gate. Take the **Wetlands/Dune Trail** leading south through the dunes parallel to the shore. After about a quarter mile, a path cuts to the right to the beach; although you can continue through the dunes, it's better to spare them wear and tear by walking the beach path. If you turn around at Deer Creek inlet, you'll make a 1.8-mile round-trip. Just south of Deer Creek inlet is **Brennan's Beach** *(swimming permitted)* and the mouth of the Salmon River.

Black Pond Wildlife Management Area

A 2-mile beach walk north from Southwick Beach State Park will take you to 526-acre Black Pond Wildlife Management Area *(315-785-2263)*. Here are high dunes and wetlands that show few signs of human impact because no trails or roads disturb the area. Admire the dunes from the beach. For a view of the wetlands, drive north on N.Y. 3 from the state park and turn left on Bolton Road to the parking area. You'll get only a look (no trails), but it's a nice one.

El Dorado Nature Preserve

North of Black Pond is El Dorado Nature Preserve, a 360-acre Nature Conservancy property *(716-546-8030)*. Take N.Y. 3 north; go west on Stony Creek Road 1.5 miles, then turn left onto Grandjean Road. When the pavement ends, take the left fork and follow the signs. (From I-81, take exit for N.Y. 193 west to N.Y. 3 north.) Here, wet meadows lie just inland from a rocky shore, and red cedar woodlands are busy with towhees and yellow warblers. A hiking trail leads from the parking area to Black Pond inlet; from there a spur goes to a bird-watching and photo blind at the lakeshore. Look for shorebirds from July through October, waterfowl and raptors in September and October. ■

Derby Hill Bird Observatory

In spring, little Derby Hill is one of the best places in the Northeast for hawk-watching. This 65-acre sanctuary has been operated by the Onondaga Audubon Society *(P.O. Box 620, Syracuse, NY 13201. 315-637-0318)* since 1975.

In the past 18 years, professional observers at Derby Hill have seen an annual average of about 6,000 sharp-shinned hawks (the 1999 count was 2,782), 8,000 red-tailed hawks, and more than 22,000 broad-winged hawks. There have been lesser numbers of red-shouldered hawks, northern harriers, Cooper's hawks, American kestrels, rough-legged hawks, northern goshawks, turkey vultures, ospreys, merlins, and peregrine falcons. In 1999, 115 bald eagles and 92 golden eagles (25 on April 25) were counted. It's common to see as many as 2,000 raptors a day in mid-April, plus a variety of other birds from warblers to sandhill cranes.

Much depends on the weather, of course: Snow, heavy rain, and strong northerly or easterly winds will discourage flying. Hawks fly best on strong southwest winds. Combine these winds with a low-pressure system approaching from the west, and you might just have to keep your head down. To get to Derby Hill from Syracuse, take I-81 north and then follow N.Y. 104 west to N.Y. 3. Drive north to N.Y. 104B. Take N.Y. 104B west 1 mile to a right turn on Sage Creek Road. When the road ends at the shore, turn right uphill to North Lookout.

Prairie smoke

Chaumont Barrens

Open from early May to early October, this 2,000-acre property of the Nature Conservancy *(TNC, 339 East Ave., Ste. 300, Rochester, NY 14604. 716-546-8030)* is unlike any other natural area in the Northeast. Termed "alvar" by scientists in Sweden, where such places were first found, this kind of landscape exists in North America only on a shallow arc from New York through Ontario, Canada, to eastern Wisconsin. A windswept land of extremes, it includes rock rubble and shallow soil, cracked and fissured limestone bedrock. It endures floods and drought and speaks of the far north even when summer sun scorches bare rock.

There is also life here (or signs of it): Tiny wildflowers such as bluets, cinquefoils, and harebells bloom among granite pebbles; trout lilies and trilliums lighten a woodland of shagbark hickory and hop hornbeam; fossil cephalopods lurk in the weathered limestone of pavement barrens; reindeer lichens grow in green-gray clumps amid the sedges and wildflowers of prairie grasslands; and stunted pines and cedars lean against the wind. Songs of thrushes, prairie warblers, and whippoorwills resound; raptors such as kestrels and red-tailed hawks circle high overhead.

Among the most eye-catching life-forms—at least during its blooming period—is a plant called prairie smoke. It grows 8 to 16 inches tall and likes dry, open sites, anchoring itself in the shallow soil covering the limestone.

Each year, in May or June, prairie smoke puts on quite a show as it releases its seeds. With their feathery plumes, the seeds are caught up by the wind and carried over the countryside.

Although scientists continue to debate the process, some of them believe that the barrens suffered a cataclysm thousands of years ago. They speculate that during the glacial recession an ice dam burst, releasing an awesome flood that swept the surface and dissolved underlying limestone along cracks and fissures. The force was so intense that the linear features it left upon the land show up in aerial photographs as patterns of vegetation. (You can hike through those areas on a 1.7-mile self-guided trail.

To reach Chaumont Barrens from I-81, take Coffeen Street and N.Y. 12F and N.Y. 12E to Chaumont; turn right on Morris Track Road for 3 miles to Van Alstyne Road; turn left and go 1.25 miles to parking lot on left.

The Thousand Islands

■ Northwest New York and southeast Ontario, where Lake Ontario flows into the St. Lawrence River ■ Best seasons summer-fall. Camping May-Oct. ■ Camping, hiking, boating, swimming, scuba diving, fishing, ice fishing, biking, cross-country skiing, snowshoeing, ice-skating, bird-watching, wildlife viewing, wildflower viewing, boat tours ■ Contact Thousand Islands International Tourism Council, P.O. Box 400, Alexandria Bay, NY 13607; phone 800-847-5263. www.1000islands.com

THE NAME IS AN UNDERSTATEMENT. To qualify as an official island, a bit of rock must be above water 365 days a year and support two living trees. In the headwaters of the St. Lawrence, the actual number of islands that make the grade is 1,864. Composed of granitic rock like that of the Canadian Shield and the Adirondack Mountains, they are very hard and very old—from 600 million to 1 billion years. Nearly all the islands are elongated in the direction of the river's flow. They have a similar rounded look, like loaves, but they're asymmetrical; the upstream ends are steep, while the downstream ends slope gently. Their common appearance indicates that glaciers crept upstream, heading southwest, parallel to the river, and crawled over them.

Today, the pink granite bones of the islands are cloaked in tall pines, softened by sandy coves, worn by waves, and capped with grand summer homes, so their basic form may not be obvious. The islands also seem to rise from the river abruptly, without proper foundation, as if they had been taken by surprise. Perhaps they were. It's believed that the Great

Family camping area, Wellesley Island State Park

View from Skydeck observation tower in Canada

Lakes (or their ancestors) drained to the south before the onset of the last glaciation; as the ice receded, the lakes changed course and flowed northeast, drowning the landscape and creating the **St. Lawrence.**

This powerful river is one of the largest in North America. The outlet for all five Great Lakes, the St. Lawrence carries an amazing volume of water (246,000 cubic feet per second) 760 miles from Lake Ontario to the Atlantic Ocean. At some points, it is 2 miles wide. Incidentally, the river was "discovered" by French explorer Jacques Cartier, who named it for the saint. Native Americans had discovered it centuries before, and they called the area Manatoana, or "garden of the great spirit."

To get the lay of the land—and the best views around—take a drive across the **Thousand Islands International Bridge.** Opened in 1938, it connects US I-81 and Canada's Highway 401. It also leads to Canada's superscenic **Thousand Islands Parkway** (Hwy. 2). From the bridge, the Skydeck observation tower, and the parkway (paralleled by a 22-mile-long paved bike path), you'll get a semi-aerial view of the great expanse of the St. Lawrence and its sprinkling of islands.

In the 1870s, President Grant and other notables made the Thousand Islands the summer playground of the rich and famous. Wealthy Easterners built summer "cottages" with dozens of rooms. For the first time, fishing became fashionable. Nowadays, although most of the islands are still privately owned, public parks and local outfitters open the pleasures of the islands and angling to wider use. You'll find plenty of things to do here. There are one- to three-hour boat tours on catamarans and cruisers; boat charters for cruising or world-class salmon fishing, sea kayaking, sailing, and scuba diving (the clear waters hold intriguing wrecks); and hot-air balloon flights complete with champagne.

What to See and Do

Wellesley Island State Park

From the Thousand Islands International Bridge, you can access 2,636-acre Wellesley Island State Park (*44927 Cross Island Rd., Fineview, NY 13640. 315-482-2722. www.nysparks.com. Adm. fee in summer*).

The park is big and the camping is dense (429 sites; 12 cottages), but Wellesley Island is a terrific family camp. It offers every facility from marina to nine-hole golf course—plus playing fields and a recreation barn for the kids, a big nature center, and miles of trails—so no member of the family need ever feel at a loss for something to do.

Wellesley's location in the middle of the St. Lawrence, with many campsites located on the riverfront, is ideal. If you don't have a boat, rent one (*315-482-6503*) to explore the area and angle for northern pike, walleye, bass, and the region's famous muskies. You can catch panfish from shore.

Take a break from fishing, swimming, or boating to visit the 600-acre **Minna Anthony Common Nature Center** (*1 mile W of administration office*). At the center's museum, exhibits on geology, the St. Lawrence River, wetlands, waterfowl, and island wildlife provide a good overview of your surroundings. A butterfly house, open in summer, is a special treat. Staff naturalists present a full environmental education program that includes nature walks, family outings, workshops, crafts, and a very popular river trip (*fee*) in a 36-foot voyageur canoe of the type used by early French traders. The center is open year-round, with cross-country skiing lessons in winter and maple sugaring in March.

The best trails in the park are right here on the grounds of the nature center: Eight miles of interconnecting trails (mostly easy walking) meander around a peninsula overlooking **Eel Bay, the Narrows,** and **South Bay.** The trails are short—from 0.3 to 1.25 miles—but they cover fields, woodlands, a pond, and granite knobs spiked with pitch pines. Using a map from the center, you can put together a substantial hike, and you might spot a bear or a porcupine along the way. Deer are abundant; foxes and coyotes are seen on occasion.

Smaller Parks near Alexandria Bay

Wellesley Island is the biggest state park in the Thousand Islands region, but New York maintains

Revealing Rocks

Deep road cuts along N.Y. 12 north of Alexandria Bay dramatically expose the underlying rocks of the area. The oldest rocks can be seen as the lowest strata in cuts just north of town, where the Frontenac Arch rises and the younger rocks have been worn away. The most intriguing is the Alexandria Bay cut a few miles northeast at Cranberry Creek. Here Precambrian gneisses 1.1 billion years old are topped by Cambrian Potsdam sandstone—white, quartz-rich rock 500 million years old. The angular unconformity between the layers represents a time gap of 600 million years. What happened in the missing years is one of geology's little mysteries.

A few miles farther north, another important cut runs uphill through a scarp at Chippewa Bay between the village of Chippewa Bay and the Cedar Point overlook. Here the lower beds are part of the Cambrian Theresa formation (500 to 570 million years old), a thin-bedded sandstone containing fossil worm burrows and broken shells. The upper beds are again Potsdam formation. The gneisses exposed in the arch at Alexandria Bay are below the surface at Chippewa Bay, an indicator of the downswing of the Frontenac Arch.

20 other parks with campgrounds in the area. At Alexandria Bay, the heart of vacationland, the 241-acre **Keewaydin State Park** (*43165 NYS Route 12, Alexandria Bay, NY 13607. 315-482-3331. Adm. fee*) stands on the grounds of a former private estate. A large summer home was built on the site in 1894, but it was demolished in 1964. Here you can live like the former gentry: A large swimming pool, a marina (*315-482-3720*) with boat rentals, and two gazebos overlooking the **American Narrows** of the St. Lawrence afford languid relaxation and the pleasure of watching gigantic Great Lakes freighters pass by on the river.

To escape civilization and savor quintessential island life, turn your boat toward 13-acre **Mary Island State Park** (*36661 Cedar Point State Park Dr., Clayton, NY 13624. 315-654-2522. Adm. fee*) off the east end of Wellesley Island, about 2 miles from Keewaydin, northwest of Alexandria Bay. Accessible only by boat, Mary Island offers 14 woodsy, riverside tent sites, picnic tables, and good fishing. The rest is up to you. Two other anglers' parks are accessible only by boat: **Cedar Island** (*315-654-2522*) has 17 campsites and a historic gazebo, and **Canoe-Picnic Point** (*315-654-2522*) offers six rustic cabins, 25 campsites, and an extensive nature trail; both of these state parks are on **Grindstone Island**.

A few miles northeast of Alexandria Bay is 56-acre **Kring Point State Park** (*5950 Kring Point Rd., Redwood, NY 13679. 315-482-2444. Adm. fee*), with 99 campsites and eight cabins, many of them waterside. One of the state's oldest parks, established in 1898, it occupies a skinny peninsula between Goose Bay and the St. Lawrence River—a choice location. The

Voyageur canoe in Wellesley Island State Park

point draws ducks, geese, and shorebirds, and just offshore is the Nature Conservancy's **Ironside Island** (see sidebar opposite), site of the largest great blue heron rookery on the river. Kring Point State Park opens the first Saturday in May and closes Columbus Day.

Robert Moses State Park

The second largest park along the St. Lawrence River, after Wellesley Island, is 2,322-acre Robert Moses State Park (*P.O. Box 548, Massena, NY 13662. 315-769-8663*). To reach the park, you have to drive *under* the St. Lawrence Seaway—through a tunnel beneath the Eisenhower Lock(see opposite), about 3 miles north of Massena. When you finally arrive, you'll find 168 camping sites, 15 cabins, and a 42-slip marina. Depending on the season, you can go hiking, orienteering, swimming, biking, cross-country skiing, ice fishing, ice skating, or snowmobiling.

Part of Robert Moses State Park is on the mainland, not far from the seaway ship channel and the locks through which the enormous lakers pass. Another part of the park is on big **Barnhart Island,** fronting the Moses-Saunders Power Dam and 25-mile-long artificial **Lake St. Lawrence,** a by-product of the immense hydro-electric project developed here in the 1950s. (Robert Moses was chairman of the New York State Power Authority in 1954, the year the seaway and power projects began, so his name pops up throughout the landscape.)

A well-groomed urban fantasy of "nature," this state park boasts rolling lawns of green, green grass. (The lawn-mowing budget must be immense.) Yet this is an amazingly good place to watch wildlife— probably because it is an island. Very much at home at the edge of the woods, white-tailed deer and woodchucks stand around on the grass like so many lawn ornaments. Walk along the **Robert Moses Nature Center Trail** and you may spot beavers, raccoons, or coyotes. Canada geese, turkeys, and pheasant laze about the lawn beside the lake, where at dusk you'll see wigeon and mergansers cruising.

Robert Moses State Park is a good place to fish, too. As the last light of evening fades, you'll see fishermen hunkered in their rowboats on Lake St. Lawrence, still waiting with admirable optimism for the big one to strike.

St. Lawrence Seaway

Built between 1955 and 1959 as a joint U.S.-Canadian effort, the St. Lawrence Seaway is a deep-draft waterway from Lake Superior to the Atlantic Ocean. Today, in the regional economy of the U.S. Great Lakes, the seaway is credited with generating 2.2 billion dollars in personal income and 1.9 billion dollars in business revenues each year. These substantial economic facts will justify your passing some time in a good old-fashioned way—watching the ships go by.

A system of 15 enormous locks enables oceangoing ships— up to 740 feet in length and 78 feet abeam—to climb 602 feet on the 2,350-mile voyage from the Atlantic to Duluth, Minnesota. More than 2,000 vessels make the transit each year, and thousands of visitors flock to the seaway's **Dwight D. Eisenhower Visitor Center** (*off NY 37 in Massena, near the entrance to Robert Moses State Park*) to see them pass through the gigantic **Eisenhower Lock.** The center offers historical exhibits and an interesting video

Birds of the St. Lawrence

The Audubon Society has identified a 42-mile stretch of the upper St. Lawrence River, from Wilson Bay on Cape Vincent (where the river begins) downriver to Chippewa Bay, as an Important Bird Area (IBA). The area encompasses a range of wetland and upland habitats; some are on large islands such as Wellesley and Grindstone, others on the small islands of Chippewa Bay.

The IBA is a major breeding ground for a remarkable range of birds, including common terns, bitterns, ospreys, and cerulean warblers. Wilson Bay is the largest breeding site in the state for black terns, and Ironside Island holds the state's largest rookery of great blue herons. The area is also critical to migrating and wintering waterfowl, harboring large concentrations of redheads, canvasbacks, common mergansers, and common goldeneyes. Six or more bald eagles winter annually near Wellesley Island.

on the mammoth construction project, but the great attraction is the observation deck above the lock. (Admission is a bargain at only 25 cents.)

For information on the seaway, call 315-764-3200, or visit the Seaway Corporation's home page (*www.dot.gov/slsdc*). To find out when ships will be passing through the Eisenhower Lock, you can call 315-769-2422. ∎

Adirondack Mountains

Lake Placid, New York

UNLIKE THE ELONGATED range of the Appalachians, the Adirondacks of northern New York are a circular mass of mountains. Even older than the Appalachians, they are composed of Precambrian crystalline igneous and metamorphic rock at least 1.1 billion (some say 3 billion) years old. This is known as basement rock, a geologic term for the oldest material in a given area. In most cases, such rock underlies sedimentary layers, but in the Adirondacks it reaches all the way to the mountaintops.

How the rock got there is not a mystery to geologists who study the long, complex history of the Adirondacks. Here's a simplified version of what happened: About 1.3 billion years ago, two of the enormous tectonic plates underlying Earth's crust collided, causing the ancestral Adirondacks to rise. Over the next several hundred million years, these mountains eroded down to the rocks that made up their roots. Later, as tectonic activity caused crustal material to collide and then pull apart, the rocks stretched and fractured along northeast-trending faults.

The whole area eventually was covered by a shallow sea that deposited the limestone and sandstone sediments we now see as the rock strata surrounding the Adirondacks. Then, about 500 million years ago—or, some say, as recently as 20 million years ago—a circular area of Earth's mantle began to rise, causing an upwarp in the layers of sediment. It's as if a giant inside the Earth were pushing up the crust to give himself a little more headroom. Geologists believe the thrust came—and continues to come—from a current of partially molten material rising from deep within the mantle. The resulting dome, about 160 miles wide, is now about a mile high (its perimeter can be seen in the wrinkling sedimentary rocks around the edge). As the dome rose, erosion carried away its soft, overlying sedimentary layers. It continues to rise today, at a pace faster than the rate of erosion, making a net gain in elevation of about one-tenth of an inch every year.

Next in the chain of events was the onslaught of glaciers. Thick sheets of ice overrode the mountains, stripping away soil, rounding the peaks, and grinding them down to ancient, hard rock—the so-called basement rock. The Ice Age left quite a legacy in New York: Alpine glaciers, remnants of the great ice sheets, carved bowls (cirques) and jagged ridges (arêtes) on the tall peaks of the Adirondacks. At lower elevations, the retreating ice dumped tons of rock and gravel across geologic faults, building natural dams that trapped water and created lakes and ponds, such as today's Lake George, Schroon Lake, Long Lake, and Indian Lake. The glaciers also strewed vast amounts of gravel across huge outwash plains and dropped large boulders, called erratics, far from where they once stood. In their wake, the ice sheets left 50 lakes more than a mile wide and thousands of smaller ones; 30,000 miles of streams and rivers, flowing from the mountains in all directions; and countless wetland complexes of marsh, swamp, and bog.

After the Ice Age, thin acidic soils slowly built up on the glacially scoured rocks. Pioneer vegetation took root and grew to deep-climax forest where moose roamed and eagles flew. People came here, too, and thus began a long saga that would lead to the establishment of the largest park in the lower 48 states: Adirondack Park.

The Algonquian people once hunted in the region's deep forests, as the Iroquois did later. The first European to arrive—Samuel de Champlain—and other French explorers and traders opened a rich fur trade with the Indians. In the 18th century, a few British military posts and small colonial settlements appeared along Lake Champlain and Lake George; they served as settings for some of the first battles of the Revolutionary War. After the war came those familiar ax- and gun-wielding profiteers who clear-cut forests for the timber, tanning, and paper industries. They also killed wildlife for food and profit. As forests fell, deer moved in, preferring sunny edge habitat. They carried brainworm, which wiped out the moose not already fallen to hunters. The hunters then began to exterminate the deer, marketing them downstate as "mountain mutton." They finished off the wolves, lynx, and beavers, too.

By 1850, politicians and journalists were speaking out against the destruction of public resources. Soil erosion and flooding increased, causing New York merchants to demand protection for the headwaters of commercial waterways, such as the Hudson River and the Erie Canal. At the same time, unspoiled areas of the Adirondacks were becoming resorts for the wealthy; the Vanderbilts, Morgans, and Carnegies built romantic "Great Camps" of rustic splendor where city men practiced the "manly" pastimes of fishing and hunting under the supervision of local guides. (The Great Camp, a cross between a log cabin and a Swiss chalet, established a style of American rustic architecture that persists to this day.) Such influential people prevailed upon the state legislature to establish the Adirondack Forest Preserve in 1885 and Adirondack Park in 1892; the forest preserve would lie within the park's borders. Then in 1895, feeling a need for stronger measures, the legislature extended constitutional guarantees to keep the Adirondack and Catskill Forest Preserves "forever wild." Any development in the Adirondacks, such as the construction of I-87 in the 1960s, now requires the support of a majority of New York citizens and both houses of the state legislature.

Today the Adirondacks are an extraordinary mix of public and private lands. The forest preserve, which consisted originally of 680,000 acres in scattered parcels, has grown to 2.7 million acres, making it twice the size of Delaware and the largest complex of public lands in the eastern United States. Adirondack Park comprises just under 6 million acres—the 2.7 million acres of the forest preserve plus nearly 3.3 million acres that remain in private hands. Much of the private land still belongs to timber companies that continue to log the forest, producing ongoing controversy; some private land belongs to the 130,000 people who make their homes here. Both the High Peaks Wilderness and Main Street Lake Placid are part of Adirondack Park, a unique arrangement that is puzzling to visitors. So beautiful are these forested mountains, strung with crystalline lakes and streams, that 1,200 miles of waterway are designated wild, scenic, and recreational rivers; every major roadway through the park is officially a scenic byway.

In the 20th century, managers faced the problem of restoring the Adirondacks. A rash of wildfires 100 years ago and a disastrous blowdown 50 years ago set things back. Nevertheless, the forests—mostly northern hardwoods such as sugar maple, beech, and yellow birch—have revived. Above 2,500 feet, the hardwoods give way to the boreal forest of red spruce and balsam fir. Above 4,000 feet only balsam fir carries on, crumpling eventually into krummholz (crooked wood), the dwarf fir forest stunted by the wind. Stands of paper birch mark the sites of old forest fires. Beavers, fishers, pine marten, bald eagles, and peregrine falcons have been reintroduced to the Adirondacks. About a hundred moose have wandered in from Vermont and Canada, black bears have increased to 4,000, and plans are under way to reintroduce the lynx—the lithe, high-elevation cat.

Since the 1960s, with the building of the Northway (I-87), managers have struggled to integrate increasing demand for recreation with the "forever wild" mandate. They have developed the Gore Mountain and Whiteface Mountain ski areas, Mount Van Hoevenberg Sports Complex, and 42 campgrounds, some packed with RVs. But they maintain 1.3 million acres as wild forest, where only some roads and trails are open to automobiles, snowmobiles, and mountain bikes. Another one million acres hold 17 designated wilderness areas, from which motorized vehicles and bicycles are banned. The result is a delicate balance. An outdoor playground for millions, crossed by an interstate highway, is probably not what the early forever wild advocates had in mind. Yet the Adirondacks, cited 150 years ago as the worst example of human ruination of the environment, are now a state treasure holding the largest tracts of true wilderness in the eastern states. Here you can practice figure skating at an Olympic venue or play a round of golf; you can also paddle a canoe far into a watery maze, accompanied only by the laughter of loons. ■

Adirondack Park

■ About 6 million acres ■ Northern New York ■ Year-round ■ Camping, hiking, orienteering, boating, canoeing, swimming, fishing, biking, mountain biking, cross-country skiing, ice-skating, bird-watching, wildlife viewing ■ Contact the park, Box 3000, Paul Smiths, NY 12970, phone 518-327-3000; or P.O. Box 101, Newcomb, NY 12953, phone 518-582-2000, www.northnet.org/adirondackvic or www.dec.state.ny.us/website/dlf/publands/adk

THE MISSION OF THE **Adirondack Park Visitor Interpretive Centers** at Paul Smiths *(N.Y. 30, 12 miles N of Saranac Lake)* and Newcomb *(N.Y. 28N, 14 miles E of Long Lake)* is twofold—providing environmental education as well as traveler orientation. Both of the official visitor centers offer maps and information. Both feature films and natural history displays describing Adirondack ecology and wildlife. In summer, both regularly offer interpretive trail walks, canoe trips, and a program packed with wildlife lectures (including a live raptor program), astronomy classes,

Mountain biking near Lake George

orienteering, and traditional basket weaving. At both centers, you'll find miles of self-guided trails that will introduce you to the diverse habitats of the Adirondacks. If you like short walks, don't miss the **Heron Marsh Trail** at Paul Smiths. In winter, the 10 miles of trails at Paul Smiths become cross-country-ski trails, while over at the Newcomb center, park personnel lend snowshoes to visitors who want to walk the trails.

These two visitor centers are great resources, but because they are well inside the park, you have to plan in advance. With six million acres at your disposal, you would be wise to do some research before you visit: Check the websites or call one of the official visitor centers. Local visitor centers at Lake George (see pp. 244-47) and all the larger communities within the park can also be helpful. Other great sources of information are the park's many outfitters, from whom you might rent a canoe, a mountain bike, fishing tackle, or skis. They know the best places to go in their parts of the park, and they can tell you how the fish are biting. While planning, don't forget that much of Adirondack Park is rugged wild forest or wilderness; a hike here is not your usual walk in the park. ■

Lake George

■ 44 square miles ■ Northern New York, off I-87 in southeast corner of
Adirondack Park ■ Best seasons spring-fall ■ Camping, hiking, walking, guided
walks, boating, sailing, sea kayaking, canoeing, swimming, fishing ■ Contact Lake
George Regional Chamber of Commerce, P.O. Box 272, Lake George, NY
12845; phone 518-668-5755 or 800-705-0059. www.lgchamber.org

MOST TRAVELERS ENTER Adirondack Park at the southeast corner, by way of
the I-87 Northway. The town on the doorstep is Lake George. Although
it's a small town of fewer than a thousand people, it has so much glitz
and neon that travelers in search of the wilderness may feel like turning
around. (The town of Lake George is within the park, but it's on private
lands where "forever wild" clearly has a different meaning, especially on
Saturday nights.) The Lake George you're looking for is the dazzling body
of water concealed by all those motel signs. Thomas Jefferson called the
lake the most beautiful body of water he had ever seen—200 years ago.
Now, private cottages and resorts line a good deal of the lakeshore, but
parts of the lake still look much as they must have to Jefferson.

Lake George, named for that king the 13 Colonies repudiated, is the
largest lake in the Adirondacks. A long, skinny body of water, it occupies
a deep fault blocked at both ends by glacial deposits. It trends northeastward for 32 miles, varying in width from 1 to 3 miles. It has 109 miles of
rocky shoreline and covers 44 square miles. Fed by immense underground
springs, it is wondrously clear, cold, and deep blue—though sadly threatened by pollution from overdevelopment along the shore. Its outlet is at

No Flies on Me

The Adirondacks' greatest defense
against human invasion is the
notorious blackfly. Most active from
mid-May through June, the blackfly
seems dedicated to inflicting misery
on humans; it's aided by battalions
of insect relatives known collectively
as no-see-ums. Wearing long pants
(tucked into your socks) and long-
sleeved shirts is the best defense.
(Some people are certain that light
colors repel insects.)

Don't use perfumed toiletries—
shampoos, deodorants, aftershaves,
colognes, or hair sprays—because
they often prove irresistible to biting insects. The essential substitute

substance is insect repellent, known
in the North Woods as bug dope.

The usual recommendation is a
lotion or spray that includes DEET
(diethyl-meta-toluamide). You can't
use DEET on infants, however, or
on children if it makes up 25 percent or more of the product. Many
people use Avon's Skin-So-Soft
Bath Oil, a pungent preparation
that turns bugs away.

Some Adirondackers prefer an
old-fashioned pine-tar-based bug
dope, such as Ole Woodsman. It
smells more authentically woodsy,
and the scent lasts and lasts and
lasts, giving you something to
remember your vacation by.

Boating on Lake George

the north end, where it descends 220 feet eastward through Ticonderoga Creek to Lake Champlain on the New York-Vermont border. The lake draws its extraordinary beauty from that clear indigo water scattered with more than 200 tiny wooded islands; the small coves rippling the irregular shore fringed with evergreens; and the long mountains rising to the east and west, forested in maples and dappled with dark conifers.

What to See and Do

For superb views of the lake, the Adirondack high peaks, and Vermont's Green Mountains, don't miss **Prospect Mountain.** You can drive to the top on **Veterans Memorial Highway,** but you'll have better views if you walk the 1.7-mile moderate trail from Lake George village to the 2,000-foot summit. *(Trailhead is a walkway over the Northway, off Smith St.)*

But don't stop there. The Lake George area has more than 60 miles of hiking trails, including a trail along the ridges of the **Tongue Mountain Range** on the west side of the lake. On the east side of the lake, 40 miles of trails lead along the shore and climb to remote mountain ponds and peaks, including beautiful **Buck Mountain** (see p. 246) and neighboring **Black Mountain,** at 2,646 feet the tallest of all.

Before you do any hiking, stop at the Adirondack Mountain Club (ADK) headquarters *(814 Goggins Rd., Lake George, NY 12845. 518-668-4447. www.adk.org)* and buy one of the ADK's indispensable guides to Adirondack Mountain trails. (These are serious mountains, and trail markers may be confusing or obscure. Even very experienced hikers should not set out without a trail guide or topo maps, a compass, and current information on trail conditions.) If your backcountry skills are dodgy, join a guided one-day hike regularly offered by the local ADK chapter (call headquarters for information).

Lake George regatta

Buck Mountain Hike

Although it is not the tallest peak
in the mountains that shelter
Lake George, Buck Mountain
affords marvelous views for hikers.
The 6.6-mile (round-trip) trail
is not difficult, but it has some
moderately steep climbs. From
Lake George take N.Y. 9L for 7.4
miles along the eastern shore
to Pilot Knob Road; turn left,
drive 3.3 miles, and park at the
well-marked Buck Mountain
trailhead on the right.

Follow the yellow DEC
(Department of Environmental
Conservation) trail markers and
light blue horse-trail markers.
You'll pass through a hardwood
forest of maple, oak, and birch and
see old logging roads. Turn left
at the first fork, staying with the
yellow markers. You will cross
Butternut Brook a couple of times,
walk along it for a while, go across
another stream, and follow the
trail to an intersection with a
sign for Inman Pond and Lower

Hogtown. Here you take the left
fork north for 2.1 miles to the
summit of Buck Mountain. The
trail follows a cut in a hillside,
then turns sharply right uphill
(where a logging road enters from
the left). The forest opens out
into scrubby oak and a bog of
wildflowers before coming into
white pine and blueberries on
the rocky top.

Gradually you achieve the bare
2,334-foot summit, all the more
dramatic because the mountain
seems to spring directly from the
lake's deepest part. Views open in
all directions: Crane Mountain is
to the west; Gore Mountain and
flat-topped Blue Mountain are
to the northwest. On a clear day,
the jagged peak you'll see between
Crane and Blue Mountains is
Snowy Mountain, 43 miles away.

Hike this trail in spring if you
can. The forest is still open enough
to afford good views on the way
up, and wildflowers are in bloom.
Also make sure you get a complete

trail guide from the ADK before setting out.

Other Activities

If you want to swim, try **Lake George Beach** *(fee),* also called Million Dollar Beach; **Shepard Park** or **Lake Avenue Beach** in Lake George village; or dozens of public beaches around the lake. To tour, you need a boat or canoe *(Lake George Boat Rental 518-668-4828).* If you're a landlubber, take a one- to four-hour cruise from the village *(518-668-5777 or 800-553-2628. www.lakegeorgesteamboat .com),* or charter a fishing boat for a day on the water with trophy lake trout, landlocked Atlantic salmon, and northern pike providing extra excitement. If you're

handy on the water, you can rent just about any kind of craft in Lake George village. (Paddlers beware: During peak season in July and August, the lake is abuzz with powerboats and jet skis; avoid the congested south end.)

A boat will set you up for the ultimate Lake George experience —island camping. Get a permit at one of the island-camping head-quarters: Long Island for the south part of the lake, Glen Island for the central part, Narrow Island at Huletts Landing for the north. Glen and Narrow Islands lack campsites themselves, but Long Island has 90 campsites, and there are more than 20 other state-owned islands where you can camp. With luck, you might get one all to yourself. ∎

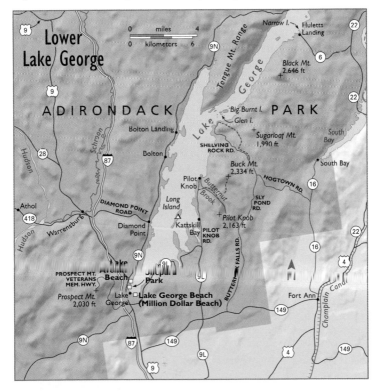

Lake Champlain Valley

■ Northern New York, eastern part of Adirondack Park ■ Best seasons
spring-fall ■ Boating, canoeing, swimming, windsurfing, biking ■ Contact
Lake Champlain Visitors Association, R.R. 1, Box 220, Crown Point, NY 12928;
phone 518-597-4646. www.lakechamplainregion.com

ABOUT 25 PERCENT OF Adirondack Park lies within the Champlain Valley,
which once served as a major corridor for Native Americans and later as a
setting for French and British military operations. Today, Lake George (see
pp. 244-47) and **Lake Champlain** form the "east coast" of the Adirondacks
and are a nautical playground for visitors. Powerboats, water skis, and jet
skis are big on Lake George, while larger Lake Champlain, swept in summer by strong southerly winds, is spectacular for sailing and windsurfing.

Traveling the lower fringe of the Adirondacks through the pastoral
Champlain Valley is a pleasant way to reach the north country. From Lake
George village, take N.Y. 9N north along the western shore of Lake George
to the north end at Ticonderoga. There a slight diversion east and south
on N.Y. 22 will take you to **Fort Ticonderoga**—first British fort captured
in the Revolution. Continue north on merged N.Y. 9N/22 through Crown
Point to Westport. Along the way you'll have good views of the southern
part of Lake Champlain, one of the country's largest freshwater lakes; it
is 121 miles long and 12 miles across at its widest, covering 490 square
miles in all. You will also get glimpses of the high Adirondacks rising to
the west and views of the Green Mountains across the water in Vermont.

If you're traveling with a bike or a cartop boat, this is the place to use
it. Bike the 23.7-mile loop from Westport north on N.Y. 9 to Essex and
return on N.Y. 22. You'll be pedaling through rolling farmlands with
mountains on both sides. Using the lakeshore roads of the **Champlain
Bikeway** *(www.champlainbikeways.org)* through New York, Quebec, and
Vermont, you can make a complete 350-mile circuit of the lake. The
paddle from Westport to Essex is also memorable, because you round
the sheer palisades at Split Rock Point. But be careful: Paddle only in
calm weather; always stick close to the shelter of the western shore; and
paddle south to north to catch prevailing winds. With no boat of your
own, you might take a cruise out of Westport on the *Philomena D (518-
962-4356 or 800-626-0342. www.westportmarina.com)*.

Leaving Westport, N.Y. 9N/22 diverges. Briefly follow N.Y. 22 north,
then bear right on N.Y. 9; it rejoins N.Y. 22 at Essex on the lakeshore. If
you're without bike or boat, pause at **Essex** (New York's best preserved
historic town) for a very pleasant summer day's diversion. Take the 20-
minute ferry ride from historic Essex across the lake to Vermont, and
return. The trip is refreshing, and the views are magnificent.

From Essex follow N.Y. 22 north. It will parallel I-87 briefly before
crossing the Ausable River (see pp. 250-51). Turn west on N.Y. 9N to
follow the twisting Ausable into the heart of the Adirondacks. ■

Lake Champlain shore

Ausable River

THE MOST ILLUSTRIOUS trout stream among the Adirondacks' more than 6,000 miles of rivers is the legendary Ausable. Follow the course of this lively little river, heading upstream as you drive N.Y. 9N west from Lake Champlain to the high peaks region. If you're an angler, keep your rod and waders handy; you'll see many irresistible stretches of river. If you're new to the sport, check out some of the fly-fishing schools in the area.

But every natural feature of the Adirondacks is rich in possibilities, and there's more to the Ausable than fish. Before heading west to the high peaks region, take N.Y. 9 northeast to Lake Champlain once more to camp or swim at **Ausable Point,** where the river flows into the lake. Launch your canoe or kayak for a paddle into 5 miles of meanders in the delta of the Ausable and the marshes at the mouth of the Little Ausable River. This is the **Ausable Marsh Wildlife Management Area,** a quiet haven for wood ducks, mergansers, blue-winged teal, common goldeneyes, and other waterfowl.

Drive west again on N.Y. 9, and near the junction of I-87 you will discover another aspect of the river at **Ausable Chasm** (518-834-7454 or 800-537-1211. www.ausablechasm .com. Fee). Here the stream plunges over falls and rapids and snarls through a deep and narrow sandstone gorge as twisted as the river itself. From mid-May through Columbus Day, you can walk a narrow mile-long path beside the churning waters of the gorge and then finish your trip with a quick three-quarter-mile guided raft ride down the flume. Above the chasm and waterfalls, the river quiets to a classic riffling mountain stream, sparkling between mountains. At Au Sable Forks, the river divides into the two streams of its headwaters; both are worth following, and both will take you to Lake Placid (see pp. 254-59).

On the **East Branch** route, you will want to stop at the **Mount Van Hoevenberg Sports Complex** (see p. 259), on N.Y. 73 between Keene and Lake Placid. N.Y. 9N follows the East Branch upstream to Keene (at the junction of N.Y. 73). In spring, when the water is up, this is a snappy canoe and kayak stream with Class II water and a dodgy Class III boulder patch. In the low water of summer, it's a placid stream that affords first-class fly-fishing.

On the **West Branch** route, you will want to take the **Whiteface Mountain Veterans' Memorial Highway** (see p. 260) off N.Y. 86 to the summit of Whiteface Mountain and stop also at Whiteface Mountain ski area. N.Y. 86 follows the smaller West Branch along some impassable, boulder-strewn stretches of shallow water to N.Y. 73, but the last 8 miles between N.Y. 73 and a take-out just above Monument Falls is a peaceful canoeing stream that flows between wooded banks and works up Class I riffles. For many years, a 5-mile stretch between Wilmington and Lake Placid has been dedicated to catch-and-release fly-fishing only; this is *the* place to take on trophy trout.

No matter which branch of the Ausable River you've followed, at N.Y. 73 turn west to **Lake Placid,** the center of the high peaks region. Either way, in the space of a 40-mile drive you've seen the many faces of a single Adirondack stream. ■

Elephant Head formation, Ausable Chasm

Mount Marcy and the High Peaks

■ 226,000 acres ■ Northern New York, northeast region of Adirondack Park
■ Best seasons spring-fall ■ Camping, hiking, backpacking ■ Contact New York
State Department of Environmental Conservation, Region 5, Route 86, Box
296, Ray Brook, NY 12977; phone 518-897-1200

ADIRONDACK PARK HOLDS more than 2,000 mountains, but it's the high
peaks of the northeast region you're likely to see on picture postcards.
At 5,344 feet and rising, New York's highest is Mount Marcy, known
more poetically to Native Americans as Tahawas, the Cloud Splitter.
Almost due south of Lake Placid, Mount Marcy is surrounded by other
high peaks of the northeast-trending MacIntyre Mountains, the crux
of this 226,000-acre wilderness.

Across the summit of Mount Marcy runs the divide between the
Hudson and St. Lawrence Rivers; just to the southwest, at the base of the
cone, lies **Lake Tear of the Clouds,** the highest lake source of the Hudson
River. Slightly northwest stands **Algonquin Peak,** reaching 5,115 feet,
and nearby, 44 other peaks rise above 4,000 feet. Among them are Gray
Peak, Mount Skylight, Mount Haystack, Basin Mountain, Gothics,
Armstrong Mountain, Upper Wolfjaw Mountain, Macomb, South Dix,
Hough Peak, Nippletop, Dial Mountain, Santanoni Peak, Panther Peak,
Mount Marshall, Iroquois Peak, Wright Peak, Porter Mountain, Cascade
Mountain, and Big Slide Mountain. The names coalesce in a dense
cluster, just where the contour lines multiply and smudge together on
the "Trails of the Adirondack High Peaks Region" map produced by the
Adirondack Mountain Club *(518-668-4447).* The map looks like a cat's
cradle of lines and loops, circling and doubling back in impossible knots
and squiggles that seem to quit in the middle of a rare blank space.
Hundreds of miles of hiking trails wind through this region; four trails
ascend Mount Marcy alone.

Birds of the High Peaks

When you hike the high peaks
region, keep your binoculars
handy. Mountains above 3,500 feet
provide habitat for seldom-seen
subalpine bird species such as
Bicknell's thrush, Swainson's thrush,
and blackpoll warbler. The conifer
forests that are characteristic of
this elevation in the region support
breeding communities of boreal
chickadees, gray jays, red crossbills,
white-winged crossbills, three-
toed woodpeckers, black-backed
woodpeckers, and spruce grouse.
The last, a threatened species
in New York, is down to only
about 200 individuals. The spruce
grouse is distinguished from
the more common ruffed grouse
by tan (not black-banded) tail-
feather tips and red combs over
the eyes of the male. The common
loon is known to breed here, as
is that sharp-eyed tenant of the
high places, the peregrine falcon.

Mount Marcy

If a quest for solitude draws you to hiking, think twice about hiking Mount Marcy. The Cloud Splitter's trails are overused and worn, barely accommodating the 10,000 people who hike them each year. On summer holiday weekends, lean-tos are so crowded that smart hikers carry tents.

The Adirondack Forty-Sixers *(www.adk46r.org)*, a group of people who've hiked all 46 of the preserve's mountains over 4,000 feet, know that each peak affords fabulous views. Try a long day hike on second highest Algonquin Peak. It's easy to reach: You can drive to the trailhead *(parking lot of Adirondack Mountain Club's Adirondak Loj)* at the end of Heart Lake Road, which runs south off N.Y. 73 at North Elba, 3.2 miles east of Lake Placid. The round-trip hike is 8 miles, with a vertical rise of 2,936 feet. Near the summit, the route is steep, rising over bare rock amid scrubby balsam and spruce and the sphagnum moss that carpets the vertical bogs of alpine summits. Above tree line, with less than half a mile to go, the scrub gives way to cushions of fragile alpine vegetation.

For an offbeat and awesome hike from the same trailhead, work out a shuttle and do a one-way hike on 10.6-mile **Indian Pass Trail** through **Indian Pass** (674-foot vertical rise), the high, boulder-strewn fault that bisects the high peaks. The narrow valley, the rugged terrain, the dark, moss-covered canyon, the chaos of fallen rock, and the cliffs towering 1,000 feet above will all make for a hike as dramatic and memorable as any mountain summit. Then take another look at your trail guides and maps, and set your sights on smaller peaks in more remote regions of the park—perhaps the **Siamese Ponds Wilderness, West Canada Lakes Wilderness,** or the **Pigeon Lake Wilderness.** ■

Lake Placid

■ Northern New York, northeast section of Adirondack Park ■ Year-round
■ Camping, hiking, rock climbing, boating, fishing, biking, horseback riding, downhill skiing, cross-country skiing, snowshoeing, ice-skating ■ Contact Lake Placid/Essex County Convention and Visitors Bureau, 216 Main St., Lake Placid, NY 12946; phone 518-523-2445 or 800-447-5224. www.lakeplacid.com

IN 1895 MELVIL DEWEY (creator of the Dewey decimal classification system) opened a summer resort called the Lake Placid Club, and a few years later he added a winter-sports season. Ever since, little Lake Placid (population 2,800) has been a popular resort. It's also one of only three places in the world to have hosted the Winter Olympic Games twice—in 1932 and 1980; Innsbruck, Austria, and St. Moritz, Switzerland, are the two others. The town of Lake Placid is in the middle of the high peaks region, oddly enough on Mirror Lake. The lake named Placid is next door.

 The "urban" center of the high peaks region, Lake Placid is the headquarters for outfitters and guides who rent equipment, give instruction, provide maps, and lead trips in almost every outdoor activity you can

Lake Placid

imagine. Ice climbing, ski jumping, downhill skiing, backcountry skiing, snowshoeing, snowboarding, tobogganing, bobsledding, ice skating, and ice fishing are popular in winter. Other times of year are great for camping, hiking, boating, bushwhacking, canoeing, kayaking, fly-fishing, mountain biking, bike touring, horseback riding, waterskiing, in-line skating, skateboarding, tennis, and golf. You can tour the Olympic venues, take a carriage ride around Mirror Lake, cruise on Lake Placid, or enjoy a sight-seeing flight. (In winter, don't miss the toboggan chute on Mirror Lake.) You can also buy a trail guide, some bug dope, a pizza—then gather up your gear and head for the backcountry.

What to See and Do

Olympic Sports Venues

The Lake Placid Olympic facilities are under the management of the Olympic Regional Development Authority *(518-523-1655)*. Together with a 16-million-dollar U.S. Olympic Training Center, they now operate year-round, hosting competitions and performances and training world-class athletes. Many facilities are open to visitors on self-guided or guided tours; a

Taking a break near Heart Lake

few will even let you strut your stuff. Admission fees are charged at every venue, so if you plan to visit several, think about buying a general admission passport. If your top sport is spectating, call the Olympic Authority Events Hotline *(518-523-1655 or 800-462-6236)* for performance and competition schedules.

Olympic Center

Near the visitors bureau in Lake Placid village, the Olympic Center holds four ice rinks: the 1932 Arena, the 1980 Arena, the USA Rink, and the Lussi Rink, the last named for the legendary coach who guided Dick Button to the Olympics. The center claims to have "the greatest amount of ice surface in the world." Outside is the 400-meter **Sheffield Olympic Speedskating Oval**—with a hockey rink in the middle. In summer, you can watch frequent figure-skating performances and competitions here. Serious skaters can train on and off the ice *(check www.orda.org for professional training programs and costs)*, taking courses in technical skating, dancing, ice dancing, pairs, freestyle, yoga, nutrition, and more.

The **Lussi Rink** is open from June to September for public skating. For less than the cost of a movie, you can rent skates and practice your triple toe loops. Sign up for a 25-minute group lesson or private session with the facility's professionals *(for public skating program, phone the center at 518-523-1655)*. For aspiring Olympians, daily learn-to-skate classes are available for all ages—and what a place to

In-line skaters and distant ski jumps

start! In winter, you can skate midweek either at the center or outdoors on the speed-skating oval, hockey rink, or Mirror Lake in the center of town.

MacKenzie-Intervale Ski Jumping Complex

Two miles east of the Olympic Center on N.Y. 73 stand the 90-meter and 120-meter ski jumps used for the 1980 Olympic Games and the 2000 Winter Goodwill Games. You can watch training and competitive events here year-round. In summer, Nordic jumpers on the 90-meter hill launch from porcelain tracks and land on a plastic-covered hill. You can catch Saturday competitions in July and August. You won't be allowed to have a go, but do take the chairlift and elevator to the sky deck (the 26th floor) atop

Curious river otters

Weasels in the Woods

Several weasel species make their homes in eastern forests, where it's a privilege to encounter one of these lithe, beautiful creatures. The smallest is the elusive mink, whose pelt was once commonly seen in coats sold by fur salons. Adult males average 20 to 26 inches, including a 7- to 9-inch tail; females are an inch or two smaller; weight is from one to three pounds. Members of this species den in borrowed muskrat houses, in hollow logs, or among tree roots. Look for them prowling in wetlands and at the water's edge, though males may hunt over a 25-square-mile area. Mink are very adaptable animals that eat fish, snakes, frogs, muskrat, rabbits, and voles—whatever is in season. Biologists believe mink adapted to human intrusions by becoming nocturnal: They are now active mostly at night.

The fisher is much larger. This species hunts in the forest canopy for squirrels; it also eats snowshoe hare and porcupines. Fishers grow to 3.5 feet in length (including a 16-inch tail) and weigh between 5 and 18 pounds. These forest dwellers disappeared with eastern trees; they're now making a comeback along with the forests. Dark, furry, and fast as lightning, fishers are often mistaken for "black panthers."

River otters can be slightly larger, reaching 3 to 4 feet in length (including a 12- to 17-inch tail) and weighing 6 to 25 pounds. These powerful swimmers hunt in the water, eating fish, frogs, and other aquatic creatures. Famous for their playfulness, they love to bodysurf on muddy banks or snowy hills. They've also been seen balancing sticks on their noses and juggling pebbles. Look for otters morning and evening, fishing at the inflow or outflow of ponds and lakes or running rapids with their heads up. Watch for their haul-outs or surf chutes along stream banks.

One weasel you may want to avoid is the elegantly striped skunk. Members of this species average 2.5 feet in length and weigh about ten pounds. They eat insects and small rodents, feeding mostly at night. All weasels produce musk, but skunks are most proficient at projecting it when threatened. You'd be smart to keep your distance.

the 120-meter tower. The views of the high peaks, from a ski jumper's precipitous perspective, are spectacular. To check practice and competition schedules here and at the Kodak Sports Park, call 518-523-2202.

Kodak Sports Park

This site, next to the MacKenzie-Intervale Ski Jumping Complex, is a year-round training and competition facility for freestyle ski jumpers. In winter they launch from ramps and land on a steep, snow-covered hill. From May to October, they loop the loop and land in a 750,000-gallon heated pool—a feat that probably ought to count as a new sport (ski diving?). It's something to see. Catch a competition almost every Wednesday in July and August.

Mount Van Hoevenberg Sports Complex

The venue for cross-country skiing events at the 1980 Winter Games, Mount Van Hoevenberg (*N.Y. 73, 6 miles E of Lake Placid. 518-523-2811*) boasts 31 miles of groomed trails, averaging 18 feet in width; the trail system connects with the **Jackrabbit Trail** (see pp. 262-63). With more than 120 inches of snow each ski season, the sports complex scarcely needs its snowmaking capabilities.

When you visit, don't let the Olympic designation intimidate you. Mount Van Hoevenberg has terrain and trails (*fee*) for everyone from experts to beginners, and the ski school here offers equipment rentals and instruction at all levels. A big boon for families: On weekends you'll find a ski school and playroom for kids ages two and up, with age-based group skiing lessons and indoor playtime (*reservations recommended*).

In summer the trails belong to mountain bikers. Because hiking trails in the high peaks region are closed to mountain bikers—the trails are both too rugged and too fragile—Mount Van Hoevenberg's cross-country trail system is the center of biking in this part of Adirondack Park. The High Peaks Mountain Biking Center at Mount Van Hoevenberg (*518-523-3764*) offers rentals, instruction, and guided trips.

Two other venues at the sports complex let visitors get a taste of what it feels like to participate in an Olympic event (*fee*). In summer, test your marksmanship on the target-shooting course used by athletes in the winter biathlon. The rifles are .22 caliber, the targets 50 meters distant. The most popular activity is the heart-stopping rocket ride down the 1980 **Olympic Bobsled Run.** The "Summer Storm," a modified four-person sled, makes a half-mile run on wheels at speeds up to 50 miles an hour. In winter, the real thing goes even faster on ice. No, they won't let you drive, but a professional driver and brakeman will help you test your nerve and your Olympic potential.

The old luge run, a longtime favorite of visitors, was dismantled in 2000 to make room for the state-of-the-art combined bobsled, skeleton, and luge track opening in 2001. The complex hopes to reintroduce the luge ride for visitors. Call ahead to see what's running (*518-523-1655*). ∎

Whiteface Mountain

■ 215 acres ■ Northern New York, on N.Y. 86, northeast section of Adirondack Park ■ Best season winter. Year-round activities ■ Mountain biking, downhill skiing, freestyle skiing ■ Contact Whiteface Mountain Ski Center, Wilmington, NY 12997; phone 518-946-2223 or 800-462-6236. www.whiteface.com

SITE OF THE ALPINE SKIING events at the 1980 Olympic Winter Games, Whiteface Mountain is the only ski area in the eastern United States ever to host an Olympics. It boasts the greatest vertical drop (3,350 feet) in the East and has numerous fans—used to a lot of double black diamond off-trail and steep, tight, expert skiing—who like to remind disdainful Rocky Mountain skiers that "Adirondack" means "those who eat trees."

Whiteface Mountain offers 70 trails (41 percent expert, 39 percent intermediate, and 20 percent novice), 6 double chairlifts, 2 triple chairs, and 1 quad lift. It also operates a new high-speed, heated, eight-passenger gondola known as the Cloudsplitter, which takes skiers to the top of **Little Whiteface** (3,600 feet) in less than 10 minutes. The top tough trails are **Cloudspin** and **Wilderness,** the site of international mogul competitions; for intermediate skiers, the 3.5-mile **Excelsior** is a challenge. At the fine ski school you can rent all the equipment you need, and kids can enjoy a ski/play program.

In summer, tote your mountain bike uphill on the gondola and then pedal down. Twenty-five trails, from gentle traverses to steep technical single tracks, offer beautiful downhills with panoramic views. You can get equipment and instruction at the site. If you're not a bicyclist, take the summer gondola ride to the top of Little Whiteface, where you'll find an observation deck and picnic tables. You can walk back down on the half-mile **Stag Brook Nature Trail,** an easy amble beside the waterfalls and pools of the brook.

Whiteface Mountain Veterans' Memorial Highway

Built in 1927, this twisting two-lane, 8-mile toll road climbs 4,867-foot Whiteface Mountain—New York's fifth highest peak and the only one with road access. To reach it, take N.Y. 86 to Wilmington *(10 miles E of Lake Placid),* and go 3 miles on N.Y. 431 to the tollbooth. Several lookouts along the way to the top allow you to pull over and enjoy the expanding views. The road ends about 300 vertical feet from Whiteface Mountain's summit, which you can reach by taking an elevator or climbing a steep, rocky trail.

The road is open in daylight hours from May to October, but it closes (sometimes on short notice) in inclement weather. On a good day, the 360-degree view from the summit takes in the surrounding peaks and mountain ranges as far away as Vermont and Montreal. Beautiful in any season, the landscape is especially dazzling in fall. ■

The Cloudsplitter, Whiteface Mountain

Northville-Placid Trail

■ 133 miles long ■ Northern New York ■ Best seasons spring-fall ■ Camping, hiking, fishing ■ Contact New York State Department of Environmental Conservation, Region 5, Route 86, Box 296, Ray Brook, NY 12977; phone 518-897-1200

LONGEST TRAIL IN Adirondack Park, the Northville-Placid Trail traverses the 133 miles between Northville, in the southern part of the park, and Lake Placid, in the northern section. Although it crosses both private and state lands, much of the trail lies in some of the wildest areas of the park. It was built by the Adirondack Mountain Club in 1922–23 and is maintained today by the Department of Environmental Conservation.

Plan about 19 days to do the whole trail, which falls into five sections. Beginning at the Sacandaga River Bridge in Northville (elevation 795 feet), **Section A** of the trail climbs to the shores of Silver Lake (2,072 feet) and winds past small lakes and ponds to the village of Piseco at Milepost 34.8. **Section B** (32.85 miles), from Piseco to Wakely Dam, is the leg to do if you can do only one. From the Cold Stream Bridge parking lot it follows an old logging road 10 miles to Spruce Lake, then crosses the West Canada Lakes Wilderness to the Cedar River. This is upland country of old second-growth forest dotted with lakes. **Section C** first takes a gravel road 12 miles across the Moose River Plains from Wakely Dam to N.Y. 28/30 near Blue Mountain Lake village. It then follows streams and ridges 14.65 miles to N.Y. 28N. The short **Section D** (12.6 miles) skirts the eastern shore of Long Lake before cutting through open woods to Shattuck Clearing. **Section E** (27.87 miles) covers the most dramatic terrain, entering the heart of the mountains with views of the high peaks ahead. The trail reaches Mountain Pond (elevation 2,142 feet); at the 12.5-mile mark, it intersects a red-marked trail leading to Indian Pass and Mount Marcy (see pp. 252-53). The blue-marked Northville-Placid Trail continues over the divide between Moose and Chubb Rivers to the village of Lake Placid.

All along the way are lean-tos, and you can camp anywhere (except on private property) as long as you're 150 feet from roads, trails, and water. Don't expect to find supplies, and do be prepared for emergencies. ■

Jackrabbit Trail

■ 33 miles long and growing ■ Northern New York ■ Best season winter ■ Cross-country skiing ■ Fees on some sections of trail ■ Contact the Adirondack Ski Touring Council, P.O. Box 843, Lake Placid, NY 12946; phone 518-523-1365. www.lakeplacid.com

IF THE NORTHVILLE-PLACID Trail is the summer trail for long walkers, the Jackrabbit Trail is the winter trail for *langlaufers*. Built by the Adirondack Ski Touring Council, it's meant to connect the villages of Keene, Lake Placid, Saranac Lake, and Tupper Lake, giving access to other networks of

Mount Van Hoevenberg cross-country ski trail

trails along the way. About 33 miles are finished, with only one major gap from Saranac Lake to Tupper Lake. It links cross-country trail systems at Bark Eater Inn, Mount Van Hoevenberg, Adirondak Loj, Cascade, Lake Placid Resort, and Whiteface Club. Nobody seems to have calculated the total mileage, but spring may come before you explore all the possibilities. The trail's name honors local hero Herman "Jackrabbit" Johannsen, who pioneered Lake Placid skiing from 1916 to 1928. He died in 1987 at age 111, reportedly attributing his longevity to his lifetime credo: "Ski, ski, ski." ■

Northwest Lake Country

■ Northern New York, north-central Adirondack Park ■ Year-round ■ Camping, primitive camping, hiking, backpacking, boating, canoeing, fishing, biking, mountain biking, cross-country skiing, ice-skating, bird-watching, wildlife viewing ■ Contact Saranac Lake Area Chamber of Commerce, 30 Main St., Saranac Lake, NY 12983; phone 518-891-1990 or 800-347-1992. www.saranaclake.com

CATCH THE SILVER FLASH of sunlit water falling from your feathered paddle. See the morning mist rise to reveal a forest pond. From a warm granite ledge, watch the play of light and shadow over blue lakes clustered far below. Whatever you do in the Lake Country, you'll find its 240 lakes and ponds, 9 major rivers, and miles of brooks and streams a wondrous pleasure.

The center of Lake Country is the historic village of **Saranac Lake,** which stands (wouldn't you know) on Lake Flower at the intersection of N.Y. 86 and N.Y. 3. It marks the eastern edge of the tri-lakes loop, a circle of scenic byways that wrap Upper, Middle, and Lower Saranac Lakes. So stunning is this landscape that you can understand why tuberculosis patients in the 19th century believed they'd get better simply by coming here to *breathe*. Dr. Edward Livingston Trudeau first made the village of Saranac Lake famous as a health resort and sanatorium in the 1880s; his most famous patient, writer Robert Louis Stevenson, termed the place a "little Switzerland" before decamping for the South Pacific to escape the cold. More than a hundred buildings dating from the sanatorium period are on the National Register of Historic Places.

Today Saranac Lake is canoe country, drawing visitors who want to not only breathe the air but also find adventure. You can launch a cartop boat almost anywhere in town, or use the state-of-the-art boat launch near the municipal parking lot. Here, too, is the place to find outfitters and guides to equip and lead you through this water world.

If you go it on your own, be sure to pick up topo maps and ask for local advice. Plan to explore beyond the popular tri-lakes loop. Lake Country extends north to the town of Paul Smiths, west to Cranberry Lake, and south through Five Ponds Wilderness to Stillwater Reservoir, Raquette Lake, and Blue Mountain Lake. The effort of moving off the main-traveled roads brings rewards of solitude and true wilderness experience.

What to See and Do

Beg, borrow, rent, or buy a canoe or kayak and get out on the water. (You'll find boat liveries at Saranac Lake, Tupper Lake, Fish Creek Ponds, Raquette Lake, Blue Mountain Lake, Long Lake, Old Forge, Inlet, and at many hotels.) To hone your eye for further ventures, sign up for a paddle trip led by a naturalist; the visitor center at Paul Smiths (see p. 242), just north of Saranac Lake, offers twice-weekly trips to **Long Pond** or **Black Pond**.

Lower Saranac Lake

If you're new to canoeing or a little

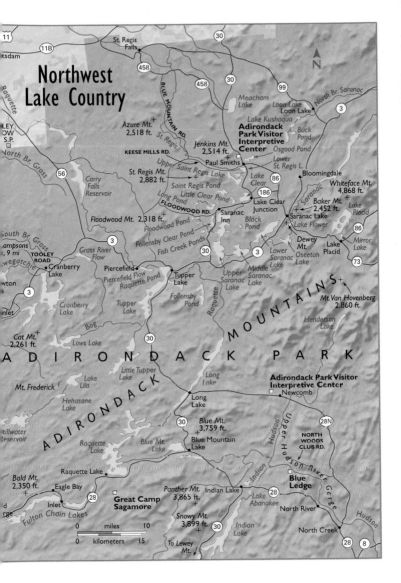

rusty, start on 2,286-acre Lower Saranac Lake, gateway to all Lake Country drainages; use the boat access (*on N.Y. 3, about 5 miles W of Saranac Lake village*) at Second Pond, which connects to Lower Saranac. It's close to civilization and popular with paddlers, so you're never far from help. Dotting the lake are many islands that serve as windbreaks and also provide beautiful primitive campsites.

Lower Saranac has 17 miles of shoreline to explore, and although the north end is disturbed by development, most of the rest of

Following pages: St. Regis Canoe Area

the shore is state-owned and wild. You'll see great variety: towering hemlocks and white cedars dominating the forests of Second Pond; sheer, cedar-covered cliffs; flat marshes astir with black ducks, ring-billed ducks, and red-winged blackbirds. You're much more likely to see wildlife—even elusive moose and black bears—from the water than from the land. You may also pass classic Adirondack Great Camps built along the shore in the late 19th century by the filthy rich. (A paddle on Lower Saranac can be either a day trip or an excursion of many days.)

St. Regis Canoe Area

More advanced backcountry paddlers should head for the pristine 18,000 acres of the St. Regis Canoe Area, known to canoeists as a pond-hopper's paradise. Dozens of ponds punctuate the area, and most of the portages are short. Many loop trips and short routes here can be done as day trips, minimizing the carry load. Everybody warms up on the classic **Seven-Carries Route,** crossing 10 lakes and ponds in 9 miles from Little Green Pond to Paul Smiths. After that, let your imagination and good maps be your guide; with a little portaging, one thing leads to another. The loop around the St. Regis Lakes requires only one half-mile carry. Other loops start from Follensby Clear, Floodwood, and Fish Creek Ponds. With longer portages, you can loop the loops.

Adirondack Canoe Classic

Marathoners should check the events schedule for the annual Adirondack Canoe Classic. This three-day race covers 90 miles of water in a northeastward-trending diagonal from the **Fulton Chain Lakes** in the southwest to Saranac Lake village. Of course, you don't have to enter the race; you could paddle just for fun on the most popular canoe path in the park.

The route starts at Old Forge and actually extends beyond Saranac Lake village to the upper reaches of the Raquette River, but you can conveniently end your trip at Blue Mountain Lake, Tupper Lake, Piercefield Flow, Saranac Inn, Paul Smiths, Saranac Lake, or many other points. For the Old Forge-Saranac Lake village 90-miler, figure about six days of paddling and camping.

More Canoeing

There's plenty of great point-to-point canoeing. The 12-mile trip from Lake Kushaqua to **Osgood Pond** requires one .75-mile carry and offers the possibility of carrying farther to Lower St. Regis Lake. Osgood Pond is the site of **White Pine Camp** (*White Pine Rd., Box 340, Paul Smiths, NY 12970. 518-327-3030. www.whitepinecamp .com; call for tour hours*), President Coolidge's summer White House.

You can make a 17.5-mile chain of the **Saranac Lakes,** from the top of Upper Saranac to the east end of Lower Saranac; by continuing through Oseetah Lake to the village of Saranac Lake, you can reach the **Saranac River,** which works up to some Class III rapids. For a long, leisurely trip, paddle 14-mile **Long Lake** to the Raquette River—the entrance is a little tricky—and float for about

Ticks and Lyme Disease

After being bitten by a tick, some people suffer the debilitating effects of Lyme disease. That's why it's wise to be prepared in eastern forests, where the threat posed by ticks is quite real. The disease—actually a bacterial infection caused by *Borrelia burgdorferi* spirochetes—was first identified in 1975 as the reason for a cluster of arthritis cases in Lyme, Connecticut. Many small rodents carry the bacteria, which are transmitted to immature ticks feeding on their bodies. As adults, the ticks feed on larger animals, especially deer. Resistant to the infection themselves, the deer transport ticks through the woods. A hiker, being another large animal in the woods, is a tempting target for ticks.

Early Lyme disease is marked by one or more symptoms: fatigue, chills and fever, headaches, muscle and joint pain, swollen lymph nodes, and a characteristic skin rash. The rash, occurring in about 60 percent of cases, begins as a solid red circle and clears in the center to resemble a bull's-eye. Symptoms that occur weeks, months, or years after a bite include arthritis and cardiac arrhythmia. That's the bad news.

The good news is that you can protect yourself from ticks, which are active from May to November and pose the greatest threat in June and July. Cover up by wearing a hat, long pants tucked into your socks, and a long-sleeved shirt tucked into your pants. Button your collar, or wear a bandanna. Light colors make it easier to spot a tick—about the size of a sesame seed. The Centers for Disease Control recommend applying an insect repellent with DEET to clothes and on all exposed skin areas except the face.

It's now known that ticks are very slow feeders and unlikely to transmit infection unless attached for 36 hours. Consequently, the best safeguard is a nightly inspection of yourself and family members. (Use tweezers to pull a tick out by its head, being careful to get the whole thing.) If you think you've been exposed to Lyme disease, a doctor can treat you with antibiotics such as amoxicillin or doxycycline.

30 meandering miles to beautiful **Tupper Lake,** site of 100-foot cliffs and the 30-foot **Bog River Falls.**

Other less traveled lakes to explore are 1,446-acre **Lake Lila** in the 7,215-acre **Lake Lila Primitive Area** and many-bayed **Cranberry Lake.** These two are good options if you like to combine paddling and hiking: At Lake Lila (elevation 1,715 feet) a 1.6-mile trail climbs 500 feet to the summit of Mount Frederick, while at Cranberry Lake, several trails lead from the shore to stands of old-growth forest and mountain overlooks. A trail also leads into the remote **Five Ponds Wilderness** from Stillwater Reservoir, but the 9-mile-long reservoir itself is open to powerboats and overused.

If you prefer white water, you can find that, too—in a stretch to match your abilities. Try the 17-mile section of **Raquette River** from Piercefield to Carry Falls. (Rapids vary with dam releases.) Only experts should try the

Backcountry camping in the St. Regis Canoe Area

Lampsons Falls area of the Grass River, the **Oswegatchie River's Middle Branch,** and the 7-mile Class IV "Silver Staircase" that runs below St. Regis Falls on the **St. Regis River.**

Camping

Lean-tos and designated primitive camping sites dot the shores of most backcountry lakes. A few lakes have primitive campgrounds, and you should use them when you can to minimize impact. If you're canoeing popular routes in July and August, bring a tent in case the lean-tos are full. Of course, wilderness camping and pack in–pack out rules apply.

If you are road camping and prefer more amenities, several state campgrounds are open to you *(518-897-1310, for information; 800-456-2267 or www. reserveamerica.com, for reservations).* The most popular campground is **Fish Creek Pond;** here the same vacationers year after year pull their RVs into line, put out their name plaques and lawn chairs, and prepare to greet camping friends old and new. A kind of urban subdivision in the Adirondacks, it's a good family camp. If you want to canoe as well, the Fish Creek Ponds loop is a great introductory tour for kids.

Fishing

Just throw your fishing gear in the canoe. You'll find trout, land-locked salmon, bass, pike, walleye, and panfish in many of these lakes, ponds, and streams. Find out about fishing regulations at www.dec.state.ny.us/huntfish. For the latest on what's biting where, call 518-891-5413. Acid rain is affecting Adirondack lakes; so far, it has been most damaging to lakes in the southwest quadrant of the park, where 200 lakes have died.

Hiking

Don't miss the chance to climb a mountain for a lofty view of the

Lake Country. You'll find plenty to choose from on your topo maps. For a substantial hike rewarded by equally substantial views, check out **Floodwood Mountain,** west of N.Y. 30 off Floodwood Road; **Cat Mountain,** south of Cranberry Lake; **Jenkins Mountain,** west from the visitor center at Paul Smiths; and **St. Regis Mountain,** southwest of Paul Smiths off Keese Mills Road. By a stroke of luck, a trail from Saranac Lake village that leads to some of the best views in the Adirondacks is both easy and short. This half-mile route ascends 900 feet to the 2,457-foot summit of **Baker Mountain.** The trail begins at Saranac Lake on the north side of Moody Pond *(from Main St., follow Pine St. to East Pine St. to Moody Pond)*. You'll travel along an old woods road for 100 yards to a stone quarry. Stay to the right of the quarry, and turn left when you've passed it. From there, the trail climbs through the forest to the summit of the peak.

This watery terrain offers innumerable trails beside lakes, ponds, streams, peaceful rivers, raging rivers, waterfalls, marshes, bogs, beaver ponds, and the like *(complete information and maps available at the visitor center in Paul Smiths)*. One good example is the **Bloomingdale Bog Trail,** a 9.8-mile round-trip stroll (or bike ride) through one of the largest bogs in the state. From Saranac Lake village, it's off N.Y. 86 about 1.5 miles north of the Adirondack Medical Center. Bird-watchers should try the bog or the 4.5-mile trail network at Indian Creek Nature Center in the **Upper and**

Roosevelt's Bird List

As a youth, Teddy Roosevelt spent three summers at Paul Smith's Hotel (now Paul Smith's College) on the shores of Lower St. Regis Lake. In 1877, when he was 18, Roosevelt published *The Summer Birds of the Adirondacks in Franklin County, NY,* the first of 18 books and other publications on natural resources that he would write in his lifetime.

Even as a teenager, T.R. made close observations and detailed descriptions that distinguished him as a skilled naturalist. *Summer Birds* lists 97 species—the eastern blue-bird, red-tailed hawk, barred owl, ruby-throated humming-bird, and downy woodpecker among them; it remains the best early ornithological record of the Adirondacks.

In September 1901, when word came that President William McKinley had died, Vice President Roosevelt and his family were hiking in the high peaks region. Roosevelt went on to become the most active conservationist President in U.S. history.

Lower Lakes Wildlife Management Area near Rensselaer Falls.

Mountain Biking

Franklin County alone offers close to 120 miles of off-road trails, ranging from 1.6 to 20 miles. With lots of beginner and intermediate trails, you can spare the adrenaline and take in the landscape. A good overnight option for beginners is the Bloomingdale Bog Trail that connects at Buck Pond campground with the 13-mile **Kushaqua Loop Trail,** then circles Loon Lake and follows the north branch of the Saranac River.

To combine biking, hiking, and high-elevation sight-seeing, try the 20-mile **Keese Mills-Blue Mountain Road Trail** from the visitor center in Paul Smiths; leave a car at the junction of N.Y. 458 and Blue Mountain Road. About 15 miles into your ride, which parallels the St. Regis River through spruce and fir forest, hike the 0.75-mile trail to the 2,518-foot summit of **Azure Mountain** *(maps and information on other trails available at Paul Smiths visitor center).*

Winter Sports

For cross-country skiing, **Dewey Mountain** *(fee)* at Saranac Lake village offers more than 9 miles of trails, with night skiing, rentals, and instruction. The visitor center at Paul Smiths offers more than 10 miles of trails *(no fee).*

There's backcountry skiing, too, but don't set out unless you have wilderness skills, a good compass, and a topo map. For downhill skiing and snowboarding, **Big Tupper** at Tupper Lake has slopes for all abilities, while **Mount Pisgah Veterans Memorial Ski Center** at Saranac Lake is a good family ski center for beginners as well as intermediates. Both facilities have night skiing.

For ice-skating, the **Saranac Lake Civic Center** maintains an outdoor rink in winter *(fee)* and offers indoor skating in summer. **Tupper Lake** has a hockey rink, too. If you'd rather fish than skate, try ice fishing at any of the 240 lakes and ponds in the area. ■

Central Adirondacks

■ Northern New York ■ Year-round ■ Camping, hiking, boating, canoeing, fishing, mountain biking, horseback riding, snowmobiling, downhill skiing, cross-country skiing, snowshoeing, bird-watching, wildlife viewing, scenic gondola rides ■ Contact New York State Department of Environmental Conservation, RD 3, Box 22A, Lowville, NY 13367; phone 315-376-3521

AFTER CLIMBING THE moderately difficult, 2-mile **Blue Mountain Trail** *(trailhead on N.Y. 30, N of Adirondack Museum in Blue Mountain Lake village),* you stand atop the 3,759-foot peak at the approximate geographical center of Adirondack Park. Far below, at the base of the mountain, lie Blue Mountain Lake and the town with the same name as the lake. To the west, the landscape rolls away, its broad, rounded mountains holding deep forests and blue-water valleys. To the southwest, the undulating green forest seems unbroken. To the south and east, the hills gather themselves again and rise as Panther Mountain, Lewey Mountain, and the rugged terrain beyond. The park's south-central areas are less celebrated than the high peaks region and the lake country to the north, but scanning Adirondack Park from this mountaintop at

Adirondack Museum

One of the country's best regional museums, the Adirondack Museum *(N.Y. 28 and N.Y. 30, Blue Mountain Lake. 518-352-7311. www.adkmuseum.org. Late May–mid-Oct.)* interprets the relationship people have with the mountains. Among its more than 20 exhibition buildings is one devoted to watercraft, featuring the elegant Adirondack guide boat, a two-ended rowboat. Other exhibits include fantastic rustic furniture—the peculiar assemblages of twigs, bark, and curly wood developed in the Adirondacks, then elevated to the status of a classic style.

Some of the exhibits are pointed reminders that the Adirondack Mountains have meant quite different things to different social classes. Here are the artifacts of the hard lives of miners, loggers, and trappers—juxtaposed with an exquisitely detailed private railroad car, complete with marble bath, typical of the railcars used by the Carnegies, Vanderbilts, Morgans, and other wealthy families.

The museum will not only give you a better understanding of the Adirondacks but also provide insight into the lives of the region's part-time and permanent residents.

dead center, it's hard to imagine why. Members of the Vanderbilt family erected their massive **Great Camp Sagamore** *(315-354-5311. Adm. fee)* to the west of Blue Mountain, south of Raquette Lake. Now that is quite an impeccable reference.

Old Forge Area

The village of Old Forge, off N.Y. 28 in the southwest part of the park, stands at the head of a long parade of 13 lakes, the **Fulton Chain Lakes.** That's the start of the Adirondack canoe route (see p. 268) linking the southwest and northern parts of the park. Like Blue Mountain Lake village, about 40 miles to the northeast, Old Forge is an important base for those using this route; both offer provisions, outfitters, campsites, and miles of hiking trails. Those who don't want to paddle can board a cruiser at Old Forge to tour the chain of lakes *(fee).*

There's also fine hiking in this region. The sweeping vistas from **Blue Mountain** are matched by views from **Bald Mountain,** near Old Forge, that take in the chain of lakes. In summer, Old Forge is also a busy mountain-biking center with miles of trials, newly dry and green, just waiting for wheels. The trails—a mix ranging from novice to expert—feed into other trails; as in the case of canoe routes, one thing leads to another. In winter, Old Forge becomes "The Snowmobile Capital of the East." From a 19th-century rail line, snowmobiles pour into the park, using miles of trails groomed from early December to March. Thankfully, wilderness areas and private lands are still off-limits. Those who head outdoors for peace and quiet should take note and plan accordingly. For information and maps of the surrounding area, contact Old Forge's visitor center at 315-369-6983.

Gore Mountain

Twenty-one miles west of I-87 *(N.Y. 28 exit)* are the 292 skiable acres of Gore Mountain *(Peaceful Valley Rd., North Creek, NY 12853. 518-251-2411 or 800-342-1234. www.goremountain.com).* Operated by the New York Olympic Regional Development Authority, Gore Mountain is "kid brother" to mighty Whiteface. It's big, with 62 trails to Whiteface's 70, and its summit is right up there at 3,600 feet, but the vertical drop is 2,100 feet, compared with Whiteface's 3,350 feet.

Gore plays to its strong suit; its wide-open cruising runs, such as **Twister** and **Sunway** on the lower part of the mountain, make it heaven for intermediate skiers. It also has more challenging slopes, with about a third of its runs in the expert category. Still, the emphasis here is on intermediate skiers and good family fun. (Gore Mountain maintains a

Summits of the central Adirondacks

nursery and has a kids' program.) Things keep moving on nine lifts, including a high-speed triple and the Northwoods, a new eight-passenger gondola. You'll find equipment rentals, as well as group and private lessons for skiers and snowboarders of all levels. Lessons for physically and emotionally challenged people can be arranged by appointment.

Like Whiteface, Gore Mountain seems blessedly old-fashioned, concentrating on skiing but providing choices for après-ski activities. There's plenty to do here in summer, too. The gondola keeps running, with service available for mountain bikers and hikers. Also on offer are mountain-bike clinics, with rentals and practice terrain at the base of the mountain. If you just want to linger over the landscape, ride the Northwoods gondola to the summit of **Bear Mountain** for one last eyeful of the Adirondacks. ■

Otter Creek Horse Trails

FOR HORSE OWNERS, the rolling, stream-crossed terrain of the foothills at the western edge of Adirondack Park *(N.Y. 12 N from Utica for 48 miles; at town of Glenfield, go E on Otter Creek Rd. and Chases Lake Rd. for about 7 miles)* is almost too good to be true.

Winding through 21,000 acres of forestland—the **Independence River Wild Forest Unit** of the Adirondack Forest Preserve and the **Independence River** and **Otter Creek State Forests**—are interlocking loops of old, sandy roads and woodland trails that add up to more than 65 miles of fine riding opportunities. Thanks to the sand deposited by enormous glaciers, which covered this area thousands of years ago, the footing is excellent for horses walking the trails.

As you ride along, you'll quickly discover that this area is wonderfully diverse. Spirea flats give way to deep mixed woodlands that are dotted with fishable ponds and threaded by creeks named for creatures living there—Little Otter Lake and Beaver Meadow Creek, for example. Approaching on horseback, you're likely to see those critters, as well as deer, bears, coyotes, foxes, turkeys, grouse, and snowshoe hare.

You will climb steep Adirondack hills and find seven designated overlooks that come with picnic tables, hitching rails, and fine views. There's an assembly area at the trailhead on Chases Lake Road; it offers trailer parking, a hundred roofed 4-foot tie stalls bedded with sand, two stud stalls, water, toilet facilities, and three mounting platforms for riders who are disabled. If you plan to camp for more than three successive nights

or in a group with more than ten people, you'll need a permit.

For more information and to obtain camping permits, get in touch with the New York State Department of Environmental Conservation at RD3, Box 22A, Lowville, NY 13367. You can also call 315-376-3521. *(Evidence of a current negative Coggins test is required for all horses, and a 30-day health certificate is needed for horses brought here from out of state.)*

Horse Trails

A number of other public horse trails wind through Adirondack Park. Here is a partial list:

Lake George Area.
The **Lake George Trail System**—on the east side of the lake, off Pilot Knob Road—is a 41-mile network of carriage and woodland roads that snake through **Lake George Wild Forest;** lean-tos provide shelter.

Pharaoh Lake Horse Trails follow 12.5 miles of sandy woodland roads through the **Pharaoh Lake Wilderness** east of Schroon Lake; lean-tos along the trails offer shelter to riders.

High Peaks.
Cold River Horse Trails are located 6 miles east of Tupper Lake off N.Y. 3. The 13- and 32-mile-loop dirt trails connect with Moose Pond Trail (10 miles) and Santanoni Trail (10 miles). Cold River has lean-tos for you and corrals for the horses.

Northwestern Lakes.
The **Saranac Inn Horse Trail System,** off N.Y. 30 near the Saranac Inn, offers an 11-mile round-trip on the Fish Pond Truck Trail; several small

Riding at Cold River Ranch

trails in the system will take you to ponds in the St. Regis Canoe Area.

Central Adirondacks.
The **Moose River Recreation Area** lies between Indian Lake and Inlet off N.Y. 28. Horses can follow a 28-mile dirt road as well as many old logging roads; campsites are available.

Get a Horse
Several outfitters in Adirondack Park offer hour-long, daylong, or overnight trail rides. Some provide guide services for longer rides and fishing or hunting trips. Here are a few to call:

Lake George Area.
Circle L Ranch, High St., Athol; 518-623-9967

High Peaks.
XTC Ranch, Forest Home Rd., Lake Clear, 518-891-5674, www.dude-ranches.com; or Wilson's Livery Stable, Alstead Hill Rd., Keene, 518-576-2221

Northwest Lakes.
Cold River Ranch, N.Y. 3, Tupper Lake; 518-359-7559

Central Adirondacks.
Adirondack Saddle Tours, Uncas Rd., Inlet; 315-357-4499 ■

Hudson River Gorge

- Northern New York, off N.Y. 28, south-central part of Adirondack Park
- Best seasons spring-fall ■ Hiking, white-water rafting ■ Contact Adirondack Park Visitor Interpretive Center, P.O. Box 101, Newcomb, NY 12953; phone 518-582-2000. www.northnet.org/adirondackvic

THE RIVER MADE FAMOUS by the Hudson River school of American painters is a broad and peaceful stream, a quiet and mature force. But upstream in the Adirondacks, not far from its headwaters in the high peaks, the young **Hudson River** acts out an impetuous adolescence. East of Blue Mountain Lake, the river follows the straight path of a fault zone that also holds Lake Abanakee, Indian Lake, and Indian River. About 4 miles northeast of Indian Lake village near the Indian River junction, the Hudson suddenly makes a right-angle bend out of the fault zone and carves a spectacular 9-mile gorge through a band of marble. When it enters another fault zone about 4 miles north of North River village, the river abruptly turns south and again follows the straightaway of the fault zone.

Once known only to lumbermen floating logs downriver, the **Hudson River Gorge** is now open to any adventurous soul who has the money for a raft trip, whether alone or with an outfitter. Outfitters usually begin their daylong trips on **Indian River** just below the Lake Abanakee dam, guaranteeing a wild 3-mile ride as the river drops 300 feet to the Hudson. In the gorge itself, long stretches of serious rapids alternate with fast-moving flat water. In the big water of April and May, the rapids become Class IV and V. By summertime—June, July, August—the river has subsided just enough to make for good family fun. Beginners can make the trip, but rafters must be at least 14 years old, in good physical condition, and able to swim.

You'll be busy paddling most of the way, but when there's a break, watch for ospreys nesting along the gorge. Notice the banded marble on the south side of the gorge, usually visible at the spring water level, and the carbonate-loving cedar trees capping the slope. On the north side, you'll see only gneiss, indicating that the Hudson made its gorge at the contact point between the two different rock faces. Most outfitters stop for lunch at the base of **Blue Ledge,** a 300-foot-high precipice at a sharp bend in the gorge. The moss-covered cliff is named for the haunting blue-gray shimmer it takes on as water flows across its face. Beyond this tranquil spot lie the river's most awesome rapids.

Nonpaddlers can hike in to get a close look at the Hudson flowing peacefully under the beautiful Blue Ledge. It's an easy 5-mile round-trip *(maps and information available at Newcomb visitor center).* North of North Creek on N.Y. 28N, take the fourth left turn onto North Woods Club Road; drive about 5 miles to the Blue Ledge trailhead on your left. Incidentally, the drive along N.Y. 28N between North Creek and Long Lake is one of the loveliest in the park. ■

Blue Ledge, Hudson River Gorge

Other Sites

Mashomack Preserve

Shelter Island is the largest of several glacially formed islands in Gardiners Bay at the eastern end of Long Island. The southeastern one-third of the island is the 2,039-acre Mashomack Preserve, part of the Nature Conservancy's "Last Great Places." Beyond a 10-mile stretch of white sand shore, 17 miles of trails lace mature oak and beech forest, salt and freshwater marshes, tidal creeks, meadows, and a pine swamp set in a series of glacial kettleholes. The preserve is rich in birds, including a rebounding breeding colony of ospreys. It's accessible by ferry (fee) from Sag Harbor or Greenport. Contact The Nature Conservancy, P.O. Box 850, Shelter Island, NY 11964; phone 516-749-1001.

Robert L. Graham/ Nanticoke Wildlife Area

This 2,500-acre state wildlife area near Laurel, Delaware, lies along the Nanticoke River—an excellent stream for flat-water canoeing and bird-watching. The river lazes through loblolly pine forests and marshes on its way to the Chesapeake Bay. Contact the wildlife area, Delaware Division of Fish & Wildlife, P.O. Box 1401, Dover, DE 19903; phone 302-739-5297.

Brandywine Creek State Park

Rolling hills, extraordinarily beautiful broadleaf woodlands, a freshwater marsh inhabited by Muhlenberg bog turtles, and a great array of upland birds make Brandywine a special place. Located 3 miles north of Wilmington, this 1,000-acre slice of the lower Piedmont is seen to advantage from its 15 miles of trails. Contact the Delaware Division of Parks and Recreation, P.O. Box 3782, Greenville , DE 19807; phone 302-577-3534.

Rock Creek Park

Mature forests of oak, cherry, and poplar cloak the ravines and ridges of the country's oldest urban natural park, located in Washington, D.C. A visitor center and nature center are just off Military Road. The park's 2,100 acres adjoin 4,400-acre Rock Creek Regional Park in Maryland; the parks support many small mammals and a great variety of birds. Ten miles of roads, 13 miles of hiking paths, and 10 miles of equestrian trails make for easy exploration. Contact the National Park Service, 3545 Williamsburg Lane NW, Washington, D.C. 20008; phone 202-426-6829.

Soldiers Delight Natural Environment Area

This 2,000-acre remnant of unusual grassland near Owings Mills, Maryland, is a prime example of serpentine barrens—isolated areas characterized by soil with high levels of nickel and magnesium silicate (or serpentine). Though a tough environment for plants, this barren supports Virginia pines and post oaks as well as littlestem bluegrass and many strange and rare plant species. Miles of trails make for good hiking in an extraordinary environment. 5100 Deer Park Road, Owings Mills, MD 21117; phone 410-922-3044.

Stokes State Forest

The uncontested gem of this 15,791-acre state forest is mile-long Tillman Ravine Trail, which runs along Tillman Brook through hemlock and hardwood forests banked with rhododendron. Adjoining High Point State Park, the forest is traversed by another 41 miles of trails. Contact the state forest, 1 Coursen Road, Branchville, NJ 07826; phone 973-948-3820.

Stuart M. Stein Memorial Preserve

The 775-acre Tannersville Cranberry Bog would look more at home in northern Canada. The southernmost low-altitude boreal bog in the east, it has been designated a national natural landmark: Here rare orchids give way to flowering heaths, and stunted black spruce and tamarack stand on hummocks of sphagnum moss in a textbook example of bog succession. Two trails provide year-round access for hikers, wildlife- and bird-watchers, and cross-country skiers. A third trail—a boardwalk through the heart of the bog—offers scheduled guided walks from May to October. Contact the Nature Conservancy, Monroe County Conservation District, 8050 Running Valley Road, Stroudsburg, PA 18360; phone 717-629-3061.

Whetstone Gulf State Park

On the northwest edge of the Adirondacks stands the isolated Tug Hill Plateau. A geologically anomalous and rugged region of shale and siltstone, it is deeply cut by the narrow, steep-sided whetstone gulf, or chasm, which is 3 miles long and 385 feet deep. The park is located off N.Y. 26, 6 miles S of Lowville. Contact the park, RD 2, Box 69, Lowville, NY 13367; phone 315-376-6630.

Raccoon Creek State Park

Only 25 miles west of Pittsburgh, this diverse 7,323-acre park centered on Raccoon Lake is popular with anglers and bird-watchers. The Wildflower Reserve at the eastern end of the park, crisscrossed by trails, is famed for its beauty and the great diversity of its Pennsylvania, southern, and midwestern species of wildflowers, ferns, and other plants. Contact the park, Pennsylvania Bureau of State Parks, 3000 SR 18, Hookstown, PA 15050; phone 724-899-2200.

Wawayanda State Park

Almost a third of this 16,615-acre park in the heart of the New Jersey Highlands is set aside in three natural areas, including Hemlock Ravine and the northern white cedar groves of Wawayanda Swamp Natural Area. Dense hardwood forests, varied wetlands, and 255-acre Wawayanda Lake make up one of New Jersey's largest parks. Contact the park, 885 Warwick Turnpike, Hewitt, NJ 07421; phone 973-853-4462.

Resources

The following is a short list of resources. Contact state and local associations for additional information. Most campsites operate seasonally, so plan ahead. Chain hotels and motels operating in the Middle Atlantic region are on p. 283.

DELAWARE

State Agencies

Delaware Division of
Fish & Wildlife
  39 Kings Highway
  Dover, Del 19901
  302-739-4431
  www.dnrec.state.de.us/fw/f
  wwel.htm
  Provides information on
  hunting and fishing licenses

Delaware State Parks
  89 Kings Highway
  P.O. Box 1401
  Dover, DE 19903
  302-739-4702
  www.destateparks.com/
  Provides camping infor-
  mation

Lodging

Delaware Tourism Office
  99 Kings Highway
  Dover, DE 19901
  800-441-8846
  www.visitdelaware.net

MARYLAND

Federal and State Agencies

Maryland State Department
of Natural Resources
  www.dnr.state.md.us/
  888-432-2267 (camping and
  cabin reservations)
  410-260-8200 (hunting and
  fishing regulations)

Outfitters and Activities

For information on the
Chesapeake Bay, contact
www.baywaves.com or
ww.chesapeake-bay.com

Potomac Appalachian
Trail Club
  118 Park Street S.E.
  Vienna, VA 21180
  703-242-0693
  http://patc.net
  Provides information and
  volunteer opportunities
  along the Appalachian Trail

Pocomoke River Canoe
Company
  312 N. Washington St.
  Snow Hill, MD 21863

410-632-3971
  Group trips, self-guided
  adventures, canoe and
  kayak rentals

Fletcher's Boathouse
  4940 Canal Rd. NW
  Washington, DC 20874
  202-244-0461
  Bicycles and boats for rent
  along the C & O Canal

Thompson's Boathouse
  2900 Virginia Ave. NW
  Washington, DC 20037
  202-333-4861
  Rents boats and bikes for
  use on the C & O Canal

Potomac Paddle Sports
  20130 Waterside Drive
  Germantown, MD 20874
  301-515-7337
  Boats and camping
  equipment

Spring Creek Outfitters
  578 Deep Creek Drive
  McHenry, MD 21541
  301-387-2034
  www.springcreekoutfitter.com
  Fly-fishing instruction and
  guide services in western
  Maryland

Outdoor Education and Resources

Chesapeake Bay Foundation
  162 Prince George St.
  Annapolis, MD
  410-268-8816; www.cbf.org
  This foundation provides
  opportunities to help
  protect the bay.

Lodging

Maryland's Department of
Natural Resources
  www.dnr.state.md.us/publi-
  clands/campinginfo.html
  Has information on campgrounds and cabins within
  state parks and forests.
  Reservations can be made
  by calling 888-432-2267.

NEW JERSEY

Federal and State Agencies

US Fish and Wildlife Service:
  Great Swamp Information
  609-646-9310

New Jersey Division of
Parks and Forestry
  501 East State Street
  PO Box 404
  Trenton, NJ 08625
  800-843-6420
  www.state.nj.us/dep/forestr
  y/parks/
  Provides camping and
  fishing information

Outfitters and Activities

Morris County Park
Commission
  PO Box 1295
  Morristown, NJ 07962
  973-326-7600
  Information on park
  activities, campgrounds, and
  boat rentals in the Great
  Swamp area

Great Swamp Outdoor
Education Center
  247 Southern Blvd.
  Chatham, NJ 07928
  Classes and guided hikes in
  the refuge

Pine Barrens Canoe Rental
  3260 Route 563
  Chatsworth, NJ 08019
  800-732-0793 or
  609-726-1515
  www.pinebarrenscanoe.com/
  Canoe and kayak rentals;
  day and overnight guided
  trips

Outdoor Education and Resources

Cape May Bird Observatory
  Center for Research &
  Education
  701 East Lake Dr.
  Cape May Point, NJ 08212
  609-884-17136
  Sponsors guided nature
  walks & birding workshops

Nature Center of Cape May
  1600 Delaware Ave.
  Cape May, NJ 08204
  609-898-8848
  Seasonal nature programs
  for children and adults

Pocono Environmental
Education Center
  R.R. 2, Box 1010
  Dingmans Ferry, PA 18328
  570-828-2319
  www.peec.org

Lodging

Cape May County
Department of Tourism
  PO Box 365
  Cape May Court House
  Cape May, NJ 08210
  800-227-2297
  www.thejerseycape.net

Camping

The New Jersey Division of
Parks and Forestry provides
a complete listing of campgrounds and cabin locations
on state lands.
  www.state.nj.us/dep/forestr
  y/parks/

Wharton State Forest
  Atsion Lake Cabin Rentals
  744 Route 206

Shamong, NJ 08088
609-268-0444
Nine century-old log cabins located on shore of Wharton's Atsion Lake

NEW YORK

Federal and State Agencies

New York State Department of Environmental Conservation (DEC)
Source for information on state lands. Provides recreational information, fishing and hunting regulations, and a list of licensed guides.
www.dec.state.ny.us/website/

Region 3 (Catskills)
845-256-3000

Region 5 (Adirondacks)
518-897-1200

Region 6 (Otter Creek Horse Trails)
315-376-3521

NYS Office of Parks, Recreation, and Historic Preservation
Albany, NY 12238
518-474-0456

Outfitters and Activities

Wildware Outfitters
171 The Commons
Ithaca, NY 14850
607-273-5158
Canoeing, camping, cross-country skiing

Cayuga Mountain Bike Shop
138 W State Street
Ithaca, NY 14850
607-277-6821
Bike rentals

House of Wheels
709 West State Street
Olean, NY 14760
716-373-2453
Biking

J & A Concessions
Route 1, Suite 1
Salamanca, NY 14779
716-354-9163
Boating, biking, cross-country skiing

Adventures for Women
PO Box 515
Montvale, NJ 07645
201-930-0557
Classes and outdoor expeditions for women

Shawangunks. Organized climbing classes in Mohonk Preserve are offered by four registered outfitters:
Diamond Sports (800-776-2577); Eastern Mountain Sports (800-310-4504);

High Angle Adventures (800-777-2546); and Mountain Skills (914-687-9643).

Town Tinker Tube Rental
P.O. Box 404
Phoenicia, NY
914-688-5553
www.towntinker.com
Full-service tube rentals for a 5-mile stretch of Esopus Creek

Onoville Marina
704 W. Perimeter Rd
Steamburg, NY 14783
814-354-2615
Canoes and fishing boats

Douglaston Salmon Run
PO Box 622
Pulaski, NY 13142
315-298-6672
Salmon and trout fishing on the Salmon River

The Boat House
2855 Aqueduct Rd.
Niskayuna, NY 12309
518-393-5711
Canoe rentals on the Erie Canal

Champagne Balloon Adventures
27 James St.
Alexandria Bay, NY 13607
315-482-9356
Soaring above the St. Lawrence

Adventure Sports Rafting Company
Main Street, P.O. Box 775
Indian Lake, NY
800-441-7238 or
518-648-5812 or
www2.telenet.net/commercial/asrc
White-water rafting tours of the Hudson River Gorge and the Moose River

Hudson River Rafting Co.
1 Main Street
North Creek, NY 12853
800-888-7238 or
518-251-3215
www.hudsonriverrafting.com
Guided white-water rafting and kayaking on several rivers, including the Ausable, the Hudson, and the Moose

St. Regis Canoe Outfitters
P.O. Box 318
Lake Clear, NY 12945
518-891-1838
Canoe and kayak rentals, instruction, shuttle services, outfitting packages, and customized trip planning in the St. Regis Canoe Area

Outdoor Education and Resources

Sagamore Institute of the Adirondacks
P.O. Box 146
Raquette Lake, NY 13436
315-354-5311
www.sagamore.org
Workshops on crafts, history, and the outdoors

Adirondack Mountain Club
814 Goggins Road
Lake George, NY 12845
518-668-4447
www.adk.org
Information on the Adirondacks including trail guides and maps, outings, and workshops

New York-New Jersey Trail Conference
212-685-9699
www.nynjtc.org
Excellent maps on the trails in both states, including the Long Path

Champlain Bikeways
c/o Lake Champlain Visitors Center
RR 1 Box 220,
Crown Point, NY 12928
518-597-4646
www.champlainbikeways.org
Information and maps for cycling around the Lake Champlain area

Camping

New York Department of Environmental Conservation
50 Wolf Road
Albany, NY 12233-5253
518-457-2500
Operates campgrounds within the state parks and forests. Reservations for all NY State facilities may be made from 2 days to 11 months in advance.

Make reservations through Reserve America
800-456-2267
www.reserveamerica.com

Lodging

Mohonk Mountain House
Lake Mohonk
New Paltz, NY 12561
800-772-6646 (reservations)
845-255-1000 (general info)
www.mohonk.com
A 2,200-acre historic Shawangunk resort located on the shores of Lake Mohonk

White Pine Camp
Paul Smiths, NY 12970

518-327-3030
www.whitepinecamp.com
This Great Camp on Osgood Pond was once the summer White House of President Coolidge. Several self-sufficient cabins.

Adirondak Loj
P.O. Box 867
Lake Placid, NY 12946
518-523-3441
Operated by the Adirondack Mountain Club, this remote lodge on Heart Lake offers cabins, dorm rooms, and regular rooms.

The Lodge on Lake Clear
Junction Rtes. 186 & 30
Lake Clear, NY 12945
800-442-2356 or
518-891-1489
www.lodgeonlakeclear.com
Rustic yet elegant accommodations on 25 acres

Bed & Breakfast Association of Greater Ithaca
800-806-4406

Ithaca Visitors Center
800-284-8422

PENNYSLVANIA

Federal and State Agencies

Pennsylvania Bureau of State Parks
PO Box 8551
Harrisburg, PA 17105-85551
888-727-2757
www.dcnr.state.pa.us
General information, campsite and cabin reservations in PA state parks

PA Department of Conservation and Natural Resources
PO Box 8767
Harrisburg, PA 17105-8767
877-444-6777
General information, campsite and cabin reservations in PA state parks

Pennsylvania Fish & Boat Commission
PO Box 67000
Harrisburg, PA 17106
www.fish.state.pa.us
Information on fishing licenses

PA Hotline for Downhill and Cross-country Skiing
800-925-7669

Rails to Trails Conservancy
Pennsylvania Field Office
105 Locust Street
Harrisburg, PA 17101
717-238-1717

Outfitters and Activities

Allegheny Outfitters
Box 1681
Warren, PA 16365
814-723-4868
Canoes and kayaks

Lehigh Gorge State Park licenses four outfitters to run the gorge: Jim Thorpe River Adventures (800-424-7238); Pocono Whitewater (800-944-8392); Whitewater Challenger (800-443-8554); and Whitewater Rafting Adventures (800-876-0285).

Laurel Highlands River Tours
PO Box 107
Ohiopyle, PA 15470
800-472-3846

Jones Outfitters, Ltd.
37 Main Street
Lake Placid, NY 12946
518-523-3468
www.jonesoutfitters.com
Fly-fishing guide services on the Ausable River

Pine Creek Outfitters
Box 130B
Wellsboro, PA 16901
570-724-3003
Rafting, canoeing, biking

Country Ski & Sports
81 Main Street
Wellsboro, PA 16901
570-724-3858
Rafting, canoeing, biking, and skiing excursions in Pine Creek Gorge area

Silver Canoe
37 S. Maple Avenue
Port Jervis, NY 12771
800-724-8342 or
914-856-705
www.silvercanoe.com
Canoe and kayak rentals, white-water rafting on Upper Delaware River

Bike World
2025 Penn Ave
Warren, PA 16365
814-723-1758

Camping

Reservations can be made for most campgrounds and cabins in Pennsylvania by calling 888-727-2757 or 517-558-2710. Pennsylvania Department of Conservation and Natural Resources website: www.dcnr.state.pa.us/stateparks/recreation/camping.htm

Allegheny National Forest Campgrounds Reservations
222 Liberty Street
Warren, PA 16365

877-444-6777
724-329-4777

Lodging

Ligonier Country Inn
Rt. 30 E., PO Box 46
Laughlintown, Pa 15655
724-238-3651

Historic Summit Inn
101 Skyline Dr.
Farmington, PA 15437
800-433-8594

The Penn Wells Hotel and Lodge
Wellsboro, PA
570-724-2111

Laurel Highlands Visitors Bureau
120 E. Main Street
Ligonier, PA 15568
800-925-7669

Hotel & Motel Chains

(In Maryland, Pennsylvania, New Jersey, and New York)

Best Western International
800-528-1234

Choice Hotels
800-4-CHOICE

Clarion Hotels
800-CLARION

Comfort Inns
800-228-5150

Courtyard by Marriott
800-321-2211

Days Inn
800-325-2525

Econo Lodge
800-446-6900

Embassy Suites
800-EMBASSY

Fairfield Inn by Marriott
800-228-2800

Hilton Hotels and Resorts
800-HILTONS

Holiday Inns
800-HOLIDAY

Howard Johnson
800-654-2000

Hyatt Hotels and Resorts
800-223-1234

Marriott Hotels and Resorts
800-228-9290

Motel Six
800-466-8356

Quality Inns-Hotels-Suites
800-228-5151

Ramada Inns
800-2-RAMADA

Red Lion Hotels
800-547-8010

Sheraton Hotels and Inns
800-325-3535

Super 8 Motels
800-843-1991

Index

About the Author and Photographer

Ann Jones has traveled to remote corners of every continent, including North America. Her latest adventure-travel narrative is *Looking for Lovedu: Days and Nights in Africa* (Knopf, 20001).

Skip Brown is a freelance photograher living near the Potomac River in Cabin John, Maryland. He is a Class V white-water kayaker, an advanced hang-glider pilot, and an avid surfer, snowboarder, and windsurfer.

Illustrations Credits

All images by Skip Brown except for the following:

National Geographic Guide to America's Outdoors: Middle Atlantic
by Ann Jones
Photographed by Skip Brown

Published by the National Geographic Society
John M. Fahey, Jr., *President and Chief Executive Officer*
Gilbert M. Grosvenor, *Chairman of the Board*
Nina D. Hoffman, *Executive Vice President, President, Books and School Publishing*

Prepared by the Book Division
William R. Gray, *Vice President and Director*
Charles Kogod, *Assistant Director*
Barbara A. Payne, *Editorial Director and Managing Editor*
Marianne Koszorus, *Design Director*

Guides to America's Outdoors
Elizabeth L. Newhouse, *Director of Travel Books*
Cinda Rose, *Art Director*
Allan Fallow, Barbara Noe, *Senior Editors*
Carl Mehler, *Director of Maps*
Caroline Hickey, *Senior Researcher*

Staff for this Book
Carolinda E. Averitt, Mary Luders, Paul Mathless, *Editors*
Joan Wolbier, *Designer*
Melissa G. Ryan, *Illustrations Editor*
Victoria Garrett Jones, Elizabeth Lenhart,
 Jane Sunderland, *Researchers*
Lise Sajewski, *Editorial Consultant*
Matt Chwastyk, Jerome N. Cookson, Sven M. Dolling, Thomas L. Gray, Joseph F. Ochlak,
 Nicholas P. Rosenbach, Gregory Ugiansky, Martin S. Walz, National Geographic Maps,
 Mapping Specialists, XNR Productions, *Map Edit, Research, and Production*
Tibor G. Tóth, *Map Relief*
R. Gary Colbert, *Production Director*
Rick Wain, *Production Manager*
Sharon K. Berry, *Illustrations Assistant*
Joyce Marshall, *Indexer*
Robert Della Vecchia, *Project Assistant*
Elizabeth B. Booz, *Contributor*
Rodger T. Faill and William D. Sevon, Pennsylvania Geologic Survey, *Consultants*

Manufacturing and Quality Control
George V. White, *Director*; John T. Dunn, *Associate Director*; Vincent P. Ryan, *Manager*;
Phillip L. Schlosser, *Financial Analyst*

Library of Congress Cataloging-in-Publication Data

Jones, Ann, 1937-
  Guide to America's outdoors. Mid-Atlantic / by Ann Jones; photography by Skip Brown.
    p. 288 cm. — (National Geographic guides to America's outdoors)
  Includes index.
  ISBN 0-7922-7748-1
    1. Middle Atlantic States—Guidebooks. 2. National parks and reserves—Middle Atlantic States—Guide
books. 3. Outdoor recreation—Middle Atlantic States—Guidebooks. I. Title: Mid-Atlantic. II. Brown,
Skip, 1957- III. National Geographic Society (U.S.) IV. Title. V. Series.
  F106 .J66 2001
  917.404'44--dc21   00-053300
                                                                                        CIP